AutoCAD® 2018 AND AutoCAD LT® 2018

ESSENTIALS

Scott Onstott

SYBEX®
A Wiley Brand

AUTODESK.
Authorized Publisher

Development Editor: Kathryn Duggan
Technical Editor: Ian le Cheminant
Production Editor: Rebecca Anderson
Copy Editor: Elizabeth Welch
Editorial Manager: Mary Beth Wakefield
Production Manager: Kathleen Wisor
Executive Editor: Jody Lefevere
Associate Acquisitions Editor: Riley Harding
Book Designer: Happenstance Type-O-Rama
Proofreader: Nancy Carrasco
Indexer: John Sleeva
Project Coordinator, Cover: Brent Savage
Cover Designer: Wiley
Cover Image: ©Natalya Vyshedko / Shutterstock

ISBN: 978-1-119-38678-0
ISBN: 978-1-119-41424-7 (ebk.)
ISBN: 978-1-119-41429-2 (ebk.)

Manufactured in the United States of America

For general information on our other products and services or to obtain technical support, please contact our Customer Care Department within the U.S. at (877) 762-2974, outside the U.S. at (317) 572-3993 or fax (317) 572-4002.

Wiley publishes in a variety of print and electronic formats and by print-on-demand. Some material included with standard print versions of this book may not be included in e-books or in print-on-demand. If this book refers to media such as a CD or DVD that is not included in the version you purchased, you may download this material at http://booksupport.wiley.com. For more information about Wiley products, visit www.wiley.com.

Library of Congress Control Number: 2017939768

10 9 8 7 6 5 4 3 2 1

ABOUT THE AUTHOR

Scott Onstott has published 13 books with Sybex prior to this one: *AutoCAD® 2017 and AutoCAD LT® 2017 Essentials, AutoCAD® 2016 and AutoCAD LT® 2016 Essentials, AutoCAD® 2015 and AutoCAD LT® 2015 Essentials, AutoCAD® 2014 and AutoCAD LT® 2014 Essentials, AutoCAD® 2013 and AutoCAD LT® 2013 Essentials, AutoCAD® 2012 and AutoCAD LT® 2012 Essentials, Adobe® Photoshop® CS6 Essentials, Enhancing Architectural Drawings and Models with Photoshop, AutoCAD®: Professional Tips and Techniques* (with Lynn Allen), *Enhancing CAD Drawings with Photoshop, Mastering Autodesk® VIZ 2007* (with George Omura and Jon McFarland), *Mastering Autodesk® Architectural Desktop 2006*, and *Autodesk® VIZ 2005* (with George Omura). Scott has worked on 20 other Sybex books as contributing author, reviser, compilation editor, or technical editor.

He also wrote, narrated, and produced the *Secrets in Plain Sight* film series (volumes 1 and 2) and seven related books, including *Tripartite, Anthology: Secrets in Plain Sight; Geometra: Coloring Book; Secrets in Plain Sight: Leonardo da Vinci; The Divine Proportion, Quantification: Illustrations from the Creator of Secrets in Plain Sight*; and *Taking Measure: Explorations in Number, Architecture, and Consciousness.*

Scott has a bachelor's degree in architecture from the University of California, Berkeley and is a former university instructor who now serves as a consultant and independent video producer. You can contact the author through his website at www.scottonstott.com.

Acknowledgments

Many people have been instrumental in making this book that you are holding in your hands or reading onscreen a reality. I would like to express my sincere gratitude to the professional team at Wiley for all their hard work.

CONTENTS

CHAPTER 6   Controlling Object Visibility and Appearance   105

CHAPTER 7   Organizing Objects   131

CHAPTER 17   Modeling in 3D   337

CHAPTER 18   Presenting and Documenting 3D Design   369

JUN   2017

INTRODUCTION

The staying power of the AutoCAD® program is legendary in the ever-changing software industry, having been around for 36 years by the 2018 release. You can rest assured that spending your time learning AutoCAD will be a wise investment, and the skills you obtain in this book will be useful for years to come.

I welcome you in beginning the process of learning AutoCAD®. It will give you great satisfaction to learn such a complex program and use it to design and document whatever you dream up. In this book, you'll find step-by-step tutorials that reveal a wide variety of techniques built on many years of real-world experience.

The first 14 chapters apply to both AutoCAD® 2018 and AutoCAD LT® 2018. AutoCAD LT is Autodesk's lower-cost version of AutoCAD, and it has reduced capabilities. Chapters 15 through 18 are for full AutoCAD users only, because they cover advanced tools not available in AutoCAD LT, including attributes, 3D navigation, 3D modeling, and rendering.

Who Should Read This Book

This book is for students, hobbyists, professional architects, industrial designers, engineers, builders, landscape architects, or anyone who communicates through technical drawings as part of their work.

If you're interested in certification for AutoCAD 2018, this book can be a great resource to help you prepare. See `www.autodesk.com/training-and-certification/certification` for more certification information and resources. This book also features appendices that can help you focus your studies on the skills you will need for the certification exams.

What You Will Learn

You'll gain a solid understanding of the features of AutoCAD in this book. Each chapter features multiple exercises that take you step by step through the many complex procedures of AutoCAD. The goal of performing these steps on your own is to develop skills that you can apply to many different real-world situations.

Although each project presents different obstacles and opportunities, I urge you to focus on the concepts and techniques presented rather than memorizing the specific steps used to achieve the desired result. The actual steps performed may vary in each geometric situation.

The best way to build skills is to perform the steps on your computer exactly as they are presented in the book during your first reading. After you achieve the desired result, start over and experiment using the same techniques on your own project (whether invented or real). After you have practiced, think about how you have achieved the desired result, and you will get the most out of this book.

Reader Requirements

You don't need any previous experience with AutoCAD to use this book. However, you'll need familiarity with either the Windows or Mac operating system and the basic skills necessary to use a graphical user interface successfully and to operate a computer confidently.

AutoCAD 2018 or AutoCAD LT 2018 System Requirements

This book was written for both AutoCAD 2018 and AutoCAD LT 2018. The following are system requirements for running either version on the different operating systems in which they are offered. See http://knowledge.autodesk .com/support/system-requirements for the most up-to-date requirements.

General System Requirements

AutoCAD 2018 runs on the following operating systems:

- ▶ Microsoft Windows 7 SP1 (32-bit & 64-bit)
- ▶ Microsoft Windows 8.1 with update KB2919355 (32-bit & 64-bit)
- ▶ Microsoft Windows 10 (64-bit only)

AutoCAD for Mac 2018 runs on the following 64-bit operating systems:

- ▶ macOS v10.12 (Sierra) or later
- ▶ OS X v10.11 (El Capitan)
- ▶ OS X v10.10 (Yosemite)
- ▶ OS X v10.9 (Mavericks)

FREE AUTODESK SOFTWARE FOR STUDENTS AND EDUCATORS

The Autodesk Education Community is an online resource with more than five million members that enables educators and students to download—for free (see website for terms and conditions)—the same software used by professionals worldwide. You can also access additional tools and materials to help you design, visualize, and simulate ideas. Connect with other learners to stay current with the latest industry trends and get the most out of your designs. Get started today at www.autodesk.com/education/free-software/featured.

What Is Covered in This Book

AutoCAD® 2018 and AutoCAD LT® 2018 Essentials is organized to provide you with the knowledge needed to master the basics of computer-aided design. The book's web page is located at www.sybex.com/go/autocad2018essentials, where you can download the sample files used in each chapter.

Chapter 1: Getting Started   You'll take a tour of the user interface and learn to identify each of its parts by name. Chapter 1 is essential reading because you'll need to know the difference between workspaces, ribbon tabs, toolbars, panels, palettes, status toggles, and so on to understand the terminology used by your colleagues and in the rest of this book. In addition, you'll learn how to match your industry's standard units to the drawings you'll be creating.

Chapter 2: Gaining Basic Drawing Skills   Learn how to navigate a 2D drawing with Zoom and Pan so that you can zero in on areas of interest. You'll learn how to draw lines, rectangles, circles, arcs, and polygons; how to cancel, erase, and undo; and how to fillet and chamfer lines. In addition, you'll use two coordinate systems to specify the exact sizes of objects you are drawing.

Chapter 3: Using Drawing Aids   Drawing aids are something you'll want to learn how to use to create measured drawings with ease. The drawing aids covered with step-by-step exercises in this chapter include grid and snap, Ortho and Polar Tracking, PolarSnap, running object snaps, the From snap, and object snap tracking.

Chapter 4: Editing Entities   This chapter teaches what you'll probably be doing most of the time in AutoCAD: editing the basic entities that you've drawn to make them conform with your design intent. Editing commands covered include Move, Copy, Rotate, Scale, Array, Trim, Extend, Lengthen, Stretch, Offset, and Mirror. In addition to these commands, you'll learn an alternative method for editing entities called *grip editing.*

Chapter 5: Shaping Curves   The landscape exercise in this chapter teaches you how to create complex curves with NURBS-based splines, curved polylines, and ellipses. By the end, you'll be able to shape curves to create almost any curvilinear form imaginable.

Chapter 6: Controlling Object Visibility and Appearance   You'll learn how to hide and reveal objects with properties and layers. Layers are essential to managing the complexity of design, and you'll use many different layer tools in this chapter's step-by-step exercises.

Chapter 7: Organizing Objects   By combining entities such as lines, polylines, circles, arcs, and text into blocks and/or groups, you can more efficiently manipulate complex objects such as chairs, mechanical assemblies, trees, or any other organizational designation appropriate to your industry. You'll learn how to create and work with blocks and groups in this chapter.

Chapter 8: Hatching and Gradients   In this chapter, you'll flood bounded areas with solid fill, hatch patterns, and/or gradients to indicate transitions between materials and to improve the readability of drawings in general.

Chapter 9: Working with Blocks and Xrefs   You'll learn how to access content from other files in the current drawing in this chapter. You'll also understand the important distinction between inserting and externally referencing content. In addition, you'll store saved content on tool palettes for simplified reuse.

Chapter 10: Creating and Editing Text   The written word is undeniably a part of every drawing. This chapter teaches you how to create both single- and multiline text, how to edit any text, and how to control its appearance through text styles and object properties.

Chapter 11: Dimensioning   You'll learn how to annotate drawings with specific measurements known as dimensions in this chapter. In addition to learning how to control measurements' appearance with dimension styles, you'll create linear, aligned, angular, and radius dimension objects.

Chapter 12: Keeping In Control with Constraints   This chapter teaches you how to add geometric and dimensional constraints to objects so that their ultimate form is controlled by mathematical formulas. The formulas in the examples are as simple as adding two dimensions or calculating the diameter of a circle from its radius.

Chapter 13: Working with Layouts and Annotative Objects   AutoCAD has two environments, which you'll learn about in this chapter on layouts: model space and paper space. You'll create floating viewports to display the contents of model space in the paper space of a layout. In addition, you'll create annotative styles and objects that always display the proper height no matter which viewport or annotation scale is selected.

Chapter 14: Printing and Plotting   From plotter drivers to plot style tables and page setups, you'll learn the intricacies of creating printed output to scale in AutoCAD. You'll plot in both model space and paper space, and you will even create electronic output that can be shared on the Internet.

Chapter 15: Working with Data   Attributes, fields, and tables are the subjects of this chapter on managing data. You'll learn how to embed nongraphical data in blocks, how to link to that data dynamically in text fields, and finally how to display and format this same data in an organized fashion in spreadsheet-like tables.

Chapter 16: Navigating 3D Models   In this chapter, you'll learn how to change your point of view while working on 3D models using the ViewCube®, the Orbit tool, and SteeringWheels® technologies. In addition, you'll compose and save perspective views with cameras to help you visualize 3D models with added realism.

Chapter 17: Modeling in 3D   You'll learn the basics of surface, solid, and mesh modeling in this chapter by building the 3D geometry you navigated in the previous chapter. Each 3D toolset has its strengths and limitations, and you'll learn to use tools in each category to get the job done.

Chapter 18: Presenting and Documenting 3D Design   By assigning realistic materials, inserting artificial and natural light sources, and rendering the scene, you'll create realistic computer-generated imagery in this chapter. By rendering in the cloud, you can keep working locally while your high-quality rendering is being processed remotely. You'll also learn how to project 2D plans, sections, and detail drawings from a model so that you can dimension and document 3D designs.

Appendix A: Making Isometric Drawings   This appendix teaches you how to make 2D isometric drawings that create the illusion of 3D objects. Isometric drawings provide a simple (and much more limited) alternative to the complexity of true 3D modeling. Isometric drawings are scaled equally in three planes separated with a common 120-degree angle between each of them.

Appendix B: Autodesk AutoCAD 2018 Certification   This appendix contains information about how to prepare for Autodesk certification exams using this book. The tables point you to the chapters where you'll find specific examples giving you practical experience with the topics covered in the exams.

The Essentials Series

The Essentials series from Sybex provides outstanding instruction for readers who are just beginning to develop their professional skills. Every Essentials book includes these features:

- ▶ Skill-based instruction with chapters organized around projects rather than abstract concepts or subjects.

- ▶ Digital files (via download) so that you can work through the project tutorials yourself. Please check the book's web page at www.sybex.com/go/autocad2018essentials for these companion downloads.

Certification
Objective
The Certification Objective margin icon will alert you to passages that are especially relevant to AutoCAD 2018 certification. See the appendix and www.autodesk.com/training-and-certification/certification for more information and resources.

CHAPTER 1

Getting Started

As we begin this book on the AutoCAD® program, I'm reminded of a quote by Chinese philosopher Lao-Tzu: "A journey of a thousand miles begins with a single step." In much the same way, learning AutoCAD is something anyone can do by taking it one step at a time. And I promise that AutoCAD is much easier than walking a thousand miles!

By buying this book, you have already taken the first step in this journey. When you finish, you will have a solid understanding of AutoCAD.

In this chapter, you'll learn to do the following:

▶ **Sign in to Autodesk® 360 on the Start tab**

▶ **Explore the AutoCAD 2018 for Windows user interface**

▶ **Set drawing units**

Sign In to Autodesk 360 on the Start Tab

Autodesk 360 is a cloud-based service that is integrated with AutoCAD. You have the option of automatically storing up to 5 GB of your drawing files in the cloud for free. The files you store in the cloud can be edited online and shared with others with your permission.

The Start tab appears when you launch the program. You can create new drawings, access existing drawings, connect to AutoCAD 360, receive notifications, and access a live chat with sales on the Try page that appears on trial versions, all on the Start tab.

Exercise 1.1: Configure Autodesk 360

To begin, launch AutoCAD 2018.

1. Click the Sign In button in the Connect section of the Start tab (see Figure 1.1).

FIGURE 1.1   Clicking Sign In on the AutoCAD Start tab

2. Sign in with an Autodesk ID or email address and password. If you don't already have an Autodesk ID, click the Create Account link and create one online (see Figure 1.2).

> ### Sign in
>
> A
>
> | Email or Username |
>
> | NEXT |
>
> NEW TO AUTODESK? CREATE ACCOUNT

FIGURE 1.2   Signing in or creating an Autodesk ID

Take advantage of free cloud storage while you use this book. Storing your files offsite in the cloud is an effective backup strategy.

▶

3. After you sign in using an Autodesk ID, the Default Autodesk 360 Settings dialog box appears. Select Sync My Settings (see Figure 1.3).

4. Click the large Start Drawing button in the Get Started section of the Start tab.

FIGURE 1.3 Setting Autodesk 360 options

This loads the full AutoCAD user interface, which you will learn about in the next exercise.

USING AUTODESK 360

Whenever you save your work in AutoCAD, a copy of your file will be uploaded to Autodesk 360 in the background. You can access this content at `http://a360.autodesk.com` (as shown here) or within AutoCAD from the A360 tab on the ribbon. You will learn about the ribbon in Exercise 1.3.

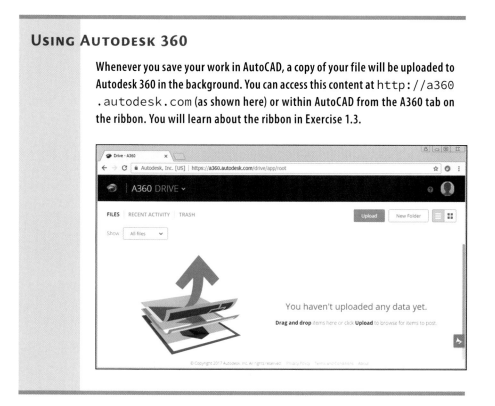

Explore the AutoCAD 2018 for Windows User Interface

AutoCAD for Mac has a user interface that is customized to the Mac experience. Although the Mac user interface is not covered in this book, its commands and capabilities are similar to those in AutoCAD for Windows (albeit with a slightly reduced set of features).

Autodesk has recently released new versions of AutoCAD, including the AutoCAD® 2018 and AutoCAD LT® 2018 software. The two Windows versions look nearly identical and function in almost the same way. The main difference between them is that AutoCAD LT doesn't support automation and some of the advanced 3D functions. Although this book was written using AutoCAD 2018 running on Windows 7, you can use it to learn any of the current versions of AutoCAD.

Exercise 1.2: Explore the Graphical User Interface

Before you can use AutoCAD, you'll need to familiarize yourself thoroughly with its graphical user interface (GUI). Figure 1.4 shows the AutoCAD 2018 (for Windows) user interface.

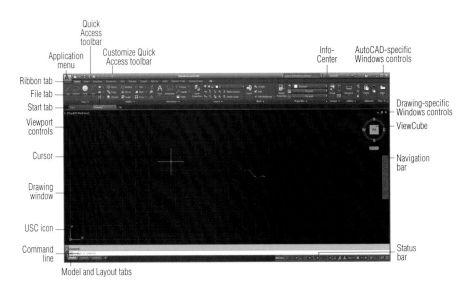

FIGURE 1.4 AutoCAD 2018 user interface

Certification
Objective

Let's now step through the basic user interface for AutoCAD.

1. Click the Application menu to open it. Type **polygon** and observe that the text appears in the search box at the top of the Application menu.

The search results (see Figure 1.5) list many related AutoCAD commands. Search is useful when you're not sure how to access a command in the interface or what its exact name is.

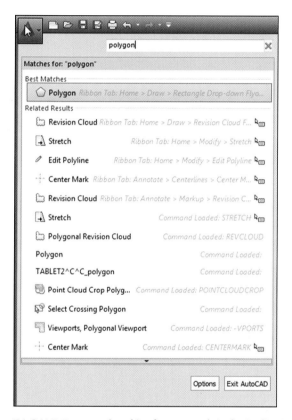

FIGURE 1.5   Searching for commands in the Application menu

2. Click the red X at the extreme right edge of the search box to make the initial Application menu interface reappear. Here you can create new or open existing drawings, export or print drawings, and more. Hover the cursor over Open and then click Drawing (Figure 1.6).

3. Select the following sample file; then click Open in the Select File dialog box:

```
C:\Program Files\Autodesk\AutoCAD 2018\Sample\
Sheet Sets\Manufacturing\VW252-02-0142.dwg
```

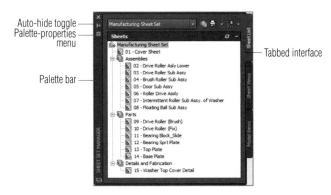

FIGURE 1.6 Opening a drawing from the Application menu

▶

Sheet sets are an optional feature in AutoCAD.

The Sheet Set Manager appears when the sample file is opened (see Figure 1.7). This palette automatically appears when you open any drawing that's part of a sheet set. AutoCAD has many palettes to organize tools and reusable drawing content.

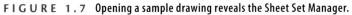

FIGURE 1.7 Opening a sample drawing reveals the Sheet Set Manager.

4. Click the Sheet Views tab along the edge of the Sheet Set Manager and observe that tabs provide a means of accessing additional interface content. In its present state, the Sheet Set Manager is a floating palette. Drag its palette bar and relocate it onscreen.

5. Click the Auto-hide toggle and watch the palette collapse to its vertical palette bar; this saves space onscreen. Hover the cursor over the palette bar and watch the whole palette reappear so that you can access its content. Now toggle Auto-hide off.

6. Click the Palette properties menu and select Anchor Left. The Sheet Set Manager palette is docked along the left edge of the user interface. You can use many options to organize the user interface to match the way you work.

7. Select Sheet Views on the tabbed interface. Double-click Detail-B under 04 – Brush Roller Sub Assy in the Manufacturing sheet set (see Figure 1.8). A new drawing appears in the drawing window.

Drag floating palettes to a secondary monitor if you have one to maximize the drawing area on your primary monitor.

Certification
Objective

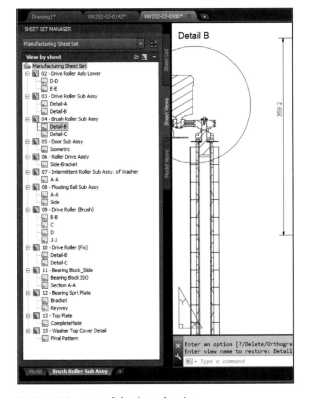

FIGURE 1.8 Selecting a drawing

8. Click the Open button in the Quick Access toolbar. Select any drawing in the Manufacturing folder and click Open. Once you open a drawing, pressing Ctrl+Home or using the GOTOSTART command brings you back to the Start tab.

The Quick Access toolbar is a convenient way to open drawings, especially when you're not using the Sheet Set Manager.

9. Move the cursor over the drawing that you opened in the previous step's tab and observe two icons. Click Model to open the drawing's model space (see Figure 1.9).

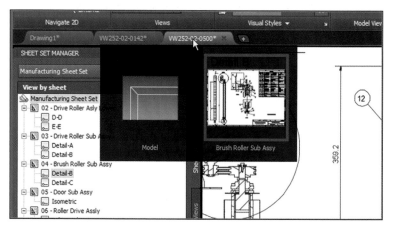

FIGURE 1.9 Accessing open drawings and their spaces

The DWG format has been updated in AutoCAD 2018, improving opening and saving performance.

10. Move the cursor over the current drawing tab and click Brush Roller Sub Assy to reopen the layout.

11. Click the Save button on the Quick Access toolbar. The drawing is saved locally on your hard drive, and a backup copy is also automatically uploaded to your Autodesk 360 account. Click the file tab of Drawing 1 and close all the sample files by typing **CLOSEALLOTHER** and pressing Enter. In addition, close the Sheet Set Manager.

AutoCAD Drawing Spaces

AutoCAD has two types of drawing spaces: paper and model. *Paper space* is a two-dimensional area analogous to, and having the dimensions of, a sheet of paper. Various sizes of "paper" can be created in individual layouts (see Chapter 13, "Working with Layouts and Annotative Objects"). *Model space*, on the other hand, is a single three-dimensional volume where everything is drawn in actual size.

Model space is typically scaled down in viewports and displayed in the paper space of layouts. Most of the drawing you will do in AutoCAD will be in model space. A drawing can have only one model space, whereas any number of layouts displaying model space through viewports can be saved in the same file.

Exercise 1.3: Control the AutoCAD Ribbon

AutoCAD has so many palettes and ribbon controls that finding the right tool for the job can seem like a job in itself. The ribbon is therefore an important feature that was introduced to AutoCAD 2010. Autodesk adopted Microsoft's ribbon standard to organize the ever-increasing number of toolbars in a single palette, making tools much easier to find. Now let's explore the various ribbon modes and identify the user interface elements of each mode (see Figure 1.10).

Certification
Objective

FIGURE 1.10   The full ribbon interface

1. Open the Customize Quick Access Toolbar menu and choose Workspace. Choose the 3D Basics workspace from the drop-down menu in the Quick Access toolbar. Close the Tool palette if it is open.

WORKSPACES

Workspaces (not to be confused with drawing spaces) are stored sets of user interface controls, which include floating palettes and the configuration of the ribbon. People use workspaces to configure the interface quickly for the task at hand.

2. Click the Minimize Ribbon button and observe that the full ribbon changes to display tabs and panel buttons (see Figure 1.11). Hover the cursor over the panel buttons. The buttons expand to reveal all the tools shown on the full ribbon.

(a)

Panel buttons

(b)

Panel titles

(c)

Ribbon tabs

FIGURE 1.11 Ribbon modes

3. Click the Minimize Ribbon button again. The panel buttons change into panel titles. Hover the cursor again over the titles to reveal each panel's tools.

4. Click the Minimize Ribbon button again. Hovering the cursor over the tabs doesn't have any effect. Click the Home tab to reveal the full panel temporarily. It disappears after you move the cursor away.

5. Verify that Cycle Through All is selected in the Minimize Ribbon button's menu and then click the Minimize Ribbon button one last time. The full ribbon interface is restored.

▶

I recommend using the full ribbon interface until you learn the location of all the tools. Use one of the minimized modes to save space onscreen.

6. Click the Edit button at the bottom of the Edit panel to reveal additional tools. Hover the mouse over one of the tools to display a tooltip that identifies the tool and describes its function. Holding the cursor a while longer reveals an image that illustrates what the tool does (see Figure 1.12).

▶

AutoCAD is based on commands. If you know the name of a command, you can type it instead of finding it in the GUI.

7. Observe that the bottom of the tooltip shown in Figure 1.12 reveals the command name (SOLIDEDIT in this case). The ribbon, menus, toolbars, and palettes are all graphical alternatives to typing commands.

8. Press and release the Alt key. Keytips appear on the ribbon (see Figure 1.13). Pressing any of the letter combinations activates that part of the GUI. Type **IN** and observe that the Insert tab is selected without moving the cursor.

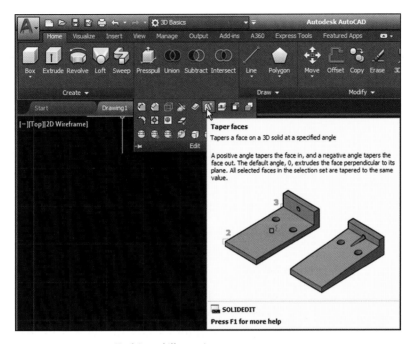

FIGURE 1.12 Tooltip and illustration

FIGURE 1.13 Keytips allow you to press keys to manipulate the ribbon with the keyboard.

If you undock the command line, it can be configured to be partially transparent and to show a number of lines of prompt history.

9. Press the F2 key to open the AutoCAD Text window. The bottom line, Command:, is called the command line. It is the active line where commands appear, regardless of whether they are typed or triggered from the GUI. The complete history of commands scrolls upward as new commands are entered. Close the AutoCAD Text window. Two lines of this command history appear at the bottom of the user interface, just above the command line that reads Type a command by default.

10. The application status bar contains a coordinate readout on the left and a number of status toggle buttons, as shown in Figure 1.14. The icons that have arrows adjacent to them open menus. Toggle off all the status bar toggles so that no icons are highlighted in blue. Open the customization menu by clicking the rightmost icon on the status bar and deselect Clean Screen, Coordinates, Isometric Drafting, and Annotation Monitor from the context menu that appears. You can control which buttons appear on the status bar using this menu.

Coordinate readout

Status toggles   Customization menu

FIGURE 1.14   Status bar

11. Type **POL** and observe how the AutoComplete feature highlights commands in alphabetical order as you type (see Figure 1.15). Use the arrow keys to move up or down through the list; press Enter when you find the command for which you are looking, or click its name in the list instead of typing the entire word.

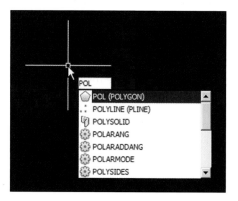

FIGURE 1.15   Command line's AutoComplete feature

12. Take a look at the InfoCenter at the top right of the screen (see Figure 1.16). Click in the search box and type **solid**.

Autodesk Exchange Apps

Search box   Search button   Help

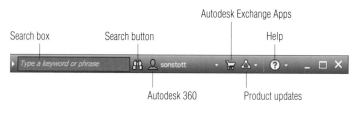

Autodesk 360   Product updates

FIGURE 1.16   InfoCenter

13. Click the binoculars icon on the right of the search field, and the AutoCAD Help dialog box appears. Multiple online books are searched, and relevant results appear in the left panel. The description of the SOLID command appears in the right panel.

14. Click the Help button on the right edge of the InfoCenter. The Help Table Of Contents page opens. All AutoCAD documentation is accessible through this interface.

15. Open the Quick Access toolbar's workspace drop-down and select Drafting & Annotation to restore the ribbon to its original configuration.

Set Drawing Units

Before you start drawing, it's important to decide what one drawing unit represents in the real world. Architects in the United States typically equate one drawing unit with 1 inch in AutoCAD. You need to choose a unit type that matches your country's industry standard.

Architectural   Most American architects will choose this type, which displays units in feet and inches. For example, 12', 6 ½" is typed as **12'6-1/2**. The hyphen is used to separate inches from fractions of an inch rather than feet from inches.

Decimal   Metric users should select this type. One decimal unit can be equal to 1 millimeter, 1 centimeter, or any metric unit that you decide.

Engineering   Like the Architectural type, engineering units feature feet and inches, but the inches are represented in decimal form—for example, 126.500 feet.

Fractional   American woodworkers often prefer to set AutoCAD drawings in fractional units of inches because that is how their work is normally reckoned. For example, 12', 6 ½" reads 150- ½" in fractional units.

Scientific   In scientific units, 12.000E+06 is broken down into two parts: 12.000 indicates 12 accurate to a precision of three decimal places, and E+06 indicates the exponential function raised to the sixth power, or $10 \times 10 \times 10 \times 10 \times 10 \times 10$, bringing the total in this example up to 12 million.

The AutoCAD Exchange website contains the Apps store, where you can access free and paid apps that add functionality to AutoCAD.

Exercise 1.4: Set the AutoCAD Drawing Units

Let's set the AutoCAD drawing units.

Certification
Objective

1. Click the New button on the Quick Access toolbar. Click the arrow button next to the Open button in the Select Template dialog box and choose Open With No Template – Imperial (see Figure 1.17).

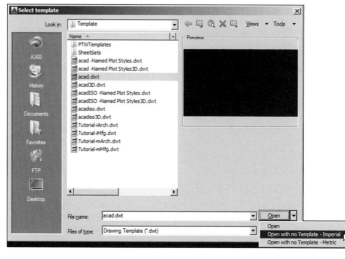

> You can press Enter or the spacebar to enter commands (command names never have spaces). Commands and their options can be typed in uppercase or lowercase.

FIGURE 1.17   Opening a drawing with no template

2. Type UN and press Enter to bring up the Drawing Units dialog box (see Figure 1.18). UN is the command alias (abbreviation) of the UNITS command. Most commands have aliases that minimize typing.

FIGURE 1.18   Setting drawing units

3. Select Architectural from the Type drop-down menu. I'm using Architectural in this book, but you should select the unit type that fits your industry when working professionally. Metric users should select Decimal length units.

4. Click the Length Precision drop-down menu and select 1/8″ (or 0.0 for metric). Set Angle Type to Decimal Degrees and Angle Precision to 0.0.

5. Click the Insertion Scale drop-down menu and select Inches (or Centimeters for metric). Click OK to close the Drawing Units dialog box.

AutoCAD 2018 has US Survey Feet as an option for insertion scale units.

◀

Now You Know

In this chapter, you learned how to sign in to Autodesk 360, open and save sample drawings, identify user interface elements, access model space and paper space, change workspaces, control the appearance of the ribbon, type commands using AutoComplete, identify commands in the graphical user interface, and set the drawing units.

CHAPTER 2

Gaining Basic Drawing Skills

This chapter teaches you how to draw basic shapes, such as lines, rectangles, circles, arcs, and polygons. You will learn how to correct mistakes, navigate two-dimensional space, and use coordinate systems to draw accurately. In addition, you'll perform your first editing tasks by joining existing lines in straight, rounded, or angled intersections.

In this chapter, you'll learn to do the following:

▶ **Navigate 2D drawings**

▶ **Draw lines and rectangles**

▶ **Cancel, erase, and undo**

▶ **Use coordinate systems**

▶ **Draw circles, arcs, and polygons**

▶ **Use Fillet and Chamfer**

Navigate 2D Drawings

Unlike in image-editing programs where zooming in results in blurry, pixelated images, you can zoom in forever in the AutoCAD® program without suffering any loss of quality. However, to avoid getting lost in space, you'll need to learn how to navigate with a variety of pan and zoom tools that you'll explore here.

Exercise 2.1: Navigate a Drawing

Begin by opening the file Ex02.1-start.dwg (see Figure 2.1), which is available for download from the book's web page at www.sybex.com/go/autocad2018essentials.

With system variables, 1 means on, and 0 means off.

1. Select the Drafting & Annotation workspace. If you don't see the Navigation bar, type **NAVBARDISPLAY** and press Enter. Type **1** and press Enter. The Navigation bar appears on the right side of the user interface (see Figure 2.1).

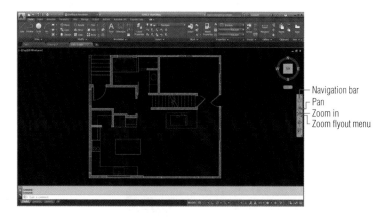

Navigation bar
Pan
Zoom in
Zoom flyout menu

FIGURE 2.1   House sample file

Certification Objective

Instead of changing the size of objects, Zoom merely increases the magnification of objects on the canvas. In is an option of the ZOOM command.

2. Click the arrow under the Zoom Extents button on the Navigation bar to open the Zoom flyout menu and select Zoom In. The Zoom In button replaces the original button (which was Zoom Extents) on the Navigation bar. The last-used tool appears on top. Click the Zoom In icon again, and the view is magnified by another factor of 2.

3. Click Pan in the Navigation bar, drag the mouse from left to right, and then press Enter to end the command.

4. For an alternative method, press and hold the mouse wheel and pan the drawing to center the refrigerator on the canvas (as shown in Figure 2.2).

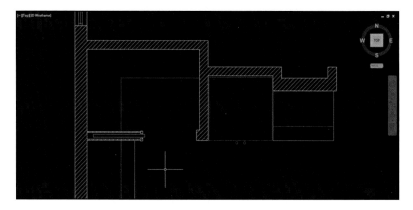

FIGURE 2.2   Navigating to focus on the refrigerator

5. Type **Z** (for the ZOOM command) and press Enter twice to activate the default option of Real Time. Drag up in the document window to zoom in until the refrigerator fills the screen and then press Esc.

6. Pan to the lower-left corner of the refrigerator by right-clicking, choosing Pan from the context menu, and dragging in the canvas. Press Esc to end the command.

7. Select Zoom Window from the Navigate panel's Zoom flyout. Click points A and B, as shown in Figure 2.3. The area of the rectangle you draw is magnified to fill the canvas.

> There are many methods for executing commands in AutoCAD so that you can find your favorite ways of working and become more efficient.

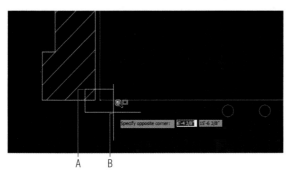

FIGURE 2.3 Zooming into a window

8. Roll the mouse wheel forward to zoom in further and drag the mouse wheel if necessary to reveal the object in the lower-left corner of the refrigerator (see Figure 2.4).

> It's not good practice to create infinitesimally small text objects; this was done only to demonstrate the unlimited zoom capability of AutoCAD.

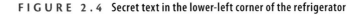

FIGURE 2.4 Secret text in the lower-left corner of the refrigerator

9. Type **E** (for the ERASE command) and press Enter. Click the "Secret text" object and press Enter.

10. Type **Z** and press the spacebar. Type **P** and press Enter to execute Zoom Previous. Press Enter again to repeat the previous command (ZOOM), type **P**, and press Enter again. Repeat this process until you can see the entire refrigerator.

COMMAND-LINE OPTIONS

Most commands have options appearing on the command line when they are invoked. You can choose an option by typing its blue letter and pressing Enter, by clicking the highlighted option on the command line itself, or by pressing the down-arrow key and selecting the option from a dynamic input menu in the drawing window.

The default option is indicated in angled brackets, which in the case of the ZOOM command is real time. You initiate the default option by either clicking Enter or pressing the spacebar.

Column sort order is persistent in AutoCAD 2018, so if you sort by date, it remembers the next time you use Open or Save.

11. To see everything that has been drawn, you can use the Extents option of the ZOOM command or, better yet, use this special shortcut: Double-click the mouse wheel. Position the cursor over the bathroom sink and roll the mouse wheel forward to zoom in. Notice that the view stays centered on the sink without your having to pan (see Figure 2.5). Drag the mouse wheel to make slight panning adjustments if necessary to center the target object onscreen.

12. Practice zooming into the kitchen sink, the stove, and the bathtub using the various methods shown in this section. Save your work. Your model should now resemble Ex02.1-end.dwg, which is available among this chapter's companion files.

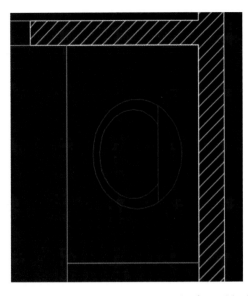

FIGURE 2.5 Directing navigation by positioning the cursor over the bathroom sink while zooming

Draw Lines and Rectangles

The drawing commands you'll probably use the most in AutoCAD are LINE and RECTANGLE. You will begin by drawing some lines and rectangles without worrying yet about entering measurements.

Exercise 2.2: Draw Lines

Lines are the backbone of AutoCAD. Let's begin drawing lines. To start, open the file Ex02.2-start.dwg from this chapter's companion files.

1. Press **Z** and Enter twice to accept the command's default option. Position the cursor over the lower-right portion of the floor plan and drag upward to zoom so that the empty space of the living room fills the canvas.

2. Turn off all status toggles in the application status bar if they are not off already. Status toggles are highlighted in blue when they are on and appear in gray when they are off (see Figure 2.6). The exception to this rule is Graphics Performance, which is always blue if your graphics card's hardware acceleration is active. Open the Customization menu (last icon on the right) and toggle off Graphics Performance.

> You will use some of the status toggles in Chapter 3, "Using Drawing Aids."

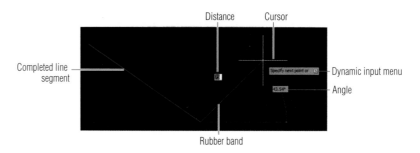

FIGURE 2.6   All status toggles turned off

3. Type **L** (for LINE) and press Enter. Click two arbitrary points to define a line object (see Figure 2.7).

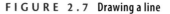

FIGURE 2.7   Drawing a line

4. Click another point to draw your second segment. The prompt on the command line reads as follows:

   ```
   LINE Specify next point or [Undo]:
   ```

   Press the down-arrow key and then click Undo in the dynamic menu that appears near the cursor. The last point you clicked is undone, but the rubber band continues to be connected to the cursor, indicating that you can keep drawing lines.

5. Click two more points and then type **C** (for the Close option) and press Enter to create a closing segment between the first and last points. The Close option automatically terminates the LINE command.

6. Press the spacebar (or Enter) to repeat the last command (LINE). Click two arbitrary points to create a single line segment. Right-click to open the context menu and then select Enter with a left-click to complete the LINE command.

7. Open the Application menu and click the Options button at the bottom. Click the User Preferences tab in the Options dialog box that appears. Under the Windows Standard Behavior section, select Right-Click Customization and then, in the new dialog box, select Turn On Time-Sensitive Right-Click (see Figure 2.8). Click Apply & Close and then click OK in the Options dialog box.

Time-Sensitive Right-Click is just that: an option. Try it to see whether you find drawing lines in this way more efficient.

Right-Click Customization

☑ Turn on time-sensitive right-click:
    Quick click for ENTER
    Longer click to display Shortcut Menu
    Longer click duration: 250   milliseconds

Default Mode
If no objects are selected, right-click means
    ○ Repeat Last Command
    ● Shortcut Menu

Edit Mode
If one or more objects are selected, right-click means
    ○ Repeat Last Command
    ● Shortcut Menu

Command Mode
If a command is in progress, right-click means
    ○ ENTER
    ○ Shortcut Menu: always enabled
    ● Shortcut Menu: enabled when command options are present

[Apply & Close]   [Cancel]   [Help]

FIGURE 2.8   Turning on Time-Sensitive Right-Click for more efficient drawing

8. Select the Home tab in the ribbon, and click the Line tool in the Draw panel. Click two points, and draw another line. Right-click quickly to terminate the LINE command.

9. Right-click again to repeat the last command, and then click two points on the canvas. Next, slowly right-click (holding down the right mouse button for longer than 250 milliseconds, to be precise), and you'll see the context menu shown in Figure 2.9. Left-click the word *Enter* in this menu to complete the LINE command.

Enter
Cancel
Recent Input   ▸

Undo

Snap Overrides   ▸

🖑 Pan
🔍 Zoom
Ⓢ SteeringWheels

▤ QuickCalc

FIGURE 2.9   This context menu appears when you hold down the right mouse button longer than 250 milliseconds.

10. Save your work. Your model should now resemble Ex02.2-end.dwg, which is available among this chapter's companion files.

Exercise 2.3: Draw Rectangles

Line segments are treated as individual objects, whereas the four line segments comprising a rectangle are treated as a single entity. Although rectangles can obviously be drawn with the LINE command, specialized commands such as RECTANG are more efficient for constructing specific shapes, and they offer more options. Let's experiment now with this feature. To begin, open the file Ex02 .3-start.dwg from the Chapter 2 companion files.

Certification
Objective

1. Click the Rectangle tool in the Draw panel and then click two oppo-site corner points on the canvas. Unlike the LINE command, this command automatically terminates when the rectangle is drawn.

2. Press Enter to repeat the last command. This time pay attention to the prompts in the Command window.

> Pay close attention to the prompts in the Command window to see what options are available and what specific input is requested at each step.

   ```
   RECTANG Specify first corner point or
   [Chamfer Elevation Fillet Thickness Width]:
   ```

   You have the opportunity to use any of the options listed in the square brackets before you even begin drawing the rectangle. However, in this case you will use the default option, which comes before the word or.

3. Click the first corner point in the document window. A new prompt appears.

   ```
   RECTANG Specify other corner point or
   [Area Dimensions Rotation]:
   ```

   At this point a new command prompt shows another default option before the word or, as well as a few options in square brackets. You will again take the default option in this prompt, which is to specify the other corner point.

4. Click the other corner point, and the rectangle is drawn. In addition, the command is automatically terminated.

> Do not type " when using Imperial units or cm when using metric units; input numbers only. It is acceptable to input the foot symbol (') when using Architectural units.

5. Type **REC** (for RECTANG) and press the spacebar. Type F and press Enter to execute the Fillet option. The command prompt reads as follows:

   ```
   Specify fillet radius for rectangles <0'-0" >:
   ```

6. Type 2 (or 5 for metric) and press Enter.

7. Click two points to draw the rectangle. The result has filleted corners (see Figure 2.10).

First click

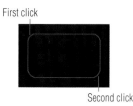

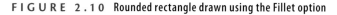

Second click

FIGURE 2.10   Rounded rectangle drawn using the Fillet option

8. Draw another rectangle and observe that it also has rounded corners. Some options such as the fillet radius are sticky; they stay the same until you change them. Zero out the Fillet option by pressing the spacebar, typing F, pressing Enter, typing 0, and pressing Enter again. Click two points to draw a sharp-edged rectangle.

9. Save your work. Your model should now resemble Ex02.3-end.dwg, which is available among this chapter's companion files.

DRAWING RECOVERY MANAGER

Occasionally something goes wrong with AutoCAD and it crashes. The next time you launch AutoCAD, the Drawing Recovery Manager will automatically appear, allowing you to recover drawings that were open (and possibly corrupted) when the program unexpectedly came to a halt. You can recover damaged files at any time with the RECOVER command.

Cancel, Erase, and Undo

Making mistakes in AutoCAD is entirely acceptable if you know how to cancel, erase, or undo what you've done wrong.

Exercise 2.4: Correct Mistakes

This exercise will show you how to cancel, erase, and undo. To begin, open the file Ex02.4-start.dwg from this chapter's companion files.

1. Type L and press Enter. Click two points on the canvas and then press the Esc key; the LINE command is terminated, but the single

segment you just created remains. The Esc key will get you out of any running command or dialog box.

Certification
Objective

2. Type E and press the spacebar. Click the line created in step 1 and then right-click; the segment is erased.

3. Click the Line tool in the Draw panel, click four points on the canvas (making three segments), and then right-click to finish the LINE command.

4. Click each of the segments, one at a time. Blue grips appear on the lines' endpoints and midpoints (see Figure 2.11). Grips are used for editing, and you'll learn more about them in Chapter 4, "Editing Entities." In the meantime, it's helpful to know that if you press the Delete key, the lines are gone.

The virtually unlimited number of undo and redo actions in AutoCAD means that it is a forgiving program. However, you can't undo past the point when you opened an existing file; in other words, undo and redo actions are stored not in the file but rather in volatile random access memory (RAM).

FIGURE 2.11 Selecting lines before deleting them

5. Click the Undo arrow on the Quick Access toolbar. The lines you deleted in step 4 reappear.

6. Click the Redo button, and the lines disappear again.

7. Undo again and, without issuing any command, click two points around the same three lines to create a selection window completely surrounding them. Press the Delete key to erase the selected objects.

8. Click the Undo button's menu arrow. A list of all the commands you've issued in this session appears. Select Erase from the menu to undo the previous step.

9. Save your work. Your model should now resemble Ex02.4-end.dwg, which is available among this chapter's companion files.

Use Coordinate Systems

AutoCAD uses the same Euclidean space you learned about in geometry class, but don't panic—I don't expect you to remember any theorems! You can draw objects in Euclidean space using the following coordinate systems: Cartesian, polar, cylindrical, and spherical. (The last two are rarely used, so they won't be covered in this book.)

Cartesian coordinates are useful for drawing rectangles with specific length and width measurements. Polar coordinates are used most often for drawing lines with specific lengths and angles, with respect to horizontal. Once you learn coordinate system syntax, you can use the systems interchangeably to draw accurately in any context.

In the Cartesian system, every point is defined by three values, expressed in terms of distances along the x-, y-, and z-axes. In two-dimensional drawings, the z-coordinate value of all objects is 0, so objects are expressed solely in terms of x- and y-coordinates (see Figure 2.12).

Certification Objective

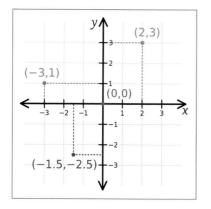

FIGURE 2.12 Cartesian two-dimensional coordinates

Exercise 2.5: Use Absolute Coordinates

Coordinates can be absolute or relative, no matter which coordinate system is used. Let's first focus on drawing a line using absolute coordinates. To begin, open the file Ex02.5-start.dwg from this chapter's companion files.

1. Click the Line tool on the Draw panel. The prompt in the Command window reads as follows:

   Certification Objective

   ```
   LINE Specify first point:
   ```

   Type **0,0** and press Enter. The origin point of Euclidean space has coordinates 0 in x and 0 in y, which is written as 0,0.

2. Now the prompt in the Command window reads as follows:

   `LINE Specify next point or [Undo]:`

   Type **3',0** (or **90,0** for metric) and press Enter. Right-click to finish the `LINE` command.

3. Save your work. Your model should now resemble `Ex02.5-end.dwg`, which is available among this chapter's companion files.

Exercise 2.6: Use Relative Coordinates

Calculating where every object is in relation to the origin point (which is what absolute coordinates require) would be far too cumbersome in practice. Therefore, relative coordinates are used more frequently. Let's explore how to use them. To begin, open the file `Ex02.6-start.dwg` from this chapter's companion files.

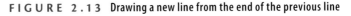

Certification
Objective

The @ symbol tells AutoCAD to consider the previous point as the origin point, relatively speaking.

You will use the last point entered as the first point in a new line. A rubber band connects the right end of the horizontal line to the cursor.

1. Click the Line tool on the Draw panel. Click an arbitrary point in the middle of the living room. The coordinates of the point you clicked are unknown; thankfully, with relative coordinates you won't ever need to find out what they are.

2. Type **@3',0** (or **@90,0** for metric) and press Enter twice.

3. Press Enter to repeat the last command. You'll see this prompt:

   `LINE Specify first point:`

4. Right-click in the drawing canvas and hold (for longer than 250 milliseconds) to open the context menu. Select the first coordinate value from the Recent Input menu (see Figure 2.13).

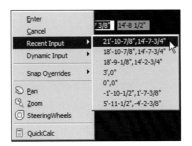

FIGURE 2.13 Drawing a new line from the end of the previous line

5. Type **@0,6'** (or **@0,180** for metric) and press Enter. A line measuring 6' (or 1.8m) is drawn vertically along the y-axis.

6. Type @-3',0 (or @-90,0 for metric) and press Enter. Type @0,-6' (or @0,-180 for metric) and press Enter twice to complete a rectangle.

7. Click the Rectangle tool on the Draw panel and then click an arbitrary point at the bottom of the living room. The prompt reads as follows:

```
RECTANG Specify other corner point or
[Area Dimensions Rotation]:
```

8. Type @3',6' (or @90,180 for metric) and press Enter. The same rectangle that you more laboriously drew with lines is already done.

9. Save your work. Your model should now resemble Ex02.6-end.dwg, which is available among this chapter's companion files.

Exercise 2.7: Use Polar Coordinates

Polar coordinates are another useful way of measuring Euclidean space. In polar coordinates, points are located using two measurements: the distance from the origin point and the angle from zero degrees (see Figure 2.14). East is the default direction of zero degrees.

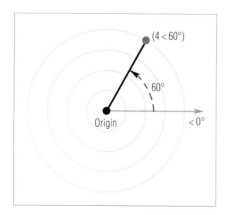

FIGURE 2.14 Polar coordinates

Let's explore how to use polar coordinates. To begin, open the file Ex02 .7-start.dwg from the Chapter 2 companion files.

1. Click the Line tool on the Draw panel. Click an arbitrary first point in the living room; then type @3'<45 (or @90<45 for metric) and press Enter to end the LINE command.

It is very efficient to use RECTANG with Cartesian coordinates.

By default, zero degrees is toward the east or right side of the canvas. In addition, positive angles are typically measured counterclockwise from east. These defaults can be set in the UNITS command.

The < or less than symbol (hold Shift and press the comma key) represents angular measure in AutoCAD. Think of the < symbol as a graphic representation of an angle.

2. Press Enter to repeat the last command. Click an arbitrary first point, move the cursor up and to the left, type 3' (or 90 for metric), and press Enter twice. A 3' (or 90 for metric) line is drawn at an arbitrary angle.

SPECIFYING ANGLES WITH THE CURSOR

Direct distance entry is the relative coordinate method of using the cursor to determine an angle, rather than typing in a specific number of degrees following the < symbol. Direct distance entry is most efficiently used with Ortho and Polar modes, which you'll learn about in Chapter 3, "Using Drawing Aids."

3. Press L and then press the spacebar. Click an arbitrary first point, type @4'<180 (or @120<180 for metric), and press Enter. The line is drawn to the left from the first point because 180 degrees is the same direction as angle zero but leads in the opposite direction.

4. Type @3'<–90 (or @90<–90 for metric) and press Enter. Negative angles are measured clockwise from angle zero by default. Press C and then Enter to close the 3:4:5 triangle you've just drawn.

5. Type **UCSICON** and press Enter. *UCS* stands for *user coordinate system*. You, the user, can change the coordinate system's orientation. Type on and press Enter. An icon indicating the directions of the positive x- and y-axes is displayed in the lower-left corner of the canvas (see Figure 2.15).

The AutoCAD LT® program has only one coordinate system that cannot be changed. AutoCAD LT users can skip ahead to the next section.

FIGURE 2.15 UCS icon in the default orientation

6. Type **UCS** and press Enter. The prompt in the Command window reads as follows:

```
UCS Specify origin of UCS or [Face Named Object
Previous View World X Y Z ZAxis] <World>:
```

There is much you can do with the UCS, but here you will simply rotate the UCS about its z-axis (the axis coming out of the screen). Type **Z** and press Enter.

7. Type **90** and press Enter to rotate the coordinate system. Observe that the UCS icon has changed to reflect the new orientation (see Figure 2.16).

FIGURE 2.16 Rotating the UCS about its z-axis

8. Type **PLAN** and press Enter. The prompt in the Command window reads as follows:

    ```
    PLAN Enter an option [Current ucs Ucs World] <Current>:
    ```

    The option in the angled brackets, <Current>, is what you want, so press Enter to make this selection. The house is reoriented with respect to the current UCS (see Figure 2.17).

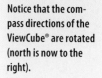

Notice that the compass directions of the ViewCube® are rotated (north is now to the right).

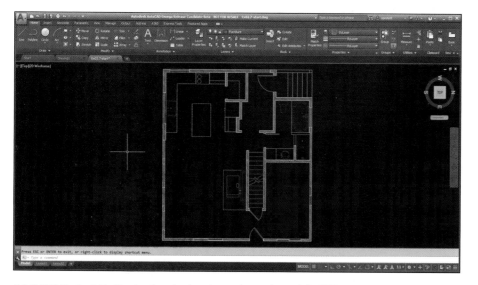

FIGURE 2.17 Reorienting the drawing to the xy plane of the UCS

ROTATING THE PLAN TO MATCH THE UCS

User coordinate systems are usually associated with 3D modeling, but there is one transformation especially useful for 2D drafting: rotation around the z-axis. If you are drawing a building wing or mechanical part that is at an angle with respect to the horizontal plane (especially when the angle isn't an increment of 90 degrees), try rotating the UCS's z-axis and then use the PLAN command to reorient the drawing to the new horizontal.

9. Click the Line tool on the Draw panel. Click an arbitrary first point in the living room, type @3'<45 (or @90<45 for metric), and press Enter twice to end the LINE command. The new line has a different orientation with respect to the original line you drew in step 1 (see Figure 2.18).

Line drawn in step 9   Line drawn in step 1

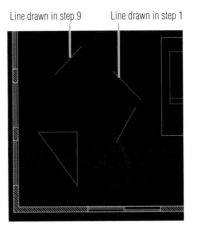

Observe that north is up again in the ViewCube.

F I G U R E   2 . 1 8   Angles are relative to the coordinate system in which they are drawn. Both lines were drawn at a 45-degree angle but in different coordinate systems.

10. To restore the current coordinate system to its original state, called the *world coordinate system* (*WCS*), type **UCS** and press Enter twice. Then type **PLAN** and press Enter twice more. The plan is oriented to the WCS as it was initially.

11. Save your work. Your model should now resemble Ex02.7-end.dwg, which is available among this chapter's companion files.

Draw Circles, Arcs, and Polygons

Arcs are sections of circles. Polygons are regular figures made of straight segments such as a triangle, square, pentagon, or hexagon. A polygon with a large number of segments may look like a circle but is fundamentally different.

There are many options for creating circles, arcs, and polygons. AutoCAD provides these options to make it easier to create accurate shapes based on all the types of geometric situations that typically arise in drawings.

Exercise 2.8: Create Circles

Let's draw some circles on the kitchen stove to represent the burners. To begin, open the file Ex02.8-start.dwg from this chapter's companion files.

1. Zoom into the stove in the kitchen. Two of the burner circles are missing, and you will draw them.

2. On the Home tab, take a look at the Layer drop-down menu in the Layers panel and observe that Furniture is the current layer (because you see its name without having to open the drop-down). Open the Layer drop-down menu and select Equipment as the current layer (see Figure 2.19).

> Drawn objects appear on whichever layer is current. Think of layers as invisible sheets of tracing paper that you draw on. You'll learn more about layers in Chapter 6, "Controlling Object Visibility and Appearance."

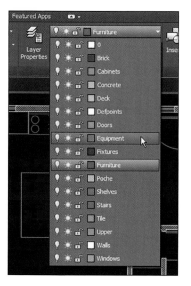

F I G U R E   2 . 1 9   Making the Equipment layer current

3. You will use preexisting points as guides in drawing the burners. However, the points are difficult to see right now because they are represented as single pixels. Expand the Utilities panel on the Home tab and select Point Style or type **PTYPE** and press Enter. In the Point Style dialog box, select the X icon and click OK (see Figure 2.20).

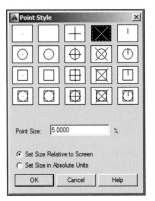

Drawing objects by eye is not good enough in AutoCAD. Always use object snaps to connect objects precisely.

F I G U R E   2 . 2 0   Changing the point style so that points are more visible

Certification
Objective

4. Click the Circle tool on the Draw panel. Before you click a center point, hold down Shift and right-click to open the Object Snap context menu.

5. Select Node from the context menu (Figure 2.21), and then click point A (shown in Figure 2.22). The prompt in the Command window reads as follows:

Note that typing the inch symbol is unnecessary. Never type m, cm, or mm to represent metric units.

```
CIRCLE Specify radius of circle or [Diameter] <0f-0g>:
```

Type 3 (or 8 for metric) and press Enter to create a circle with a radius of 3" (or 8 for metric).

6. Right-click to repeat the last command. The prompt in the Command window reads as follows:

```
CIRCLE Specify center point for circle or
[3P 2P Ttr (tan tan radius)]:
```

Object snaps listed in the context menu must be selected each time they are used. You will learn how to set up running object snaps in Chapter 3.

Type **2P** to indicate the two-point option and press Enter. Hold down Shift and right-click to open the Object Snap context menu. Select Node and then click point B (shown in Figure 2.22).

7. Hold Shift again, right-click, and choose Node. Click point C (shown in Figure 2.22), and the CIRCLE command is completed.

FIGURE 2.21   Object Snap context menu

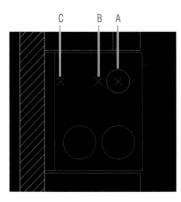

FIGURE 2.22   Drawing a circle by locating its center using node snap

8. Click the arrow under the Circle tool in the Draw panel and select 3-Point. Shift+right-click and select Tangent. Click the circle you drew in the previous step.

9. Hold Shift, right-click again, and type **G**. Notice that this letter is underlined in the word *Tangent* in the context menu (refer to Figure 2.21). Click the circle on the bottom left.

10. Type **TAN**, press Enter to invoke the Tangent object snap, and click the circle on the lower right. You can type the first three letters of any object snap as an alternative to using the context menu. AutoCAD draws a circle precisely tangent to the three others (see Figure 2.23).

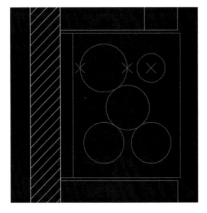

FIGURE 2.23 Drawing circles with various options

11. Erase all three point objects and the last circle you drew to leave the four burners of the stove.

12. Save your work. Your model should now resemble Ex02.8-end.dwg, which is available among this chapter's companion files.

Exercise 2.9: Create Arcs

Arcs have more options than circles because of the complexities of the geometric situations in which arcs can be drawn. In the next set of steps, you will use one such arc option to draw a door swing. To begin, open the file Ex02.9-start.dwg from this chapter's companion files.

1. Pan and zoom into the bathroom by dragging and rotating the mouse wheel.

2. Select Doors from the Layer drop-down menu in the Layers panel.

Certification Objective

3. Click the Arc tool's drop-down flyout menu in the Draw panel, which is indicated by the arrow under the word Arc. Select Center, Start, End. This is the sequence in which information must be entered.

4. Type **INT**, press Enter to invoke the Intersection object snap, and click the center point A shown in Figure 2.24.

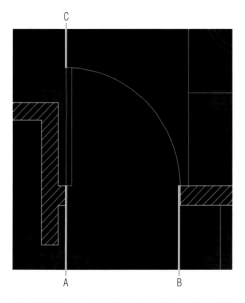

FIGURE 2.24 Drawing a door swing with an arc option

5. Hold Shift and right-click. Select Endpoint from the context menu and click the start point B (shown in Figure 2.24).

6. Type **END**, press Enter, and click the arc endpoint C (shown in Figure 2.24). The arc appears, and the command is completed.

7. Save your work. Your model should now resemble Ex02.9-end.dwg, which is available among this chapter's companion files.

CONTROLLING ARC AND CIRCLE SMOOTHNESS

Arcs and circles are defined with perfect curvature in AutoCAD, but sometimes they appear blocky on the screen. The system variable VIEWRES controls how smoothly arcs and circles are drawn onscreen. Adjust this on the View tab under the Visual Style panel's expansion menu. Set the resolution to the maximum VIEWRES value by typing **VIEWRES**, pressing Enter twice, typing **20000**, and pressing Enter again. Type **REGEN** and press Enter to make this change take effect on the screen.

AutoCAD automatically renders high-quality representations of circles, arcs, ellipses, and elliptical arcs on systems with graphics cards supporting DirectX 11, regardless of the drawing's VIEWRES setting. Type **GRAPHICSCONFIG** and

(Continues)

CONTROLLING ARC AND CIRCLE SMOOTHNESS   *(Continued)*

press Enter to see whether your system supports this feature, which is called High Quality Geometry (for capable devices) in the Graphics Performance dialog box.

Graphics Performance

Hardware Setup

Video Card: NVIDIA GeForce GT 750M

Driver Version: 9.18.13.4725   Virtual Device: DirectX 11

Effects Settings

Hardware Acceleration   On

Disable hardware acceleration only if you are experiencing graphics issues or have an incompatible video card.

☑ **High quality geometry (for capable devices)**
Renders curves and lineweights in high quality and improves anti-aliasing performance in 2D wireframe.

☑ **Smooth line display**
Removes the jagged effect on the display of diagonal lines and curved edges in 2D wireframe.

☑ **Advanced material effects**
Increases details and realism of certain materials applied to 3D surfaces.

☑ **Full shadow display**
Displays 3D object shadows in the viewport.

☑ **Per-pixel lighting (Phong)**
Increases details and realism when working with 3D objects and lighting effects.

☑ **Uncompressed textures**
Uses more video memory to display better quality textures.

Restore Defaults   Tuner Log   OK   Cancel   Help

Exercise 2.10: Draw Polygons

When you want to draw triangles, squares, pentagons, or any figure having equally sized edges, use the POLYGON command. You can draw these shapes inside or outside a circle or specify the edge length, as shown in the following steps. To begin, open the file Ex02.10-start.dwg from the Chapter 2 companion files.

1. Select the Home tab if it's not already active. Make the Furniture layer current by selecting it from the Layer drop-down menu in the Layers panel.

2. Zoom into the living room.

3. Click the Rectangle tool's drop-down flyout and select the Polygon tool. The prompt in the Command window reads as follows:

```
POLYGON Enter number of sides <5>:
```

4. Type 4 and press Enter to draw a square.

5. The command prompt now reads as follows:

```
POLYGON Specify center of polygon or [Edge]:
```

Type E and press Enter to specify an edge length and direction. Click a point somewhere in the living room as the first endpoint of the edge, type @2'<0 (or @60<0 for metric), and press Enter to specify the second endpoint of the edge relative to the first one, using polar coordinates in this case. A 2' (or 60 in metric) square appears.

6. Press Enter to repeat the last command, type 6, and press Enter to draw a hexagon. Click a point in the living room where you want to center the hexagon. The prompt now reads as follows:

```
POLYGON Enter an option [Inscribed in circle
Circumscribed about circle] <I>:
```

7. Press Enter to accept the default Inscribed In Circle option.

8. Type 1' (or 30 for metric) as the radius of the circle and press Enter. A hexagon fitting inside a 1' (or 30 in metric) radius circle appears (see Figure 2.25).

FIGURE 2.25 Drawing polygons

9. Save your work. Your model should now resemble Ex02.10-end.dwg, which is available among this chapter's companion files.

Use Fillet and Chamfer

Fillet and Chamfer are tools that create transitions between objects. Fillet creates arcs, and Chamfer creates lines. Fillet is most commonly used for a purpose for which it probably wasn't designed—joining separate lines so that they intersect at their endpoints, without creating arcs at all.

Exercise 2.11: Join Nonparallel Lines

Fillet and Chamfer can be used to join lines that are crossing as well as lines that don't meet. Chamfer doesn't work on parallel lines at all, but Fillet will create a half-circle connecting the endpoints of parallel lines, regardless of the fillet radius. Let's explore the FILLET and CHAMFER commands. To begin, open the file Ex02.11-start.dwg from this chapter's companion files.

1. Position the cursor on the canvas and type **CHA** (for CHAMFER) or select Chamfer under the Fillet icon in the Modify panel. Press Enter and then press the down-arrow key to expand the command's options.

> If you do not see prompts onscreen, then press the F12 key to toggle on *dynamic input*.

2. Press the down-arrow key three more times and press Enter to select the Distance option in the Dynamic Input display (see Figure 2.26). Type **1'** (or **30** for metric) and press Enter twice to input equal first and second distances, which are 1' (or 30 for metric) each.

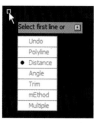

> Fillet and chamfer previewing works only if When A Command Is Active is selected on the Selection tab of the Options dialog box (OPTIONS command). This option should be selected by default.

FIGURE 2.26 Displaying a command-line option on the canvas with dynamic input

3. Click one line and then hover the cursor over the second line; you'll see a preview of the chamfer that will be created. Click the second line to perform the chamfer and complete the command. (The chamfer is shown in the middle of Figure 2.27.)

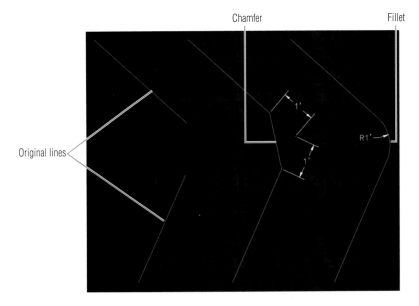

Chamfer   Fillet

Original lines

FIGURE 2.27 Chamfered and filleted lines

4. Type F and press Enter to execute the FILLET command. Press the down-arrow key and choose Radius from the Dynamic Input display. Type 1' (or 30 for metric) and press Enter.

5. Click the first line and then position the cursor over the second line; the fillet preview shows onscreen. Click the second line to commit to that particular radius. (A fillet is shown at the right of Figure 2.27.)

6. Save your work. Your model should now resemble Ex02.11-end .dwg, which is available among this chapter's companion files.

Certification
Objective

◄

Fillet radius and cham-
fer distances are sticky;
they stay the same
until you change them.

Exercise 2.12: Join Crossed Lines with Fillet

When lines cross, there are multiple fillet and chamfer possibilities on different sides of the intersection. In the case of crossing lines, you must select the lines on the portions that you want to keep, as shown in these steps. To begin, open the file Ex02.12-start.dwg from this chapter's companion files.

1. Type F and press Enter. Press the down-arrow key to access the Dynamic Input display and select Radius. Type 0 and press Enter. Now Fillet will not create an arc at all.

2. Click the points A and B, as shown in Figure 2.28. The lines are joined at their endpoints, and the remaining portions of the lines beyond their intersection point are trimmed away.

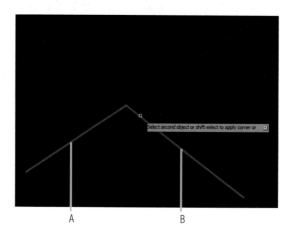

A   B

FIGURE 2.28   Filleting lines with a zero radius joins them together precisely.

3. Save your work. Your model should now resemble Ex02.12-end.dwg, which is available among this chapter's companion files.

Now You Know

In this chapter, you learned how to pan and zoom around 2D drawings and draw lines, rectangles, circles, arcs, and polygons. You have filleted and chamfered sets of lines, used absolute and relative coordinate systems, and created objects using specific measurements. In addition, you now know how to cancel, erase, and undo, as well as how to correct your mistakes.

CHAPTER 3

Using Drawing Aids

The drawing aids in the AutoCAD® program are like the triangles, compasses, and engineering scales of traditional drafting. Drawing aids are essential modes and methods of entering data that, once mastered, allow you to create measured drawings with ease. I highly recommend learning all of the drawing aids because they will make you a more productive draftsperson. Most drawing aids can be toggled on or off from the application status bar. Additional settings and dialog boxes are accessible by right-clicking the individual status bar toggles.

In this chapter, you'll learn to do the following:

▶ **Use Grid and Snap**

▶ **Employ Ortho and Polar Tracking**

▶ **Use PolarSnap**

▶ **Select running object snaps**

▶ **Harness the From snap**

▶ **Apply object snap tracking**

Use Grid and Snap

Certification
Objective

The most basic drawing aid, *Grid*, makes the canvas in AutoCAD look like graph paper. You can adjust the grid's measured size and the spacing of its major lines to simulate many types of graph paper.

Snap constrains your ability to draw objects so that they automatically start and end precisely at grid intersections. Grid and Snap are most helpful when used together so that you can draw objects that snap to the grid. Figure 3.1 shows some of the status bar toggles you'll be learning about in this chapter.

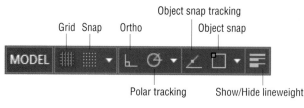

FIGURE 3.1 Various status toggles

Exercise 3.1: Draw with Grid and Snap

In the following steps, you will experiment with Grid and Snap by drawing lines using these aids:

1. Click the New button on the Quick Access toolbar.

2. Choose the acad.dwt template (or acadiso.dwt metric template) from the Select Template dialog box and click Open.

3. Open the Customization menu (on the extreme right of the status bar) and select Units and LineWeight. Deselect Isometric Drafting, Annotation Visibility, Autoscale, and Annotation Scale. Click in the drawing window to close the Customization menu. Change Units to Architectural if you are using Imperial units; leave Decimal selected if you are using metric units.

> Grid spacing is usually equal to or an increment of the snap interval.

4. Type **DS** and press Enter to open the Drafting Settings dialog box. Change Grid X spacing to 1" (or 10 for metric) and press Tab; Grid Y spacing updates with the same value. Set Major Line Every to 12 for Imperial (or 10 for metric) so that you'll see darker grid lines every foot. Notice that Snap spacing is set to 1/2" (or 10 mm) by default. Select Snap On and verify that the Grid Snap and Rectangular Snap radio buttons are selected in the Snap Type area (see Figure 3.2). Click OK.

> Zoom or pan as necessary as you are working to locate grid intersections in the drawing window.

5. Click the Line tool in the Draw panel on the ribbon's Home tab. Click the first point close to the origin point of the UCS icon, located in the lower-left corner of the drawing window. Click the second point, 2' (or 600 in metric) above the first point, by clicking the second intersection (or sixth intersection in metric) of major grid lines. Right-click to end the LINE command.

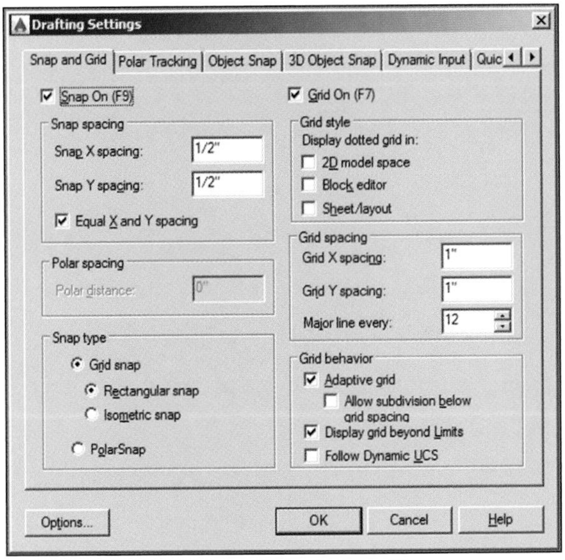

FIGURE 3.2   Setting up grid spacing and toggling on Snap

6. Click the Lineweight icon in the status bar so that the button is highlighted in blue.

7. Right-click the Lineweight icon, and choose Lineweight Settings from the context menu. Open the Default drop-down list, select 0.012" (or 0.30 mm) (see Figure 3.3), and click OK.

You'll learn how to control lineweight with layers in Chapter 6, "Controlling Object Visibility and Appearance."

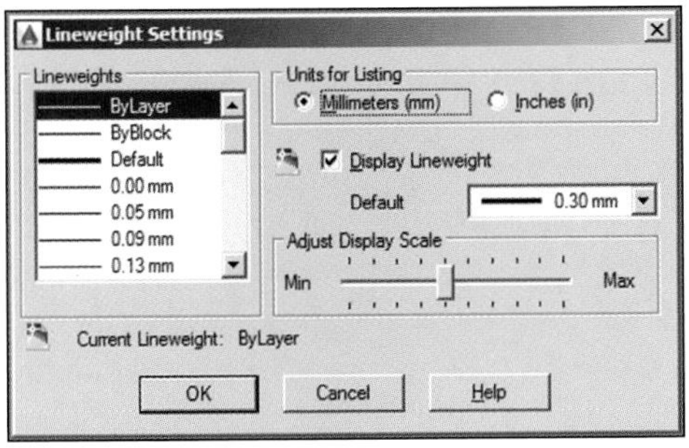

FIGURE 3.3   Adjusting the default lineweight settings

8. Type L and press Enter twice to continue drawing from the last point. Toggle Grid off in the status bar. Move the cursor horizontally to the right from the point at which the rubber band is anchored. Click the drawing canvas when the dynamic input value reads 2'-0" (or 600 mm), as shown in Figure 3.4, and press Enter.

Snap can be used independently of Grid; the grid is merely a visual drawing aid.

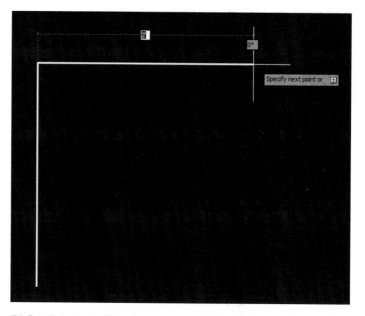

FIGURE 3.4   Using Snap to gauge distances without typing specific measurements

9. Save your work.

Your model should now resemble Ex03.1-end.dwg, which is available among this chapter's companion files.

TRANSPARENT COMMANDS

Status bar buttons can be toggled on or off and their settings adjusted while another command is running. Commands that operate while another command is running are called *transparent commands*. Typing an apostrophe before a command forces it to be run transparently. For example, while drawing a line, type **'Z** and press Enter. The ZOOM command is run transparently, and when it is done, the LINE command resumes. The following transcript shows this command sequence:

```
Command: L
LINE Specify first point: 'Z
'ZOOM
>>Specify corner of window, enter a
scale factor (nX or nXP), or
```

```
[All/Center/Dynamic/Extents/Previous/
Scale/Window/Object] <real time>:
>>>>Specify opposite corner:
Resuming LINE command.
Specify first point:
```

Employ Ortho and Polar Tracking

Ortho mode aids in drawing orthogonal (horizontal or vertical) lines. Polar Tracking is more flexible than Ortho mode, with the ability to constrain lines to increments of a set angle. A list of common angles—45, 90, 135, 180, and so on—is included on Polar Tracking's context menu. The traditional square and a set of triangles from traditional drafting are analogs to Ortho and Polar Tracking modes in AutoCAD.

◄

When Polar Tracking is set to 90, 180, 270, 360, it functions identically to Ortho mode.

Exercise 3.2: Draw with Ortho and Polar Tracking

Let's try Ortho and Polar Tracking modes by drawing a series of line segments. You'll use Ortho when the segments are 90° apart and Polar Tracking when the segments are drawn at other angles. Begin by opening the file Ex03.2-start.dwg from this chapter's companion files.

1. Type **L**, position the cursor over the right endpoint of the horizontal line, and click to establish the first point of a new line.

2. Toggle off Snap mode by pressing the F9 key.

3. Toggle on Ortho mode by clicking the Ortho toggle in the status bar or by pressing the F8 key.

The dash is a necessary separator between whole and fractional inches.

◄

4. Move the cursor down from the last point, type **10-3/4"** (or **240** for metric), and press Enter. Ortho mode constrains the line vertically, and typing in an explicit value obviates the need for Snap.

5. Toggle off Ortho mode by clicking its status bar button. Toggle on Polar Tracking by clicking the adjacent button on the right. Right-click the Polar Tracking button, and choose 45°, 90°, 135°, 180° from the context menu.

Certification
Objective

6. Move the cursor around and observe that green dashed lines appear in eight locations around a circle (in 45° increments). Move the cursor to the right relative to the last point, type **2'** (or **600** for metric), and press Enter (see Figure 3.5). Press Esc to terminate the LINE command without deleting the last segment drawn.

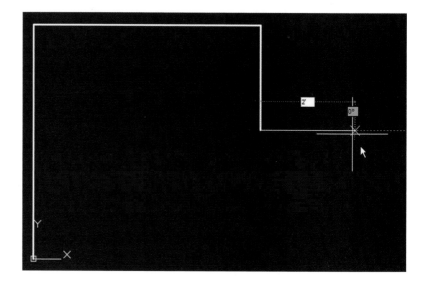

FIGURE 3.5 Drawing a line using Ortho mode and direct distance entry

7. Save your work.

Your model should now resemble Ex03.2-end.dwg, which is available among this chapter's download files.

Just like Ortho mode, Polar Tracking guarantees that the last line drawn was perfectly aligned to the set increment; you merely had to move the cursor in the general direction you wanted to direct the new line. Ortho and Polar Tracking save you from having to type in angles or coordinate values explicitly or to even think about coordinate systems.

Use PolarSnap

PolarSnap includes a kind of snap that is customized for Polar Tracking. Instead of being tied to a spatial grid (as with Snap), PolarSnap is based on relative polar coordinates.

Exercise 3.3: Draw with PolarSnap

As you'll see in the steps that follow, PolarSnap is useful for drawing measured lines on angles other than horizontal or vertical. Begin by opening the file Ex03.3-start.dwg from this chapter's companion files.

1. Toggle on Snap by clicking its icon on the status bar. Right-click the same button and choose Snap Settings from the context menu.

2. Select the PolarSnap radio button in the Drafting Settings dialog box. Type **1"** (or **10** for metric) in the Polar Distance text box (this dialog was shown in Figure 3.2). Click OK.

3. Type L and press Enter. Type **4',1'1-1/4** (or **1200,360** for metric) and press Enter to input the absolute coordinates of the end of the lower horizontal line.

4. Move the cursor down at a 45° angle from east, and observe the Snap values that appear with Dynamic Input onscreen. Click when the value is 6" (or 150 mm) (see Figure 3.6).

> You can avoid having to type distances by using Polar Tracking with PolarSnap.

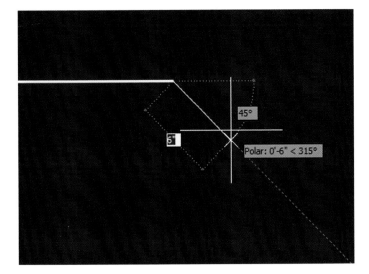

FIGURE 3.6 Drawing a line using Polar Tracking and PolarSnap

5. Move the cursor vertically down and click to draw a line when the value reads 1' (or 300 mm). Right-click to end the LINE command.

6. Press the spacebar to repeat the LINE command. Type **0,0** (or **100,200** for metric) and press Enter to input the first endpoint of the new line.

7. Toggle off Snap mode by clicking its icon on the status bar, thus disabling PolarSnap.

8. Move the cursor horizontally to the right until it overshoots the last line drawn in step 5. Click to draw the line without worrying about its length (see Figure 3.7). Right-click to complete the command.

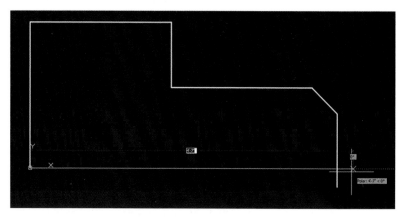

FIGURE 3.7 Drawing a horizontal line that overshoots the vertical line

9. Type **F** (for Fillet) and press Enter. Verify that Radius is set to 0 in the Command window and then click the vertical and horizontal lines on the portions of the lines that you want to keep (marked A and B in Figure 3.8).

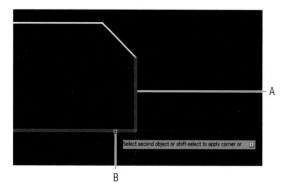

FIGURE 3.8 Filleting with a zero radius to form a corner

10. Save your work.

Your model should now resemble Ex03.3-end.dwg, which is available among this chapter's companion files.

Select Running Object Snaps

The lines you have drawn thus far are all precisely connected because they were chained together as they were drawn or their coordinates were known. Aside from these special circumstances, lines must be connected using object snaps to ensure accuracy.

You learned to use the Object Snap context menu in Chapter 2, "Gaining Basic Drawing Skills," and now you will use that as a jumping-off point to learn a far more efficient method called *running object snap.*

Exercise 3.4: Draw with Running Object Snaps

As you will see in the steps that follow, with running object snaps, frequently used object snaps can be turned on continuously. That way, you don't have to invoke them explicitly every time you want to use object snaps. Begin by opening the file Ex03.4-start.dwg from this chapter's companion files.

1. Using Polar Tracking, but without invoking Snap or Object Snap, draw a line using points A to B in Figure 3.9 as a guide. Click each point as accurately as you can because I want you to see that you can't make it perfect without using Object Snap.

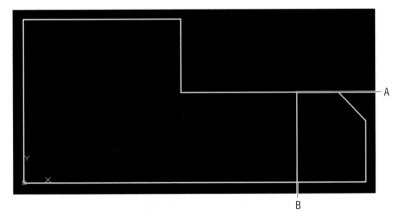

FIGURE 3.9   Drawing a line without Object Snap

2. Press **Z** and then Enter. Click two points to define a tightly cropped zoom window around point A. Zoom in again if necessary until you can see that the endpoint of the line you just drew is not on the horizontal line (see Figure 3.10). No matter how carefully you clicked point A in the previous step, the line you drew will not be on the edge (it will either fall short of it or overshoot it).

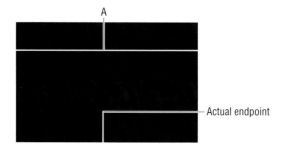

FIGURE 3.10 Zooming in reveals that the lines do not meet.

3. Select Zoom Previous from the Navigation bar's Zoom menu. Click Zoom Previous again if necessary to return to the original view.

4. Click the line drawn in step 3, and press the Delete key.

5. Toggle on Object Snap on the status bar. Right-click the same icon and choose Object Snap Settings from the context menu. Click the Clear All button and then select Endpoint, Midpoint, and Perpendicular (see Figure 3.11). Click OK.

Certification Objective

You can toggle on one object snap type at a time using the Object Snap icon's menu. Choose Object Snap Settings from this menu to access the Select All and Clear All buttons.

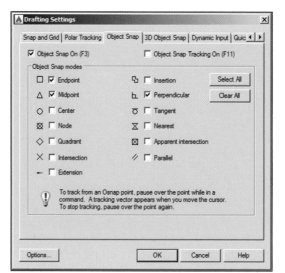

FIGURE 3.11 Turning on a few Running Object Snap modes

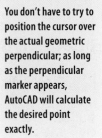

6. Toggle off Polar Tracking on the status bar. Click the Line tool on the Draw panel. Move the cursor close to point A in Figure 3.12 and wait for the green endpoint marker to appear. When it does, click to snap the first point of your line precisely to this point.

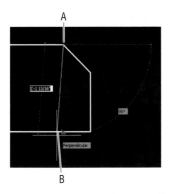

F I G U R E   3 . 1 2   Drawing a line using running object snaps

7. Move the cursor down to point B and wait until the green perpendicular marker appears. When it does, click the drawing canvas to select the second point of the line. Press Esc to end the command. This line is connected precisely at both ends because Object Snap was used.

8. Zoom into point A or B in Figure 3.13 and verify that the lines are connected perfectly. Click Zoom Extents in the Navigation bar to return to the initial overall view.

You don't have to try to position the cursor over the actual geometric perpendicular; as long as the perpendicular marker appears, AutoCAD will calculate the desired point exactly.

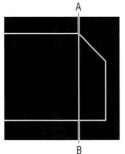

F I G U R E   3 . 1 3   Overriding running snaps with the Nearest snap

Nearest should be used with caution as a running snap mode because it conflicts with other snap modes. Choosing None in the Snap context menu overrides any running snaps (with no snap).

9. Type L and press Enter. Hold down Shift, right-click to open the Object Snap context menu, and choose Nearest. Object snaps invoked from the context menu override any running object snaps. Click point A, shown in Figure 3.14. Nearest ensures that the new line is attached somewhere along the edge of the horizontal line.

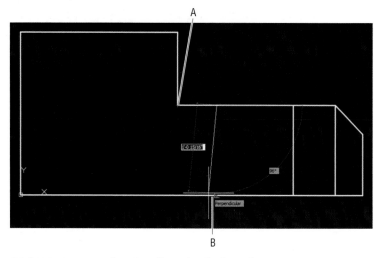

FIGURE 3.14 Drawing a line using the From object snap

10. Move the cursor close to point B, as shown in Figure 3.14, and click when the perpendicular marker appears. Press Esc to end the LINE command.

11. Save your work.

Your model should now resemble Ex03.4-end.dwg, which is available among this chapter's companion files.

Harness the From Snap

Rather than snapping to an existing geometrical feature (such as an endpoint, midpoint, intersection, and so on), how do you snap a set distance and direction from one? Answer: Use the From snap, as shown in the following exercise.

Exercise 3.5: Use the From Snap

Begin by opening the file Ex03.5-start.dwg from the Chapter 3 companion files.

1. Type **L** and press Enter. Hold Shift and right-click to open the Object Snap context menu. Select From in the context menu.

2. Click point A shown in Figure 3.14. This is the point from which you will specify a displacement. Type **@6<0** (or **@150<0** for metric) to specify the displacement to the first point of the line and press Enter.

3. Move the cursor to point B and wait for the running perpendicular snap marker to appear. When it does, click to specify the second point of the line. Press Esc to end the LINE command. You've drawn a line starting exactly 6" (or 150 mm) over from the corner.

4. Select the line you just drew and press the Delete key.

5. Save your work.

Your model should now resemble Ex03.5-end.dwg, which is available among this chapter's companion files.

Apply Object Snap Tracking

Object snap tracking is for situations where you want to snap to a point that has a geometric relationship with two or more snap points. As you'll see in the following steps, using object snap tracking saves time when compared with drawing temporary construction lines that must later be deleted.

Exercise 3.6: Use Object Snap Tracking

Begin by opening the file Ex03.6-start.dwg from this chapter's companion files.

1. Click the Circle tool on the Draw panel.

2. Toggle on Object Snap Tracking by clicking its icon on the status bar. Verify that Ortho mode is on. (If it isn't, press F8.)

Certification
Objective

3. Move the cursor over point A in Figure 3.15. When the running midpoint snap marker appears, move the cursor horizontally to the right to establish the first tracking line. Do not click yet.

4. Move the cursor over point B in Figure 3.15, and wait for the Midpoint marker to appear. Move the cursor down vertically to establish the second tracking line. Again, do not click yet.

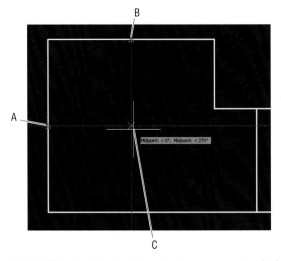

FIGURE 3.15 Locating a circle's center point with object snap tracking

5. Move the cursor down until both tracking lines intersect. When they do, click point C to set the center point of the circle. Type **9** (or **220** for metric) and press Enter to create a circle with a radius of 9" (or 220 mm).

6. Click the Rectangle tool on the Draw panel. Move the cursor over the endpoint marked A in Figure 3.16 and, without clicking, move the cursor down to establish the first tracking line.

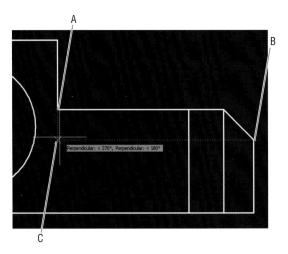

FIGURE 3.16 Drawing a rectangle by tracking its first corner

7. Move the cursor to point B in Figure 3.16 to track another endpoint. Move the cursor horizontally back to the intersection with the first tracking line, and click to establish the first corner of the rectangle (point C).

8. Type @1',-6 (or @280,-160 for metric) and press Enter. The rectangle and drawing are complete (see Figure 3.17).

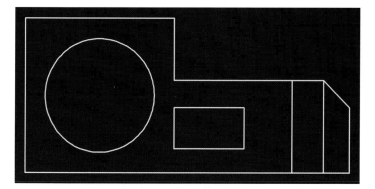

FIGURE 3.17 Completed mechanical part

9. Toggle off Lineweight.

10. Save your work.

Your model should now resemble Ex03.6-end.dwg, which is available among this chapter's companion files.

Now You Know

In this chapter, you learned how to draw with Grid and Snap when your geometry conforms to a spatial grid; how to use Ortho and Polar Tracking to draw horizontal, vertical, and angled lines; how to use PolarSnap when angled lines are measured in set increments; how to use running object snaps to save time connecting objects; how to use the From snap to draw in relation to another object; and finally, how to use object snap tracking to snap to points implied by the position of other snap points.

CHAPTER 4

Editing Entities

Drawing in the AutoCAD® program is not just about creating lines, rectangles, circles, and other shapes. Most of your time will be spent editing entities. Although AutoCAD provides the basic tools for transforming shapes (such as Move, Copy, Rotate, and Scale), more complex editing tools (such as Array, Trim, Extend, Lengthen, Stretch, Offset, Mirror, Break, Join, and Overkill) are also available.

In this chapter, you'll learn to do the following:

▶ **Create selection sets**

▶ **Use Move and Copy**

▶ **Use Rotate and Scale**

▶ **Work with arrays**

▶ **Use Trim and Extend**

▶ **Use Lengthen and Stretch**

▶ **Use Offset and Mirror**

▶ **Edit with grips**

Create Selection Sets

All editing commands operate on one or more drawing entities. In complex drawings, you have to plan how you will select only those entities you want to edit while leaving all other entities unaffected. You will learn a number of techniques for adding and removing entities from the selection set, which is the collection of entities your chosen editing command acts upon.

To edit objects, you must first select them. In complex drawings, selecting would be tedious if you had to click one object at a time. In the following exercise, you will learn several efficient selection methods that you can use at any Select objects: prompt, which appears in every editing command.

Exercise 4.1: Create a Selection Set at the *Select Objects:* Prompt

Begin by opening the file Ex04.1-start.dwg (a fictitious office building; see Figure 4.1) from this chapter's companion files, available for download from the book's web page at www.sybex.com/go/autocad2018essentials.

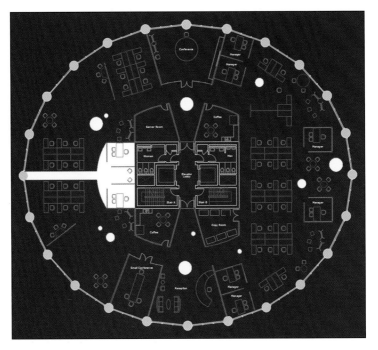

F I G U R E 4 . 1 Office building start file

1. Zoom into Stair A in the building core.

2. Click the Erase tool on the Modify panel on the ribbon's Home tab. The prompt in the Command window reads as follows:

   ERASE Select objects:

   This is the same way almost every command begins—with the opportunity to create a selection set.

Certification Objective

3. Click point A and then B, as shown in Figure 4.2. Observe that a transparent *implied window* appears between these points. The objects that are selected are only those completely contained within the borders of the blue window. This particular selection includes the

stair arrows, handrails, and three lines representing stair treads near the break lines.

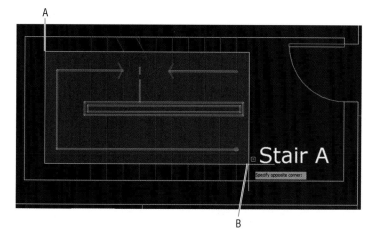

FIGURE 4.2 Drawing an implied window

4. Type **R** (for Remove) and press Enter. The command prompt reads as follows:

   ```
   ERASE Remove objects:
   ```

5. Click point A and then B, as shown in Figure 4.3. When you click the first point on the right (A), release the button, and move the cursor to the left (at B), a transparent green *crossing window* appears between the points. Whatever the green window crosses is selected. The crossing selection removes the handrail and two of the stair treads because the selection was made at the Remove objects: prompt.

Certification
Objective

In AutoCAD 2018, you can begin a selection window in one area of your drawing and then pan and/or zoom to another offscreen area and keep selecting.

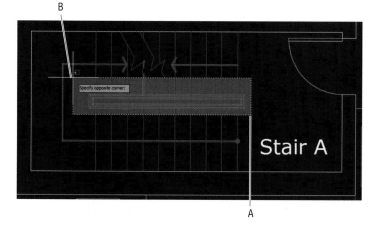

FIGURE 4.3 Drawing a crossing window to remove objects from the selection set

6. Click point A and then point B, as shown in Figure 4.4. This implied window selects the short line segment trapped in the break line and removes it from the selection set.

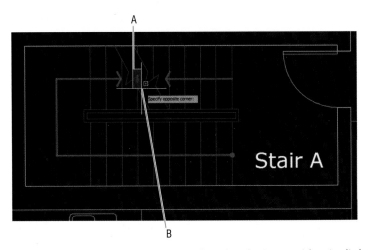
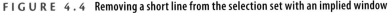

FIGURE 4.4   Removing a short line from the selection set with an implied window

7. Type **A** (for Add) and press Enter. The command prompt again reads as follows:

   ```
   ERASE Select objects:
   ```

8. Click both of the break lines to add them to the selection set. All of the break line segments are selected in two clicks because the break lines are polylines.

9. Hold Shift and click the break lines again. They are removed from the selection set without being at the Remove objects: prompt.

10. Press Enter to complete the ERASE command.

11. Save your work.

Your model should now resemble Ex04.1-end.dwg, which is available among this chapter's companion download files.

Exercise 4.2: Create a Selection Set Before Deciding on a Command

In addition to creating a selection set at any Select objects: prompt, you can create a selection set first and then decide which command to use afterward. (Additional Dynamic Input prompts are available onscreen when you select objects first.) Let's explore these additional selection methods.

Begin by opening the file Ex04.2-start.dwg from this chapter's companion files.

1. Click point A, as shown in Figure 4.5. Press the down-arrow key to expand the Dynamic Input menu onscreen. Select WPolygon.

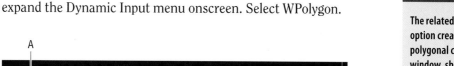

The related CPolygon option creates a polygonal crossing window, shown in transparent green. The Fence option allows you to draw a multisegmented line that selects whatever it crosses.

FIGURE 4.5 Selecting WPolygon selection mode from the Dynamic Input menu

2. Click points B through H, as shown in Figure 4.6. The transparent blue polygon you are drawing functions the same as an implied rectangular window; the difference is the polygonal window offers more flexibility because you can shape it. Only those objects completely contained within the borders of the blue window will be selected.

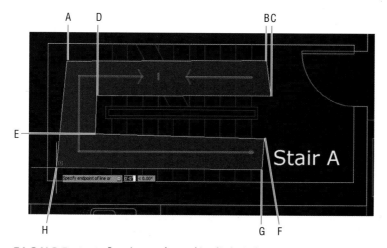

FIGURE 4.6 Drawing a polygonal implied window to create a selection set

3. Press Enter to make the selection. Square blue dots appear on the selected objects—these are called *grips*, and you will learn to use them later in this chapter. Press Esc to deselect.

4. Toggle on Ortho mode in the status bar. Without being concerned with measurements or accuracy, draw a line under the word *Stair*, a circle around the letter *A*, and a rectangle around the entire section, in that order (see Figure 4.7).

FIGURE 4.7   Drawing a few objects to learn about the selection buffer

5. Type **SELECT** and press Enter. Select the circle and the line and press Enter. The SELECT command is used merely to make a selection. The grips for the circle and line appear; press Esc to deselect.

6. Click the Erase icon on the Modify panel. At the Select objects: prompt, type **P** (for Previous) and press Enter. The circle and line are selected because they comprise the set of objects that was selected previously. Press Enter again to delete these objects.

> You can select the entire drawing by typing **all** at any Select objects: prompt.

7. Press the spacebar to repeat the last command (ERASE). Type **L** (for Last) and press Enter. The rectangle is selected because it was the last object you created. There can be only one last object. Press Enter again to delete the rectangle.

8. Press Ctrl+W to toggle on selection cycling.

9. Click the dot at the end of the stair direction line (shown in Figure 4.8). This dot is at the confluence of the horizontal stair direction line and the vertical tread line. When Selection Cycling is on, you are presented with the Selection dialog box whenever your selection is ambiguous. Hover the cursor over the items in the list, and each one is highlighted in blue on the drawing canvas. Select the line in the list that highlights the stair direction line, as shown in Figure 4.8, and then press Esc.

Click this dot.

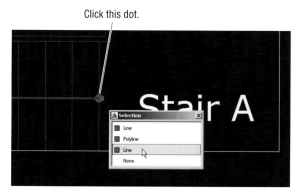

FIGURE 4.8 Selection cycling

10. Press Ctrl+W to toggle selection cycling off.

11. Select one of the vertical tread lines in Stair A by clicking it. Right-click and choose Select Similar from the context menu that appears. All lines on the same layer are selected; you might have to zoom out to see both stairs (see Figure 4.9). Other object types on the same layer remain unselected because they were not similar enough. Press Esc.

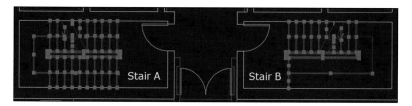

FIGURE 4.9 Selecting similar objects en masse

12. Save your work.

Your model should now resemble Ex04.2-end.dwg, which is available among this chapter's companion download files.

SELECTING SIMILAR OBJECTS

Type **SELECTSIMILAR**, press Enter, type **SE**, and press Enter again to open this command's Settings dialog box. Here you can choose criteria to determine which object properties must match in order to be selected by this useful command: Color, Layer, Linetype, Linetype Scale, Lineweight, Plot Style, Object Style, or Name.

(Continues)

SELECTING SIMILAR OBJECTS *(Continued)*

Use Move and Copy

MOVE and COPY are the most commonly used commands in AutoCAD. As you'll see in the following steps, they are similar in that they require both a distance and a direction to indicate where you plan to displace the selected objects.

Exercise 4.3: Move and Copy

Begin by opening the file Ex04.3-start.dwg.

> The disadvantages to moving by dragging are that the displacement is unmeasured, you don't see the selection moving, and you can't use Object Snap to maintain accuracy.

1. Pan to the upper-right quadrant of the building and zoom into the furniture grouping that needs to be filled in.

2. Click the chair that is not in front of a desk to select it. Position the cursor over the selected chair but not over its grip. Drag the chair while holding down the left mouse button to move it closer to the upper desk; see Figure 4.10.

3. To position the chair more precisely, click the Move tool on the Modify panel. Select the chair you just moved in the previous step and press Enter. The command prompt reads as follows:

   ```
   MOVE Specify base point or [Displacement] <Displacement>:
   ```

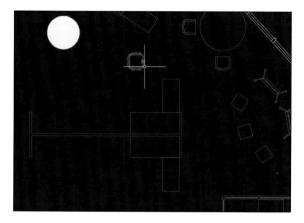

FIGURE 4.10   Moving a selected object by dragging

4. Right-click the Object Snap toggle in the status bar and choose Midpoint from the context menu if it is not already selected. Click the base point at the midpoint of the front of the chair (point A in Figure 4.11).

Certification
Objective

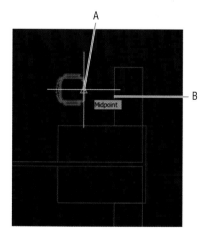

FIGURE 4.11   Selecting the base point for a move

5. Click the second point (B in Figure 4.11). The chair is moved precisely to the midpoint of the desk edge.

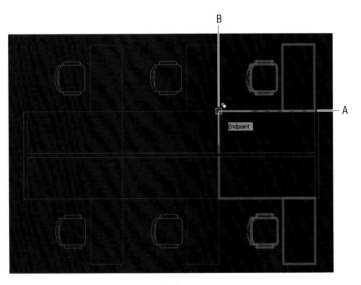

6. Press the spacebar to repeat MOVE. Type **P** and press Enter twice to select the same chair again. Type **D** and press Enter once more to choose the Displacement option. In Displacement mode, the first point is the origin point. Any coordinates you enter are relative to the origin, so typing the @ symbol is unnecessary. Type **4<180** (or **10<180** for metric) and press Enter.

7. Click the Copy tool on the Modify panel. Select the chair you just moved and press Enter. Select the midpoint of the desk (point B in Figure 4.11) as the base point and then click the midpoint of the corresponding mirror image desk below in the same furniture group as the second point. Press Enter to end the COPY command.

Certification Objective

8. Press the spacebar to repeat the previous command, select both desks and chairs with crossing windows (but not the low partition between them), and press Enter. Select point A in Figure 4.12 as the base point. Type **A** and press Enter. The command prompt reads as follows:

```
COPY Enter the number of items to array:
```

FIGURE 4.12 Copying multiple items

You must include the original object in the count of items.

9. Type **3**, press Enter, and then click point B in Figure 4.12 as the second point. Press Esc to end the COPY command.

10. Pan over to the Conference room. Type **UCS** and press Enter. Select the Object option by clicking `Object` on the command prompt. Select the inner-left wall line and watch as the crosshair cursor changes to parallel the angle of the wall (see Figure 4.13).

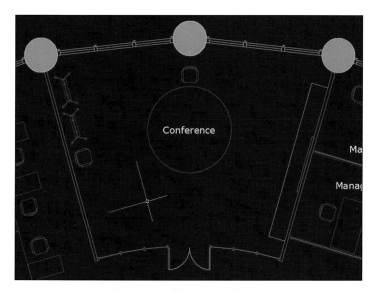

Conference

Ma

Mana

FIGURE 4.13 Reorienting the UCS to an object

11. Toggle on Ortho on the status bar if it is not already on. Type **CO** (for Copy) and press Enter. Select the chair that is against the left wall of the Conference room and press Enter. Click an arbitrary base point by clicking in the empty space of the Conference room.

12. Move the cursor down along the direction of the wall and click the Array option. The command prompt reads as follows:

    ```
    Enter number of items to array:
    ```

    Type **5** and press Enter. Move the cursor downward and observe that five ghosted chairs appear. When the spacing looks right (see Figure 4.14), click in the document window to complete the array and press Enter.

13. Type **UCS** and press Enter twice to accept the default option of World. The crosshair cursor returns to its default orientation.

14. Save your work.

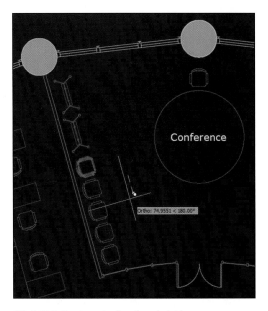

FIGURE 4.14 Copying chairs in an array

Your model should now resemble Ex04.3-end.dwg, which is available among this chapter's companion download files.

Use Rotate and Scale

The ROTATE and SCALE commands are obviously essential to drawing; each requires a base point to indicate the center from which objects are transformed. Numerically speaking, you typically rotate by degrees or scale by percentages about base points. On the other hand, you can avoid using numbers entirely by choosing the Reference options, which let you rotate or scale selection sets in relation to other objects.

Exercise 4.4: Rotate and Scale

Begin by opening the file Ex04.4-start.dwg.

Rotate

1. Navigate to Reception at the bottom of the floor plan. Click the Rotate button on the Modify panel, select the upper lounge chair, and press Enter. The command line reads as follows:

   ROTATE Specify base point:

   Click a point in the center of the chair; you don't need to snap this point because an approximation is good enough right now.

2. Toggle off Ortho (and Polar Tracking if it is on) in the status bar. Move the cursor around the point, and observe that a rubber-band line connects the base point to your cursor and a ghosted image of the chair is superimposed over the original chair representation. Move the cursor until the rubber band aligns more or less perpendicularly to the wall behind the chair (see Figure 4.15) and click.

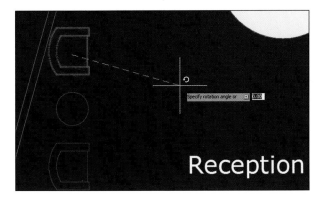

FIGURE 4.15 Rotating a chair by visually estimating the angle

3. Click the chair that you just rotated to select it without issuing an explicit command. Hold the Ctrl key, and repeatedly press the arrow keys to nudge the selected object a few pixels at a time. Nudge the chair so that it is a similar distance from the wall and the round table as compared to the other armchair in Reception. Press Esc to deselect all.

4. Zoom out and focus on the upper-left quadrant of the building. Type CO (for Copy) and press Enter. Select the furniture group shown in Figure 4.16 and press Enter. Select midpoint A as the base point, and select midpoint B as the second point. Press Esc to end the command.

5. Type **RO** (for Rotate) and press Enter. Type **L** (for Last) and press Enter twice. Select the same midpoint where the furniture group was attached to the midpoint of the shell window wall as the base point of the rotation. The command line reads as follows:

```
ROTATE Specify rotation angle or [Copy Reference] <0.00>:
```

Type **R** (for Reference) and press Enter. Instead of specifying the reference angle with a number, you will determine the angle interactively. Type @ and press Enter to input the base point of the rotation as the base point of the reference angle.

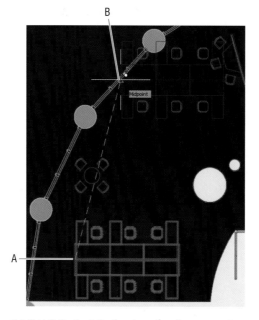

FIGURE 4.16   Copying a furniture group to a new center of rotation

Using the ROTATE
and SCALE com-
mands' Reference
options allows you to
transform with refer-
ence to other objects
without having to
input numerical angles
or scale factors.

6. Click endpoint A as shown in Figure 4.17 to specify the second point
   of the reference angle and point B to specify the second point of the
   new angle. The furniture group rotates so that it is parallel and centered on the window wall.

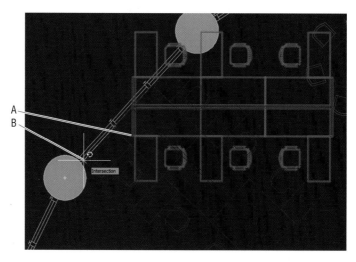

FIGURE 4.17   Rotating with the Reference option

7. Pan over to the upper-right quadrant of the building and zoom in on the oversized round table. Click the Scale icon on the Modify panel, select the circle representing the table, and press Enter. The command line reads as follows:

   ```
   SCALE Specify base point:
   ```

8. Right-click the Object Snap icon in the status bar and select Center from the context menu. Click outside the menu to close it, and then snap to the center of the circle by hovering over the circle and then moving the cursor to its center and clicking. Type **.5** and press Enter to scale the circle down to 50 percent of its original size (see Figure 4.18).

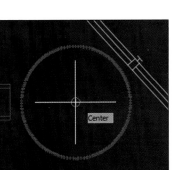

FIGURE 4.18 Scaling a circle from its center

9. Toggle on Ortho on the status bar, and move the chairs closer to the table, both horizontally and vertically.

10. Save your work.

Your model should now resemble Ex04.4-end.dwg, which is available among this chapter's companion download files.

Work with Arrays

Arrays produce single associative objects, which you can edit at any time to alter the parameters of the array. You will learn how to create two types of associative arrays: rectangular and polar.

Exercise 4.5: Create a Rectangular Array

Rectangular arrays are arranged in a grid of rows (running horizontally) and columns (running vertically).

Begin by opening the file Ex04.5-start.dwg.

1. Type **UCS** and press Enter. Type **OB** (for Object) and press Enter. Select the bottom-left edge of the table in the Small Conference room.

2. Click the Rectangular Array tool on the Modify panel. Select both chairs on the sides of the conference table and press Enter.

3. Change Columns to 1 and Rows to 5 on the temporary Array Creation tab that appears on the ribbon. Type **2′4** (**72** for metric) in the Between text box in the Rows panel and press the Tab key (see Figure 4.19).

Depending on which side of the line you selected with the UCS, you might have to enter five columns and one row if the UCS is 180 degrees out of phase.

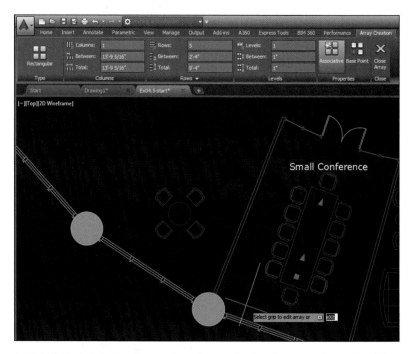

FIGURE 4.19 Creating a rectangular array by changing parameters on the ribbon

4. Select the Associative toggle in the Properties panel if it is not already blue. Click Close Array on the ribbon.

5. Select one of the new chairs and observe that all the arrayed chairs are selected as a unit. Change Rows to 4 and Between to 3' (90 for metric); the five chairs along each side of the table are replaced by four. Click Close Array.

6. Type **UCS** and press Enter twice to return to the world coordinate system.

7. Save your work.

Your model should now resemble Ex04.5-end.dwg, which is available among this chapter's companion download files.

Exercise 4.6: Create a Polar Array

Polar arrays are used for rotating and copying objects around a common central point.

Begin by opening the file Ex04.6-start.dwg.

1. Type **AR** (for Array) and press Enter. Select the chair at the top of the conference room's round table and press Enter.

2. The command prompt reads as follows:

   ```
   ARRAY Enter array type [Rectangular Path Polar]
   <Rectangular>:
   ```

3. Type **PO** (for Polar) and press Enter.

4. Hold down Shift and right-click to open the Object Snap context menu. Choose Center and click the table's center to set the center point of the array.

5. Type **12** in the Items text box on the ribbon and press Tab. Toggle on Associative, Rotate Items, and Direction if they are not already on in the Properties panel (see Figure 4.20). Click Close Array.

6. The table is a bit too large. Click the circle to select the table. Click the circle's top blue quadrant grip and move the cursor down. Type 4'6 (or **140** for metric) to set a new radius. Press Enter and then Esc.

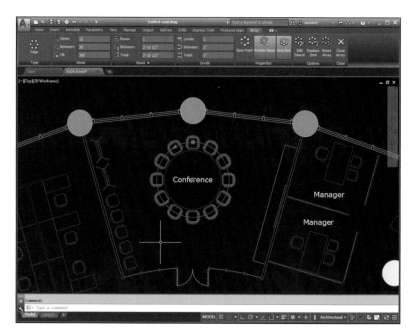

FIGURE 4.20   Creating a polar array

7. Click any one of the chairs to select the polar array. Hover the cursor over the base point grip and choose Stretch Radius (see Figure 4.21). Type 5'9 (or **175** for metric); then press Enter and Esc. The chairs more closely wrap around the smaller table.

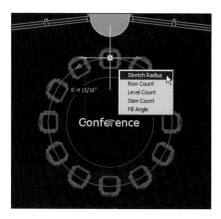

FIGURE 4.21   Editing a polar array with its grips

8. Save your work.

Your model should now resemble Ex04.6-end.dwg, which is available among this chapter's companion download files.

DIVIDE AND MEASURE

The DIVIDE and MEASURE commands do not copy objects in a rectangular grid or around a center point as does the ARRAY command. Instead, these commands are used for arraying points. DIVIDE splits up a path into any number of evenly spaced points. MEASURE lays out points at a set distance, often leaving a remainder at the end of a path. You'll use DIVIDE in Chapter 5, "Shaping Curves."

Use Trim and Extend

The TRIM and EXTEND commands are opposites. You can invoke the opposite command while running either by holding down Shift. This method is especially helpful because TRIM and EXTEND are often used together.

Certification Objective

Exercise 4.7: Trim and Measure

Begin by opening the file Ex04.7-start.dwg.

1. Navigate to Stair B in the building's core.

2. Click the Extend tool on the Modify panel (it is nested under Trim). Select the inner line of the bottom core wall and press Enter.

3. Create a crossing window by clicking points A and B, as shown in Figure 4.22. Four tread lines are extended. Click each remaining tread line, one at a time, to extend all the stair treads to the core wall. Press Enter to end the command.

Extend

◀

This line will be the boundary edge that you will extend the stair treads to meet.

FIGURE 4.22 Extending lines with a crossing window and by selecting

4. Type **TR** (for Trim) and press Enter. Select the upper and lower hand-rail lines to act as cutting edges and press Enter. Make a narrow crossing window in the center of the handrail to trim away all the treads that pass through the handrails and press Enter.

5. Type **EX** (for Extend) and press Enter. Select the inner line of the bottom core wall and press Enter. Click each of the five missing tread lines to extend them into the bottom flight and press Esc to end the command.

6. Press the spacebar to repeat the EXTEND command, select the upper and lower railings, and press Enter. Hold Shift and click each one of the treads passing through the handrail. Press Esc when you have removed all five line segments (see Figure 4.23).

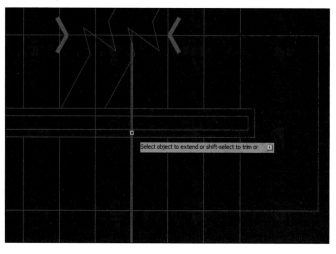

FIGURE 4.23 Trimming with the EXTEND command

7. Save your work.

Your model should now resemble Ex04.7-end.dwg, which is available among this chapter's companion download files.

Use Lengthen and Stretch

The LENGTHEN and STRETCH commands are similar in how they can increase the length of objects. However, STRETCH is the more flexible of the two, allowing you to reposition interconnected objects.

> You can hold Shift to trim in the EXTEND command or hold Shift to extend in the TRIM command.

Exercise 4.8: Lengthen and Stretch

Begin by opening the file Ex04.8-start.dwg.

1. Type **LEN** (for Lengthen) and press Enter. The command prompt reads as follows:

   ```
   LENGTHEN Select an object or [DElta/Percent/Total/
   DYnamic]:
   ```

   Type **P** (for Percent) and press Enter.

2. Type **200** and press Enter. Click the line segment on the right side of the incomplete copy machine to lengthen it toward the right. Press Esc.

3. Type **S** (for Stretch) and press Enter. The command prompt reads as follows:

   ```
   STRETCH Select objects to stretch by crossing-window
   or crossing-polygon ...
   Select objects:
   ```

   Implied windows won't work for STRETCH; only crossing windows or crossing polygons are acceptable. Click points A and B as shown in Figure 4.24 to select the objects to stretch and press Enter.

Certification Objective

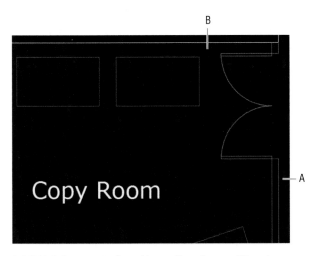

FIGURE 4.24 Stretching walls, a door, and its swing

4. Toggle on Ortho if it is not already on. Click a base point off to the right side of the door opening, well away from the geometry so that you do not inadvertently snap to anything. Move the cursor down vertically, type 2'6 (or 75 for metric), and press Enter to specify the second point. The wall, door, and swing end up more or less centered on the wall.

5. Save your work.

Your model should now resemble Ex04.8-end.dwg, which is available among this chapter's companion download files.

Use Offset and Mirror

The OFFSET and MIRROR commands are often used to create new objects. OFFSET creates an object a set distance on one side of the original object. MIRROR creates a reversed object at a distance from the original object as determined by the position of a drawn reflection line.

Exercise 4.9: Offset and Mirror

Begin by opening the file Ex04.9-start.dwg.

1. Click the Offset tool on the Modify panel. The command line reads as follows:

   ```
   OFFSET Specify offset distance or [Through Erase Layer]
   <Through>:
   ```

   Type 4 (10 for metric) and press Enter. Select the elliptical arc at the bottom edge of the Copy Room.

2. The command line asks you to specify a point to determine on which side of the selection to offset the new object. In this case, click anywhere above the elliptical arc, and a new ellipse is created such that its curvature matches the original but is spaced a set distance away. Press Esc to exit the command.

3. Type F (for Fillet), press Enter, and click the new elliptical arc and the inner line of the adjacent vertical wall on the right. Press the spacebar to repeat the FILLET command and click the elliptical arc and inner line of the adjacent vertical wall on the left. The intersections between the wall objects are cleaned up (see Figure 4.25).

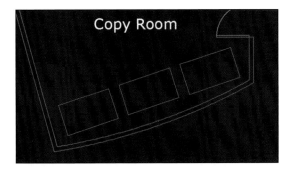

FIGURE 4.25 Offsetting and filleting walls

4. Zoom into the furniture system that is missing two desks in the upper-right quadrant of the building. Toggle on Ortho on the status bar if it is not already on. Click the Mirror tool on the Modify panel. Make crossing and individual line selections to select the desks and chairs shown in Figure 4.26 and press Enter. The command line reads as follows:

   Specify first point of mirror line:

   Click point A, and then move the cursor up and click point B to draw the mirror line. Press Enter to say no to "Erase source objects?" and to end the command.

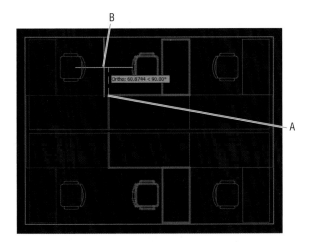

FIGURE 4.26 Mirroring furniture blocks

5. Press Enter to repeat the MIRROR command. Double-click the mouse wheel to zoom to the drawing extents. Select the furniture system indicated in Figure 4.27 and press Enter. For the first point of the mirror line, type **0,0** and press Enter.

Mirror a copy here.

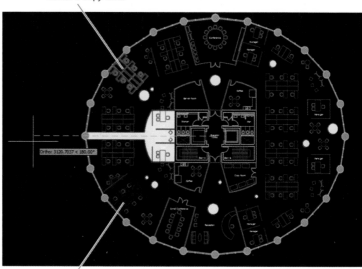

Select this group.

FIGURE 4.27 Mirroring a furniture grouping

6. Move the cursor horizontally to the left—beyond the building—and click to specify a horizontal mirror line. Press Enter to complete the command and decline to erase the source object by pressing Enter again.

7. Save your work.

Your model should now resemble Ex04.9-end.dwg, which is available among this chapter's companion download files.

Edit with Grips

Certification Objective

All objects have grips, which are the square blue symbols that appear in AutoCAD at significant points when objects are selected without issuing any command. Grips provide an alternative means of accessing a number of editing commands, including STRETCH, MOVE, ROTATE, SCALE, and MIRROR.

Exercise 4.10: Edit with Grips

Begin by opening the file Ex04.10-start.dwg.

1. Select the inner line of the window wall directly below the sofas, right-click, and choose Properties from the context menu. Make a note that the Angle property of this line is 173.77 degrees (see Figure 4.28). Press Esc to deselect.

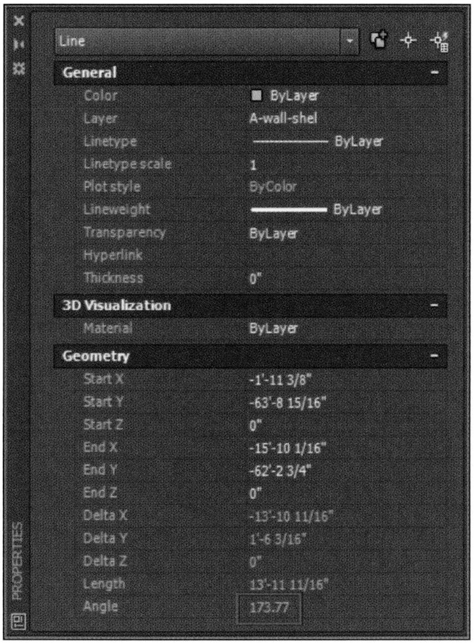

FIGURE 4.28 Examining an object's properties

2. Click both sofas and the coffee table in between them to select all three. Single blue grips appear on the sofas because they are blocks (see Chapter 7, "Organizing Objects," for more on blocks).

3. Click the grip in the center of the coffee table to activate it and turn it red. The command prompt reads as follows:

```
** STRETCH **
Specify stretch point or [Base point Copy Undo eXit]:
```

Press the spacebar. The command prompt changes to this:

```
** MOVE **
Specify move point or [Base point Copy Undo eXit]:
```

4. Press the spacebar again. The command prompt now says this:

```
** ROTATE **
Specify rotation angle or
[Base point Copy Undo Reference eXit]:
```

5. Type **'CAL** to invoke the command-line calculator transparently. Type **173.77-180** and press Enter to have AutoCAD calculate the negative rotation angle for you (−6.23 degrees in this case). Press Esc.

6. Save your work.

Your model should now resemble Ex04.10-end.dwg, which is available among this chapter's companion download files.

Now You Know

In this chapter, you learned how to use many different editing tools, including Move, Copy, Rotate, Scale, Array, Trim, Extend, Lengthen, Stretch, Offset, and Mirror. You learned several methods for selecting objects so they can be edited with these commands. In addition, you learned how to edit objects directly, without issuing commands, by editing with grips.

CHAPTER 5

Shaping Curves

From the simplest polyline that includes straight and curving arc segments to more complexly curving ellipses and splines, you can shape curves to suit any geometric situation in the AutoCAD® program. Spline objects offer the most flexibility, allowing you to shape them using fit points or control vertices. You can also create splines that seamlessly blend between existing straight or curved objects while maintaining smooth or tangent continuity.

In this chapter, you'll learn to do the following:

▶ **Draw and edit curved polylines**

▶ **Draw ellipses**

▶ **Shape splines**

▶ **Blend between objects with splines**

Draw and Edit Curved Polylines

The simplest curved objects are circles and arcs (which are just parts of circles) because they curve with a constant radius from a center point. In the following steps, you will chain a series of arcs and/or lines together in a single polyline object, which not only streamlines editing and selection, but also ensures smooth curvature between adjacent arcs.

Exercise 5.1: Draw and Edit Curved Polylines

Begin by opening the file Ex05.1-start.dwg from this chapter's companion files, available for download from the book's web page at www.sybex .com/go/autocad2018essentials. Figure 5.1 shows the landscape plan.

Certification Objective

1. Click the Polyline tool on the Draw panel of the ribbon. Click the first point, at point A, shown in Figure 5.1. Type **A** (for Arc) and press Enter.

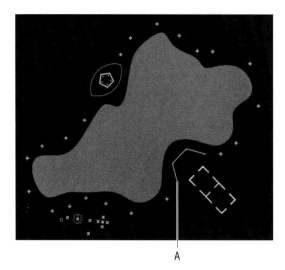

F I G U R E   5 . 1   Initial landscape plan

 2. Toggle off Ortho and Polar Tracking modes if they are on. Observe that the arc you are drawing follows the natural curvature of the lake (see Figure 5.2). The command prompt reads as follows:

```
Specify endpoint of arc or
PLINE [Angle Center Direction Halfwidth Line
Radius Second pt Undo Width]:
```

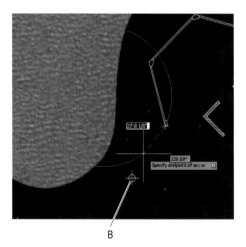

F I G U R E   5 . 2   The polyline arc follows the curvature of the lake.

> Normally, polyline arcs are defined by two points, and by using the Second Point option, you are choosing the arc to be formed by three points.

3. Type S (for Second Point) and press Enter. Click point B shown in Figure 5.2.

4. Right-click the Object Snap toggle in the status bar and turn on Node and Endpoint in the menu. Toggle off any other snap options that are selected. Toggle on Object Snap if it is off.

5. Click each subsequent node around the left half of the lake until you reach point C in Figure 5.3. Press Enter to end the PLINE command.

By turning on Node running object snap, you will be able to snap arcs to all the point objects surrounding the lake.

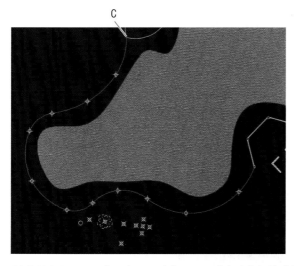

FIGURE 5.3   Drawing a polyline around the left half of the lake

6. Press the spacebar to repeat the last command. Click point D shown in Figure 5.4, type **A** (for Arc), and press Enter.

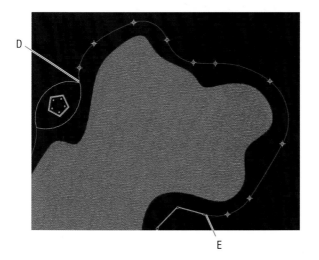

FIGURE 5.4   Drawing another polyline around the right half of the lake

7. Type S (for Second Point), press Enter, and snap to the node adjacent to point D.

8. Click each subsequent node around the right side of the lake until you reach point E in Figure 5.4. Press Enter.

The point objects in the sample file are meant to guide you in the exercise. Snapping to points typically isn't necessary when drawing curves on your own.

9. Click the Offset tool in the Modify panel. Type 6′ (or 2 for metric) and press Enter. Click the left polyline you drew around the lake in steps 1–5 and then click a point on the side of the polyline away from the lake. Click the right polyline and click outside the lake. Click the outer arc surrounding the pentagonal structure and then click outside the lake.

Certification
Objective   Trim

10. Click the Trim tool in the Modify panel. Press Enter to select all objects as potential cutting edges, and click the portions of the arcs that overlap in the top highlighted area in Figure 5.5. Zoom into the lower highlighted area, and trim the arcs at their tips so that they meet at their endpoints. Press Esc to end the TRIM command.

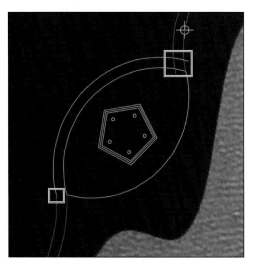

FIGURE 5.5   Trimming polylines and arcs

Certification
Objective

11. Pan to the building at the bottom of the lake. Click the lower-left polyline to select it. Click the endpoint grip, move it down a short distance, and click again (see Figure 5.6). You can't get the end of the path to open up without distorting the path farther up because it's all part of the same arc segment.

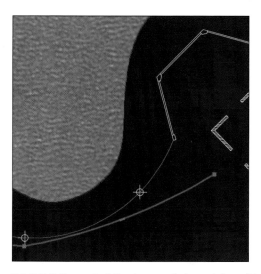

FIGURE 5.6   Adjusting an existing polyline with its grips

12. Press Esc and then click the Undo button in the Quick Access toolbar.

13. Click the Arc tool in the Draw panel, hold down Shift and right-click, and choose Nearest from the context menu. Click points A, B, and C in Figure 5.7 to shape the arc as shown.

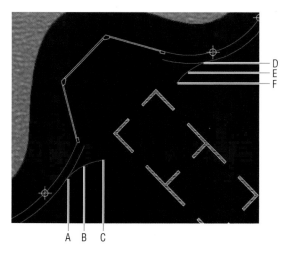

FIGURE 5.7   Drawing new short-radius arcs and snapping them along the longer existing arcs

Trim

Certification
Objective

14. Press Enter twice to end and restart the ARC command. Type **NEA** (for Nearest), press Enter, and click points D, E, and F in Figure 5.7.

15. Zoom in and trim away the portions of the original polylines that extend beyond the new arcs you've just drawn.

16. Type **J** (for Join) and press Enter. Select all five objects that comprise the outer path (three arcs and two polylines). Press Enter, and the command line reads as follows:

    ```
    14 segments joined into 1 polyline
    ```

    There are 14 segments if you include all the arcs that make up the two polylines. You are left with a single polyline marking the outer edge of the path.

17. Press the spacebar to repeat the JOIN command. Select the three objects along the inner edge of the path, which includes two polylines and the arc above the pentagon. Press Enter, and multiple segments are joined into one polyline (see Figure 5.8).

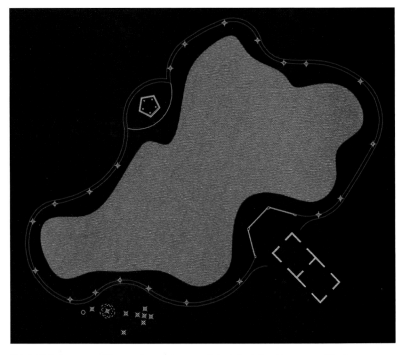

F I G U R E 5 . 8 The curving path around the lake joined into two objects

18. Save your work.

Your model should now resemble Ex05.1-end.dwg, which is available among this chapter's companion files.

Should You Use *JOIN* or *PEDIT*?

In AutoCAD 2013 and earlier, objects had to be converted into polylines and then joined using the polyline editing command called PEDIT. The streamlined JOIN command makes the older workflow unnecessary. Use it on lines, 2D and 3D polylines, arcs, elliptical arcs (sections of ellipses), and/or helices. Multiple object types can be joined at once. The resulting object type depends on what was selected.

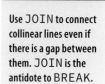

Use JOIN to connect collinear lines even if there is a gap between them. JOIN is the antidote to BREAK.

Draw Ellipses

AutoCAD can draw perfect ovals, which are mathematically known as *ellipses*. Instead of stretching a cord from two pins to a moving pencil point (which is how you draw an ellipse by hand), in AutoCAD you specify the lengths of its major and minor axes (see Figure 5.9).

The center of an ellipse is the intersection of its major and minor axes.

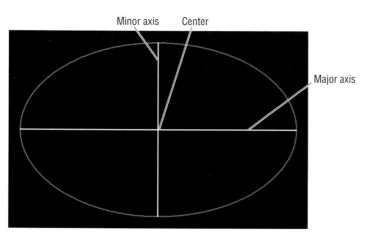

FIGURE 5.9 An ellipse's major and minor axes

Exercise 5.2: Draw Ellipses

In this exercise, you will draw an ellipse and distribute shrubs along its edge. Begin by opening Ex05.2-start.dwg from this chapter's companion files.

1. Zoom into the area in the lower left where the remaining point objects are located.

2. Type **REGEN** (for Regenerate) and press Enter. The size of point objects is recalculated when the drawing is regenerated.

Certification Objective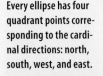

3. Open the Ellipse menu in the Draw panel and choose the Center method. Click the center point, the end of the major axis, and the end of the minor axis, shown in Figure 5.10.

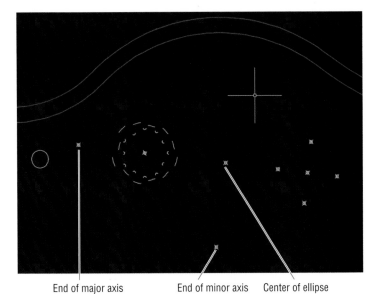

End of major axis   End of minor axis   Center of ellipse

FIGURE 5.10 Drawing an ellipse

> Every ellipse has four quadrant points corresponding to the cardinal directions: north, south, west, and east.

4. Expand the Modify panel and click the Break button. Select the ellipse. The command prompt reads as follows:

    `BREAK Specify second break point or [First point]:`

    Click First Point on the command line.

5. Right-click the Object Snap toggle in the status bar, and select Quadrant from the context menu. Click the *quadrant point* opposite the point object marking the end of the major axis (see Figure 5.10) and then click the aforementioned point object itself to break the ellipse in half. The lower half of the ellipse remains, leaving an *elliptical arc*.

> The DIVIDE command always creates one less point or block than the number of segments into which the object is divided.

Certification Objective 6. Type **DIV** (for Divide) and press Enter. Select the elliptical arc. The command prompt reads as follows:

    `DIVIDE Enter the number of segments or [Block]:`

    Click Block on the command line.

7. A block called Shrub is predefined, so at the next command prompt (shown here), type **Shrub**, and press Enter:

   ```
   Enter name of block to insert:
   ```

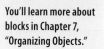

You'll learn more about blocks in Chapter 7, "Organizing Objects."

8. Press Enter to accept the default when asked if you want to align the block with the selected object. (It doesn't matter in this case because the Shrub block is a circle.)

9. Type **13** (for the number of segments) and press Enter. Twelve "shrubs" appear along the elliptical arc (see Figure 5.11).

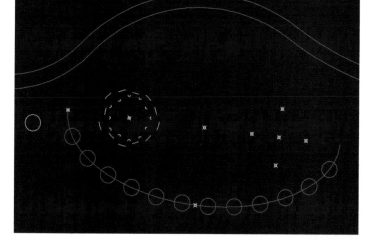

FIGURE 5.11 Dividing an elliptical arc with blocks

10. Delete the three points used in drawing the ellipse, the elliptical arc itself, and the white circle, which is the original Shrub block. You deleted the layout geometry and are now left with precisely positioned shrubs.

11. Save your work.

Your model should now resemble Ex05.2-end.dwg, which is available among this chapter's companion files.

Shape Splines

Splines are the equivalent of a French curve in traditional drafting, used for making curves of constantly changing radii. The splines in AutoCAD are NURBS-based curves (the same type used in Autodesk® Alias® Design,

Autodesk® Maya®, Autodesk® 3ds Max®, and many other high-end 3D programs). There are two types of NURBS curves:

▶ Those defined by control vertices (CVs), which don't lie on the curve except at its start and endpoints

▶ Those defined by *fit points*, which lie on the curve itself

You have more control over shaping curves with CVs, but if you want the curve to pass through specific points or want the curve to have sharp kinks, then Fit Points mode is preferable. Fortunately, it is easy to switch between CVs and Fit Points editing modes, so you can make up your mind about which method to use to suit the situation.

Exercise 5.3: Work with Control Vertices

CVs offer the most flexibility in terms of precisely shaping NURBS curves. A *control frame* connects CVs and represents the maximum possible curvature between adjacent CVs.

You will now draw a CV spline around the lake. Begin by opening `Ex05.3-start.dwg` from this chapter's companion files.

Certification
Objective

CV curves are typically
roughed in initially
and then are refined
in shape immediately
afterward.

▶

1. Toggle off Ortho, Polar Tracking, Object Snap Tracking, and Object Snap modes on the status bar if any of them are on. Type SPL (for Spline) and press Enter. The command prompt reads as follows:

```
Current settings: Method=Fit Knots=Chord
SPLINE Specify first point or [Method Knots Object]:
```

Click Method on the command line.

2. The command prompt reads as follows:

```
SPLINE Enter spline creation method [Fit CV] <Fit>:
```

Click CV on the command line. Click the first point anywhere along the edge of the lake.

3. Continue clicking points all the way around the lake. When you get close to the first point, type **C** (for Close) and press Enter. Click the spline you just drew to reveal its CVs (see Figure 5.12).

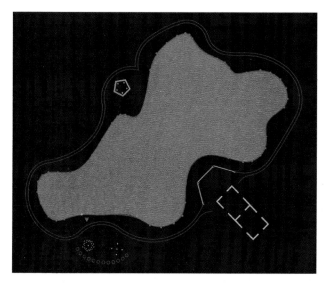

FIGURE 5.12 Drawing a rough CV spline around the lake

4. Position the cursor over a CV and observe the multifunction grip menu. Select Stretch Vertex, move the cursor, and click to relocate that particular CV.

5. Try adding and removing vertices using the corresponding choices on the multifunction grip menu (see Figure 5.13).

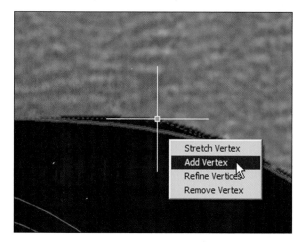

FIGURE 5.13 Adding and removing vertices from a CV spline using multifunction grips

▶

Vertices with higher weights pull the curve toward the control frame, and vertices with weights below 1 (but above 0) push the spline farther away.

6. Refining a vertex transforms one vertex into two adjacent vertices. Try refining vertices in areas where the curvature is changing rapidly.

7. Another way to affect the shape of a spline is to adjust the weights of individual CVs. Double-click the spline itself (rather than a CV or the control frame) to invoke the SPLINEDIT command. The prompt reads as follows:

```
SPLINEDIT Enter an option [Open Fit data Edit vertex
convert to Polyline
Reverse Undo eXit] <eXit>:
```

Click Edit Vertex on the command line.

8. The prompt now reads as follows:

```
SPLINEDIT Enter a vertex editing option [Add Delete
Elevate order
Move Weight eXit] <eXit>:
```

Type **W** (for Weight) and press Enter.

▶

The weights you need to enter depend entirely on exactly where you placed the CVs when creating the curve in step 2.

9. Before entering a weight value, you must select the vertex in which you're interested. Zoom out until you can see all the vertices, locate the red one, press Enter repeatedly to choose the default option (Next), and move the red CV one position at a time until your chosen CV turns red.

10. Type **2** and press Enter (see Figure 5.14). The spline will get closer to the red CV and its control frame. Type **.5** and press Enter again; the curve moves farther away from the control frame. Type a value appropriate to your particular situation and press Enter. You're setting a weight of 0.75 for the CV shown in Figure 5.14 to push it away from the control frame and more closely match the shape of the lake.

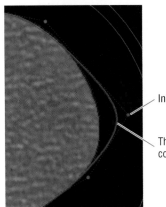

Increase the weight of this CV.

The curve is drawn closer to the control frame near the weighted CV.

FIGURE 5.14 Adjusting the weight of a CV

11. Type X (for Exit) and press Enter. Press X and Enter twice more to exit SPLINEDIT fully.

12. Continue adjusting the spline until it closely matches the outline of the lake.

13. Type **IM** (for Image) and press Enter. The External References palette appears.

14. Right-click Pond in the External References palette and choose Detach. Close the External References palette. Select the pond spline and change its color to Blue in the Properties panel. The pond is now represented by a blue curve rather than a blue image (see Figure 5.15).

You'll learn more about this palette in Chapter 9, "Working with Blocks and Xrefs."

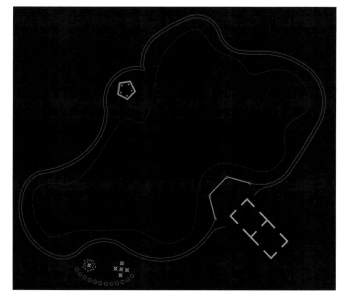

FIGURE 5.15 Pond shown as a spline rather than as an image

15. Save your work.

Your model should now resemble Ex05.3-end.dwg, which is available among this chapter's companion files.

SKETCH AND REBUILD CVS

Instead of stretching, adding, removing, refining, and/or adjusting CVs, you can sketch spline curves freehand. The SKETCH command is admittedly difficult to

(Continues)

SKETCH AND REBUILD CVs *(Continued)*

use with a mouse, so if you have a stylus and a drawing tablet, try using them for a more natural drawing feel. Unfortunately, sketching splines usually results in an uneven distribution of CVs, but this can be rectified by using CVREBUILD. The CVREBUILD command's Rebuild Curve dialog box is shown here:

Exercise 5.4: Work with Fit Points

Fit-point splines are straightforward in the sense that the fit points you click lie on (or very close to) the curve itself. Controlling the shape of a fit curve on the most basic level is a matter of adding more fit points in strategic locations. There are a few advanced options affecting the shape of a spline in between fit points (Tangent, Tolerance, Kink, and Knot Parameterization), and you will use Kink in this exercise to establish sharp points on the spline. Begin by opening the file Ex05.4-start.dwg from this chapter's companion files.

1. Zoom into the area at the bottom of the lake. More specifically, zoom into the grouping of five points. Type **REGEN** and press Enter to regenerate the display and thus automatically resize the point objects.

2. Expand the Draw panel and click the Spline Fit tool at the top left. Toggle on Object Snap mode in the status bar (with Node snap on) and click the top point, the point on the right, the point on the bottom, and then the one on the left. Type **C** (for Close) and press Enter. The fit curve looks very much like a circle, although it is not perfectly round (see Figure 5.16). This will be the start of an abstract tree representation.

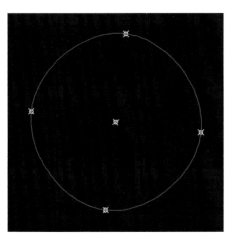

FIGURE 5.16 Snapping spline fit points to point

3. Expand the Modify panel and click the Edit Spline button. Select the curve you drew in step 2. Choose Fit Data from the Dynamic Input menu. Then choose Add from the next Dynamic Input menu that appears.

4. The prompt reads as follows:

    SPLINEDIT Specify existing fit point on spline <exit>:

    Click the top point.

5. The prompt now says the following:

    SPLINEDIT Specify new fit point to add <exit>:

    This particular command requires that you snap the new fit point, so type **NEA** (for Nearest), and press Enter. Click the curve in between the top and right points. Press Enter four times to exit SPLINEDIT fully.

6. Another way to add fit points is with the multifunction grips, although this method doesn't work on the first point. To use this feature, click the spline to select it, hover the cursor over the rightmost point, and choose Add Fit Point from the menu that appears. Hold Shift, right-click, and choose Nearest from the context menu. Click a point between the right and bottom points.

7. Repeat the previous step twice, adding additional fit points between the bottom, left, and top points (see Figure 5.17).

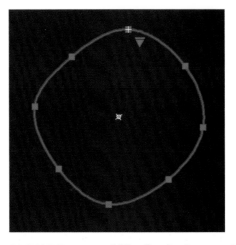

F I G U R E 5 . 1 7 Adding fit points between the initial points

8. Double-click the spline itself to invoke the SPLINEDIT command. Click Fit Data from the dynamic prompt menu. The command prompt reads as follows:

```
SPLINEDIT Enter a fit data option
[Add Open Delete Kink Move Purge Tangents
toLerance eXit] <eXit>:
```

Click Kink and then click eight points in between all the existing fit points (see Figure 5.18). Press Enter three times to exit the command fully.

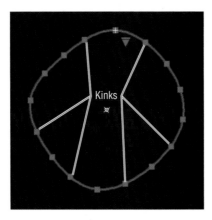

F I G U R E 5 . 1 8 Adding kinks to the fit-point spline

9. Click each kink grip, and move it in toward the center to create an abstract representation of a tree (see Figure 5.19).

FIGURE 5.19   Abstract tree created by stretching kinks in a fit-point spline

10. Save your work.

Your model should now resemble Ex05.4-end.dwg, which is available among this chapter's companion files.

Blend Between Objects with Splines

The BLEND command creates a CV spline in between two selected lines, circular or elliptical arcs, splines, or any combination of these object types. Blend curves join the endpoints of the two objects with a curve having either tangent or smooth continuity. A subtle difference exists between these types of blending.

A blend curve with tangent continuity has its control frame parallel to the control frame of the adjacent curve. Not only does a blend curve with smooth continuity have its control frame parallel to the control frame of the adjacent curve, but the control frames have equal lengths. In simpler terms, tangent continuity is smooth, and smooth continuity is "perfectly smooth."

Exercise 5.5: Blend Splines

In the following steps, you will create blend splines with two types of curvature. Begin by opening `Ex05.5-start.dwg` from this chapter's companion files.

1. Zoom and pan over to the other "tree" to the left of the tree you've drawn with kinks. Type **BLEND** and press Enter.

2. The prompt reads as follows:

```
Continuity = Tangent
BLEND Select first object or [CONtinuity]:
```

   Select a flat arc and an adjacent tight arc, and the command is finished. A CV spline with tangent continuity blends between the two arcs.

3. Press the spacebar to repeat BLEND, type **CON** (for Continuity), press Enter, type **S** (for Smooth), and press Enter again. Click two adjacent arcs to create another blend curve (see Figure 5.20).

Smooth continuity   Tangent continuity

F I G U R E 5 . 2 0   Blending between arcs with different types of continuity

4. Continue blending all the adjacent curves in the tree. Figure 5.21 shows the completed drawing.

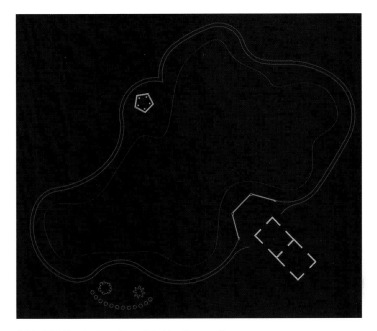

FIGURE 5.21 Completed landscape plan

5. Save your work.

Your model should now resemble Ex05.5-end.dwg, which is available among this chapter's companion files.

Now You Know

In this chapter, you learned how to draw and edit curved polylines, ellipses, elliptical arcs, and splines. You also learned the control vertex and fit point methods for editing splines, and you created smooth and tangent blend curves between existing curved elements.

CHAPTER 6

Controlling Object Visibility and Appearance

Layers control whether objects are visible or hidden. All objects have properties that control their appearance—color, linetype, lineweight, and so on. The layers to which objects are assigned usually control general object properties, but these properties can be set on a per-object basis as well. This chapter explores the many AutoCAD® tools associated with layers, illustrating their importance in managing the complexity of design.

In this chapter, you'll learn to do the following:

▶ **Change object properties**

▶ **Set the current layer**

▶ **Alter the layer assignments of objects**

▶ **Control layer visibility**

▶ **Apply linetype**

▶ **Assign properties by object or by layer**

▶ **Manage layer properties**

▶ **Isolate objects**

Change Object Properties

All objects have properties controlling their appearance. When you draw a line, you are ultimately specifying its geometric properties (the start point and the endpoint). Likewise, when you draw a circle, you are just specifying its center point and radius properties. Geometric properties are the most important factor governing how objects look and determining where the objects are in space.

In addition to geometric properties, all objects share a short list of general properties: layer, color, linetype, linetype scale, lineweight, transparency, and thickness. Although general properties are assigned on a per-object basis, they are usually controlled by using layers.

Exercise 6.1: Edit Object Properties

In this exercise, you will explore object properties in an existing drawing and then learn how to change properties and merge the layers to which objects are assigned. Begin by opening the file Ex06.1-start.dwg, which is available for download from the book's web page at www.sybex.com/go/autocad2018essentials. Figure 6.1 shows the architectural plan for a small office.

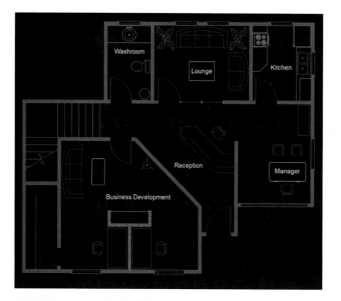

FIGURE 6.1 Small office plan

1. Zoom into the reception desk at the center of the small office plan.

2. Press Ctrl+Shift+P to toggle on Quick Properties mode.

Certification
Objective

3. Click the line of the desk immediately adjacent to the Reception text object; the Quick Properties panel appears at the top right of the selected object on the drawing canvas. Click the Desk-High layer name to activate the Layer drop-down menu (see Figure 6.2).

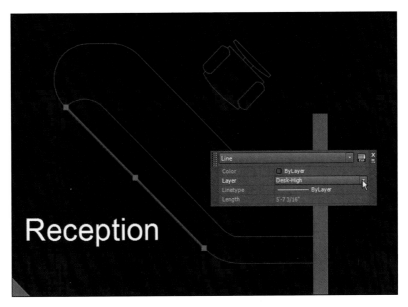

FIGURE 6.2   Targeting an object property using Quick Properties mode

4. Open the Layer drop-down and observe that the layer in blue is what is currently assigned. Select Desk (see Figure 6.3) in the drop-down and press the Esc key to exit Quick Properties mode. Press Ctrl+Shift+P to toggle off Quick Properties mode. Observe that the line whose layer property you changed now appears violet, like the other objects on the Desk layer.

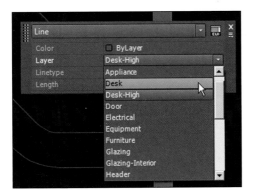

FIGURE 6.3   Assigning a different layer to the selected object

5. Expand the Layers panel and click the Merge tool. The command prompt reads as follows:

```
LAYMRG Select object on layer to merge or [Name]:
```

6. Click one of the brown lines in the upper portion of the reception desk and press Enter.

7. Click the violet line you changed to the Desk layer in step 4 and press Enter. The command history reads as follows:

```
Select object on target layer or [Name]:
******* WARNING ********
You are about to merge layer "Desk-High" into layer "Desk".
Do you wish to continue? [Yes/No] <No>:
```

> Use the LAYDEL command to delete a layer and everything on it. Be careful, though, to avoid deleting valuable information.

8. Choose Yes from the dynamic prompt menu. The Desk-High layer is deleted, and the objects that were on it have been reassigned to the Desk layer. The LAYMRG command is done.

9. Type **REGEN** and press Enter. The display is regenerated.

10. Expand the Properties panel and click the List tool. Pan over and select the Business Development text object by clicking it and pressing Enter. The AutoCAD Text window appears, displaying the following property information:

```
TEXT Layer: "Title"
Space: Model space
Handle = 71e
Style = "Standard"
Annotative: No
Typeface = Arial
mid point, X=16'-1 7/8" Y=11'-0 13/16" Z= 0'-0"
height 0'-7 1/2"text Business Development
rotation angle 0
width scale factor 1.0000
obliquing angle 0
generation normal
```

This list might be helpful if you were looking for a particular piece of information, but you can't edit any of the properties directly. Close the AutoCAD Text window.

Certification
Objective

11. Select the View tab on the ribbon and, on the Palettes panel, click the Properties tool to open the Properties panel.

12. Select the Business Development text object you selected in step 10. Many of its properties appear in the panel (see Figure 6.4). Property values that are editable are displayed on a black background when selected.

Although the LIST command shows some property information that does not appear in the Properties panel, most people prefer using the panel because much of the data is directly editable.

FIGURE 6.4 Editing a value in the Properties panel

13. Select the words *Business Development* in the Contents property, type **Marketing**, and press Enter. Press Esc to deselect the text object. The department's name has been changed. You can now close the Properties panel.

Your model should now resemble Ex06.1-end.dwg, which is available among this chapter's companion files.

Set the Current Layer

Objects are always drawn on the current layer, and there is only one current layer at any given time. Every drawing has at least one layer, layer 0 (zero), which is current by default when you create a new drawing.

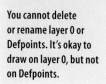

You cannot delete or rename layer 0 or Defpoints. It's okay to draw on layer 0, but not on Defpoints.

AutoCAD has another special layer, called *Defpoints*, which is automatically created when you add associative dimensions to a drawing (see Chapter 11, "Dimensioning").

Exercise 6.2: Choose the Current Layer

Begin by opening the file Ex06.2-start.dwg from this chapter's companion files.

1. Zoom into the manager's office.

2. Select the Home tab on the ribbon. Click the Rectangle tool on the Draw panel and click a point a few inches (no need to measure) from the lower-left corner of the room. Type @18,72 (or @45,180 for metric) and press Enter to create a credenza in the manager's office (see Figure 6.5).

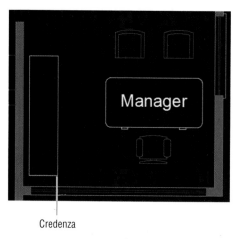

Credenza

FIGURE 6.5 Drawing furniture on layer 0

3. Press Ctrl+Shift+P to toggle on Quick Properties mode. Select the rectangle you drew in the previous step and change its Layer assignment to Furniture in the Quick Properties window that appears. Press Esc to deselect.

4. If you plan on drawing more than one object, a more efficient approach is to set the current layer before drawing so that the new object will have the proper layer assignment automatically. Open the Layer drop-down menu in the Layers panel and click on or to the right of the word *Furniture* to set this layer as current (see Figure 6.6).

FIGURE 6.6 Setting Furniture as the current layer using the drop-down menu in the Layers panel

5. Pan over to the Marketing space.

6. Click the Rectangle tool on the Draw panel and click a point a few inches (without measuring) from the lower-right corner of the room. Type @–18,72 (or @–45,180 for metric) and press Enter to create a credenza in Marketing (see Figure 6.7).

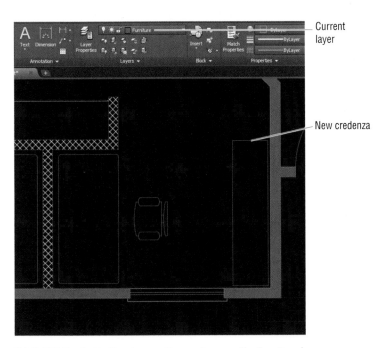

FIGURE 6.7 Drawing another credenza on the Furniture layer

7. Select the rectangle you drew in the previous step and verify that it is on the Furniture layer in the Quick Properties window that appears. Press Esc.

8. Pan over to the closet in Marketing. One of the lines representing shelves is missing. You will draw the missing line on the same layer as the existing shelf line.

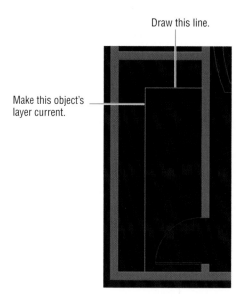

9. In the Layers panel, click the Make Object's Layer Current tool. Click the existing shelf line in Marketing's closet.

10. Toggle on Endpoint and Perpendicular running object snap modes on the status bar, if they are not already on.

11. Click the Line tool on the Draw panel and draw the line shown in Figure 6.8. Press Esc to end the LINE command.

Draw this line.

Make this object's layer current.

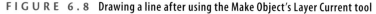

FIGURE 6.8 Drawing a line after using the Make Object's Layer Current tool

Your model should now resemble Ex06.2-end.dwg, which is available among this chapter's companion files.

Alter the Layer Assignments of Objects

Although you have already changed the layer assignments of objects using Quick Properties, there are more efficient methods, some of which do not require you to remember a layer name.

Exercise 6.3: Assign Layers

Let's explore several methods for changing the layer assignments of existing objects. Begin by opening the file Ex06.3-start.dwg from this chapter's companion files.

1. Type **DS** and press Enter. Select the Quick Properties tab of the Drafting Settings dialog box and uncheck Display The Quick Properties Palette On Selection (see Figure 6.9). Click OK.

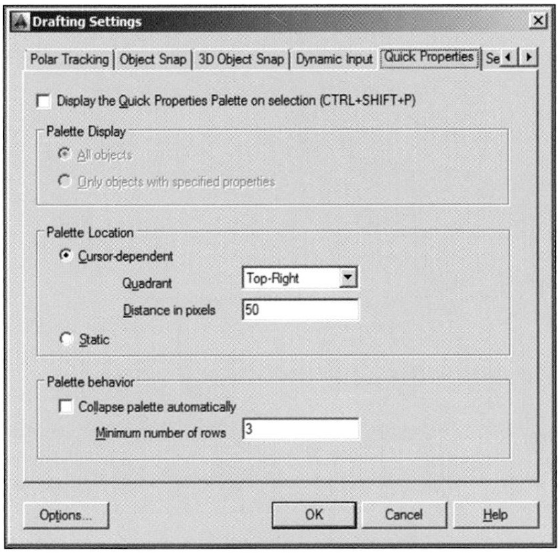

FIGURE 6.9 Drafting Settings dialog box

2. Select the coffee table in Marketing. Select the Home tab on the ribbon. Notice that the entry in the Layer drop-down in the Layers panel changes to layer 0; this does not mean that layer 0 is current (Millwork is), only that the selected item is on layer 0.

In AutoCAD 2018, you can optionally add the Layer drop-down list to the Quick Properties toolbar.

3. Open the Layer drop-down menu in the Layers group on the Home tab and click Furniture (see Figure 6.10) to change the layer assignment of the selected items. Press Esc to deselect.

FIGURE 6.10   Changing layer assignment with the Layer drop-down menu

4. Pan over to the lounge room.

5. Click the Match tool in the Layers panel, select the coffee table in the lounge, and press Enter. The command prompt reads as follows:

   ```
   LAYMCH Select object on destination layer or [Name]:
   ```

6. Click one of the sofas in the lounge and press Enter; the LAYMCH command ends. The coffee table is now assigned to the same layer as the sofas (Furniture).

7. Pan to the manager's office.

8. Click the Match Properties tool in the Properties panel on the Home tab of the ribbon. Select the credenza in the manager's office. The command prompt reads as follows:

   ```
   MATCHPROP Select destination object(s) or [Settings]:
   ```

9. Click Settings on the command line; the Property Settings dialog box appears. You can match many properties in addition to layers with this tool (see Figure 6.11). Click OK.

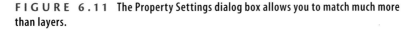

FIGURE 6.11 The Property Settings dialog box allows you to match much more than layers.

10. Click the desk in the manager's office and press Enter; the desk turns green because it is now on the Furniture layer. Press Esc to exit the MATCHPROP command.

Your model should now resemble Ex06.3-end.dwg, which is available among this chapter's companion files.

MERGING LAYERS

You can merge the contents of multiple layers into a single layer. First, select the layers you want to merge in the Layer Properties Manager (using the Ctrl key to select multiple nonsequential layers), right-click, and select Merge Selected Layers To. You are then presented with a dialog box where you can select the single destination layer from a list. The source layers are automatically purged after their contents are merged into the destination layer.

Certification
Objective

Control Layer Visibility

In traditional drafting, separate drawings would have to be made for the floor plan and the reflected ceiling plan to represent the floor and ceiling of the same space. In AutoCAD, simply displaying some layers while hiding others allows you to create some of the drawings required to describe the space graphically.

To understand better how to do this, you need to learn how to toggle layer status, isolate layers to work without distraction, and save layer states to recall the layer status of multiple layers quickly.

Exercise 6.4: Toggle Layer Status

In addition to having properties such as color, linetype, lineweight, and so on, layers have states that can be toggled, including On/Off, Thaw/Freeze, and Lock/Unlock. As you'll see in the following steps, layer states control the visibility and editability of the objects assigned to layers. Begin by opening the file Ex06.4-start.dwg from this chapter's companion files.

1. Expand the Layers panel and click the Turn All Layers On tool. You now see the switches ($ symbols), downlights, and header layers. Figure 6.12 shows the result.

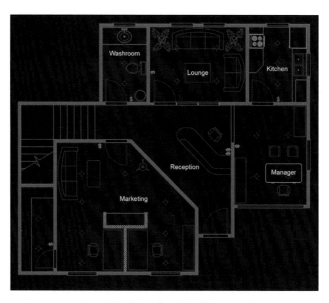

FIGURE 6.12 The floor plan with all layers

2. Open the Layer drop-down menu in the Layers panel and click the Appliance layer's lightbulb icon to toggle it off. Toggle off the Desk layer as well. Click outside the Layer drop-down menu to close it.

3. Click the Off tool in the Layers panel and click the following objects: furniture, sink, door, toilet, plant, stairs, low wall, low wall's pattern fill, text, reception desk, and the porch. Click a kitchen cabinet, and the command prompt reads as follows:

```
LAYOFF Layer "Millwork" is current, do you want to
turn it off? [Yes/No] <No>:
```

If you turn the current layer off, then anything you draw subsequently will be hidden.

4. Choose Yes from the dynamic prompt. Press Esc to end the LAYOFF command. Figure 6.13 shows the result.

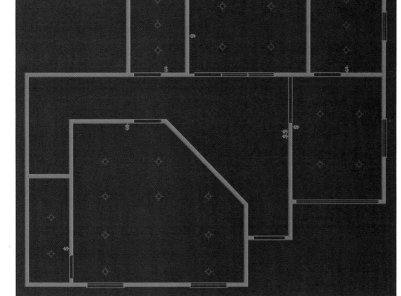

FIGURE 6.13   Reflected ceiling plan created by toggling layers off

5. Open the Layer drop-down menu in the Layers panel and set layer 0 as current.

6. Click the Zoom Extents tool in the Navigation bar. Notice that there is a gap between the bottom wall of the building and the lower edge of the drawing canvas.

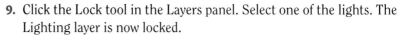

Even though it is off, the Porch layer is still defining the extents of the drawing.

7. Open the Layer drop-down menu in the Layers panel and freeze the Porch layer. Press Esc to close the drop-down menu.

8. Click the Zoom Extents tool in the Navigation bar again.

9. Click the Lock tool in the Layers panel. Select one of the lights. The Lighting layer is now locked.

10. Type **E** (for Erase) and press Enter. Click a different light, and observe a tiny padlock appear near the object. You can't select the object because it is locked.

Your model should now resemble Ex06.4-end.dwg, which is available among this chapter's companion files.

Exercise 6.5: Isolate Layers

You can quickly isolate one or more layers to work on them without the visual clutter of all the other layers. Begin by opening the file Ex06.5-start.dwg from this chapter's companion files.

1. Click the Isolate tool on the Layers panel and then make a crossing selection through one of the windows. Press Enter, and all the other layers disappear (see Figure 6.14).

F I G U R E 6 . 1 4 Isolating a couple of layers for focused work

2. Expand the Layers panel and click the Copy Objects To New Layer
tool. Select each one of the nine sill lines on the inside of the building
and press Enter. The command prompt reads as follows:

```
COPYTOLAYER Select object on destination layer or
[Name] <Name>:
```

3. Click Name on the command line. The Copy To Layer dialog box
appears (see Figure 6.15). Select Header from the Destination Layer
list, click OK, and press Enter.

◄

**There are now nine
lines on the Sill layer
and nine duplicate
lines on the Header
layer.**

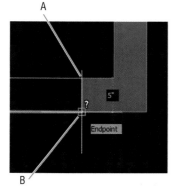

FIGURE 6.15 Selecting a layer in the Copy To Layer dialog box

4. Click the Unisolate tool on the Layers panel. The layers return to the
way they were before you used the Isolate tool.

5. Type **LAYOFF** and press Enter. Click one of the sills on the outside of
the building to turn off the Sill layer and press Enter.

6. Zoom into the entry and click the Measure tool in the Utilities panel.
Click points A and B shown in Figure 6.16 to measure the wall thickness. The tooltip reads 5" (12.7 in metric). Press Esc.

FIGURE 6.16 Measuring the wall thickness with Measure

7. Type O (for Offset), press Enter, type **5** (or **12.7** for metric), and press Enter again. Click the header line in the window opening and then click below it to offset a line on the outer edge of the wall.

8. Continue clicking each header and a point outside the building to offset a second header line in each window opening. Press Enter to end the OFFSET command when done. The reflected ceiling plan is complete.

Your model should now resemble Ex06.5-end.dwg, which is available among this chapter's companion files.

Exercise 6.6: Save Layer States

In this section, you will learn how to save collections of layer states for later recall. You have already created a reflected ceiling plan in this chapter, and you will now save it as a layer state so that you won't have to repeat all the work of toggling layer states in the future. Begin by opening the file Ex06.6-start.dwg from this chapter's companion files.

1. Expand the Layers panel and open the Unsaved Layer State drop-down menu. Select New Layer State in the drop-down menu (see Figure 6.17).

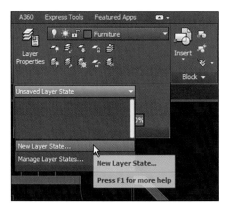

FIGURE 6.17 Saving a new layer state

2. Type **Reflected Ceiling Plan** in the New Layer State To Save dialog box and click OK. The closed drop-down now says Reflected Ceiling Plan.

3. Click the Turn All Layers On tool.

4. Click the adjacent Thaw All Layers tool.

5. Click the Freeze tool in the Layers panel and select the following objects: light, switch, header, and computer. The layers Lighting, Electrical, Header, and Equipment are frozen. Press Enter to end the LAYFRZ command.

6. Expand the Layers panel, open the Layer State drop-down menu in the Layers panel, and click New Layer State. Type **Furniture Plan** in the New Layer State To Save dialog box and click OK.

7. Open the Layer State drop-down menu and select Reflected Ceiling Plan (see Figure 6.18). All the layer states associated with the Reflected Ceiling Plan are immediately toggled.

Using LAYERP (Layer Previous) undoes the last set of changes to layers. This is different from UNDO, which affects more than layers.

Switch back to the Furniture Plan state, and you'll see the value in saving layer states (it saves lots of time).

FIGURE 6.18 Accessing saved layer states from the drop-down in the Layers panel

Your model should now resemble Ex06.6-end.dwg, which is available among this chapter's companion files.

Apply Linetype

In traditional drafting, you draw short, interrupted line segments when you want to indicate a *hidden line*. Hidden lines represent objects that are above the section plane. For example, objects such as upper cabinets, high shelves, or roof edges are shown as hidden because they are above an imaginary section line cutting the building horizontally.

In AutoCAD, lines are not interrupted (broken into multiple little pieces) to indicate hidden lines. Instead, continuous lines are assigned a *linetype*, and this style makes lines appear as if they are interrupted. One advantage to this is that you can adjust the scale of the line breaks without having to redraw myriad little lines.

Exercise 6.7: Use Linetype

Begin by opening the file Ex06.7-start.dwg from this chapter's companion files.

Certification
Objective

1. Open the Linetype drop-down menu in the Properties panel and select Other at the bottom of the menu (see Figure 6.19).

FIGURE 6.19 Accessing other linetypes

2. In the Linetype Manager dialog box that appears, click the Load button. Scroll down in the Load Or Reload Linetypes dialog box that appears and select Hidden in the list (see Figure 6.20); then click OK. Hidden now appears in the Linetype Manager dialog box because this particular linetype style has been loaded in the drawing file; click OK to close the Linetype Manager dialog box.

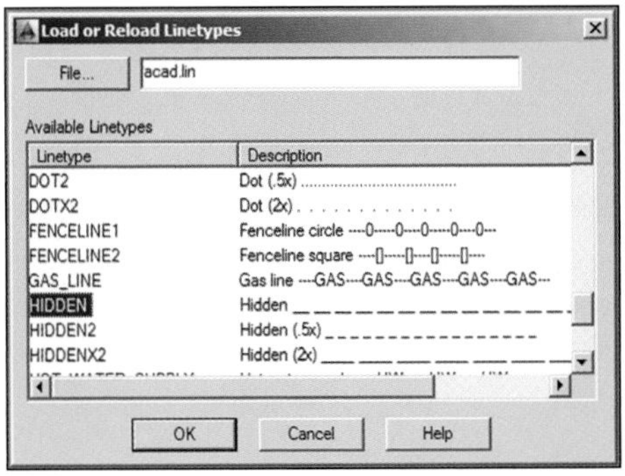

FIGURE 6.20 Loading the Hidden linetype

3. Zoom into the closet in the Marketing space, and select both lines on the Millwork layer, representing a high shelf.

4. Open the Linetype drop-down menu in the Properties panel and select Hidden from the menu. Now the two selected lines have the Hidden linetype assigned. Press Esc to deselect.

5. You still don't see breaks in the lines because the linetype scale is too small by default. Type **LTS** (for Linetype Scale) and press Enter. The command prompt reads as follows:

   ```
   LTSCALE Enter new linetype scale factor <1.0000>:
   ```

6. Type **48** (or **50** for metric) and press Enter. The lines appear with breaks indicating that the shelf is above the section plane (see Figure 6.21).

> The factor of 48 is appropriate for 1/4" scale. The factor 50 is appropriate for 1:50 metric drawings.

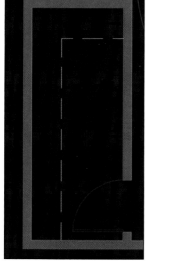

FIGURE 6.21 Hidden lines representing a high shelf in the closet

> Alter the linetype scale of specific objects by adjusting the Linetype Scale property in the Properties panel. Lower values scale linetypes smaller.

7. Select the horizontal shelf line, right-click, and choose Properties from the context menu.

8. Change Linetype Scale to 0.5 in the General section of the Properties panel (see Figure 6.22).

F I G U R E 6 . 2 2   Adjusting the Linetype Scale property

In AutoCAD 2018, you can select and snap to gaps in complex and DGN linetypes.

9. Press Esc to deselect the horizontal shelf line. The breaks in the horizontal line are half as large as those in the vertical segment (see Figure 6.23). Close the Properties panel.

Both lines' linetype scales are affected by LTSCALE.

This line's linetype scale property was changed.

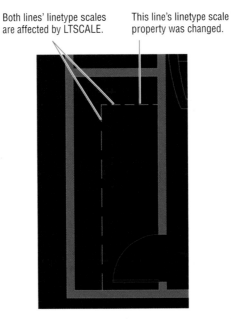

F I G U R E 6 . 2 3   Scaling the linetype of an individual object

Your model should now resemble Ex06.7-end.dwg, which is available among this chapter's companion files.

Assign Properties by Object or by Layer

Properties such as color, linetype, and lineweight are typically assigned by layer rather than by object. There is a special property value called *ByLayer* that passes control over specific properties to the properties managed by the layer to which the objects are assigned. As you'll see in these steps, using the ByLayer property is a lot easier than it sounds.

Exercise 6.8: Assign Properties

Begin by opening the file Ex06.8-start.dwg from this chapter's companion files.

1. Open the Linetype drop-down menu on the Properties panel and select Hidden (see Figure 6.24). Draw a line of arbitrary length anywhere on the canvas.

FIGURE 6.24 The Properties panel settings affect all the objects you create.

2. Open the Linetype drop-down menu on the Properties panel and select ByLayer.

3. Draw another line and observe that it has continuous linetype.

4. If you want to change the property of a specific object, use Quick Properties instead of the drop-down menus in the Properties panel. Press Ctrl+Shift+P to toggle on Quick Properties if it is currently off.

5. Select the continuous line drawn in step 2 and change its Linetype property to Hidden (see Figure 6.25). Press Esc to deselect.

6. Draw another line and verify that it has continuous linetype.

Objects should be assigned specific colors, linetypes, or lineweights only in exceptional circumstances.

Your model should now resemble Ex06.8-end.dwg, which is available among this chapter's companion files.

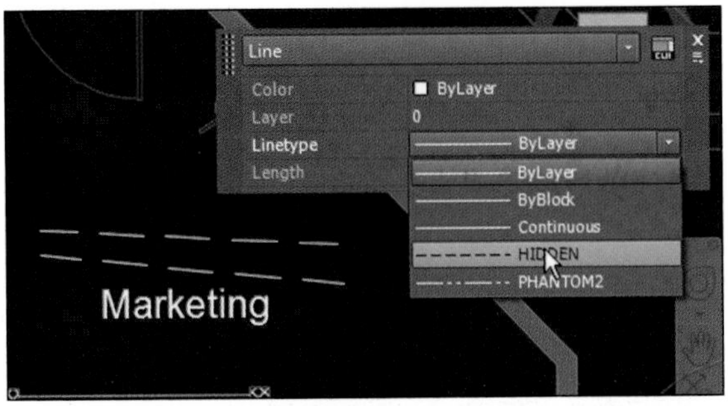

FIGURE 6.25 Changing a specific object property

Manage Layer Properties

The Layer Properties Manager is where you create layers and manage the properties that are assigned to them. Let's explore the Layer Properties Manager with a practical example.

Exercise 6.9: Control Layer Properties

Begin by opening the file Ex06.9-start.dwg from this chapter's companion files.

 1. Click the Layer Properties tool in the Layers panel. The Layer Properties Manager appears (see Figure 6.26).

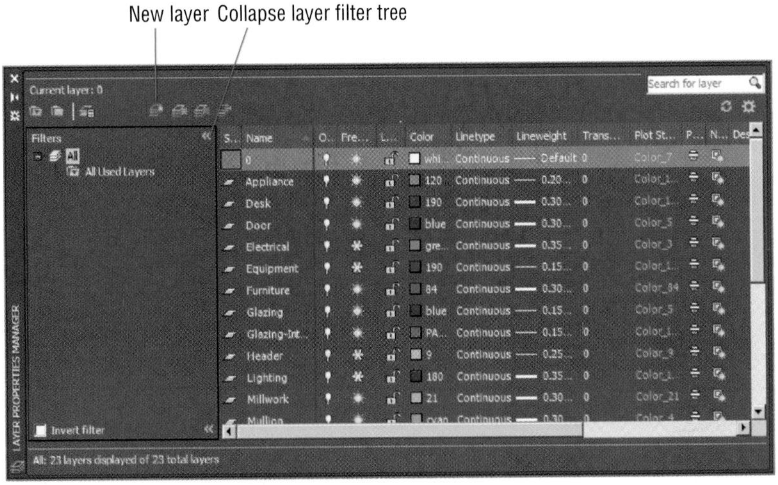

FIGURE 6.26 Layer Properties Manager

2. Collapse the layer filter tree to save some space in the panel.

3. Click the New Layer button, type **Millwork-Upper** as the new layer's name, and press Enter.

4. Double-click the blue parallelogram next to the new layer.

5. Right-click any one of the column headers to access a context menu. Choose Maximize All Columns from this menu. Figure 6.27 shows the result: The columns are all readable.

The green check mark next to the Millwork-Upper layer indicates it is the current layer.

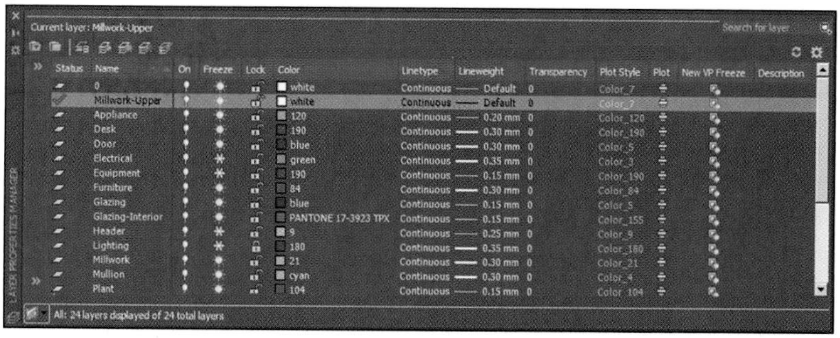

FIGURE 6.27 Maximizing the columns in the Layer Properties Manager makes them easier to read.

6. Click the Freeze column header to sort the column by that criterion (frozen state). Click the Freeze column header again to reverse the sort order. All columns are sortable.

Sorting columns is a quick way to find layers that have common properties. Drag the vertical bars between columns to resize them.

7. Click the word *Continuous* in the Linetype column in the Millwork-Upper layer. In the Select Linetype dialog box that appears, choose Hidden, and click OK.

8. Click Millwork-Upper's color swatch to open the Select Color dialog box. Click the larger red swatch where indicated in Figure 6.28 and click OK. Close the Layer Properties Manager.

The two lines appear red with the Hidden linetype because their properties are set to ByLayer, so they inherit layer Millwork-Upper's properties.

9. Zoom into the closet in the Marketing space and select both shelf lines. Change Layer to Millwork-Upper and Linetype to ByLayer in the Quick Properties window.

Your model should now resemble Ex06.9-end.dwg, which is available among this chapter's companion files.

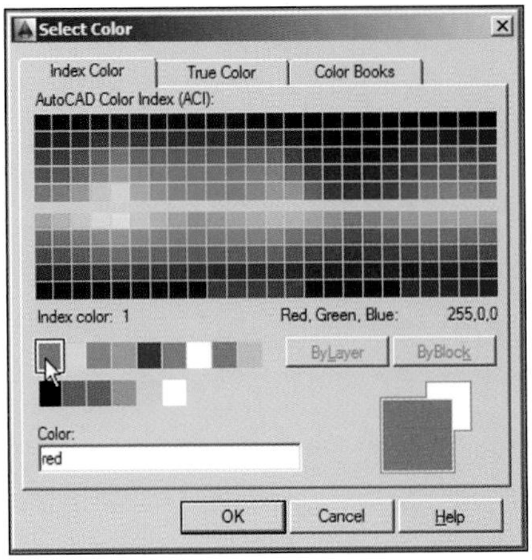

FIGURE 6.28 Selecting a layer color

Isolate Objects

In addition to object properties and layers, AutoCAD has yet another system for controlling the visibility of objects that allows you to isolate and/or hide individually selected objects. This system works completely independently of object and layer properties. It is best to isolate and/or hide objects as a drawing aid to reduce visual clutter onscreen while you are working in complex drawings.

Exercise 6.10: Isolate and Hide Individual Objects

In this exercise, you will learn how to isolate objects, hide additional objects, and finally end the object isolation to return the drawing to its initial state. This procedure is useful in situations where you want to focus on a chosen set of objects without visual distraction while you perform a task.

Begin by opening the file Ex06.10-start.dwg from this chapter's companion files.

Certification
Objective

1. Click the Isolate Objects button on the status bar and select Isolate Objects from the menu that appears. Select all of the objects inside the kitchen with a crossing selection (see Figure 6.29).

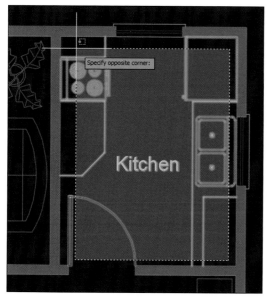

FIGURE 6.29 Isolating the contents of the kitchen

2. Click the same icon on the status bar as you did previously and select Hide Objects from the menu. Select the word *Kitchen* and the door and see them disappear.

3. Click the Stretch button in the Modify panel. Make a crossing selection from point A to B, as shown in Figure 6.30, and press Enter. Toggle on Ortho mode if it is not on already. Click an arbitrary first point, move the cursor downward a short distance to establish the vertical direction for the STRETCH command, type **12 (30 in metric)**, and press Enter.

4. Select the same icon in the status bar, which now has the tooltip Unisolate Objects, and choose End Object Isolation from the menu that appears. The hidden and isolated objects are now once again visible.

  Your model should now resemble Ex06.10-end.dwg, which is available among this chapter's companion files.

B

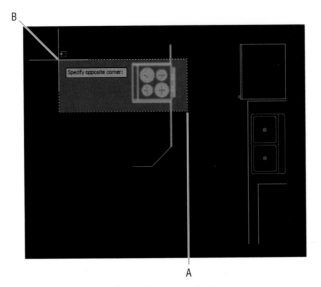

A

FIGURE 6.30   Stretching isolated objects

Now You Know

In this chapter, you learned how to change object properties, set the current layer, alter the layer assignment of objects, control layer visibility, apply linetype, assign properties by object or by layer, and manage layer properties.

CHAPTER 7

Organizing Objects

The fundamental entities in the AutoCAD® program are lines, polylines, circles, arcs, ellipses, and text. By combining these entities into blocks and/or groups, you can manipulate more complex objects, such as chairs, mechanical assemblies, trees, or any other organizational designation appropriate to your industry.

Manipulating blocks is an efficient means of working not only because it reduces the number of items requiring selection, but also because blocks can potentially control numerous references from a single definition. In this chapter, you will learn how groups are a flexible means of organizing collections of objects, which often include blocks as members. You will also learn how to select and manipulate a group as a whole or access the members of the group individually whenever needed.

In this chapter, you'll learn to do the following:

▶ **Define blocks**

▶ **Insert blocks**

▶ **Edit blocks**

▶ **Redefine blocks**

▶ **Work with groups**

Define Blocks

Before drawing and copying a series of repetitive elements, you should first define them as a block. This is because you have a higher level of organizational control over blocks than you do over individual entities. In this section, you will draw a chair and a door and then define them as blocks.

Exercise 7.1: Draw a Chair and Define It as a Block

In the following steps, you will use the drawing skills that you've learned in previous chapters to draw a chair. Then you will convert the chair into a block definition. Begin by opening the file Ex07.1-start.dwg (see Figure 7.1), which is available for download from the book's web page at www.sybex.com/go/autocad2018essentials.

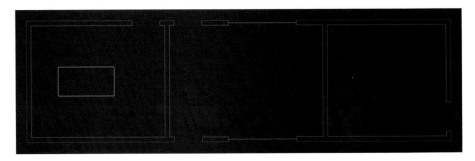

F I G U R E   7 . 1   **Three rooms**

1. Zoom into the leftmost room above the desk.

2. Click the Rectangle tool on the Draw panel and then click an arbitrary point above the desk (which is represented by the yellow rectangle) as the first corner point. The command prompt reads as follows:

   ```
   RECTANG Specify other corner point or [Area Dimensions
   Rotation]:
   ```

   Type @18,18 (or @45,45 for metric) and press Enter.

3. Click the Explode tool on the Modify panel, select the rectangle you just drew, and press Enter.

4. Click the Fillet tool on the Modify panel, and click Radius on the command line. Type 3 (or 7 for metric) and press Enter to set the fillet radius; then click the left and bottom edges to create an arc.

5. Press the spacebar to repeat the FILLET command. Click the bottom and right edges to create another arc. Figure 7.2 shows the result.

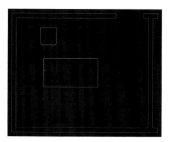

FIGURE 7.2   Using Fillet to round two corners

6. Expand the Modify panel, click the Join tool, select all the objects making up the chair you are drawing, and press Enter.

7. Toggle on Ortho mode on the status bar.

8. Select the polyline you joined in step 6. Hover the cursor over the top-middle grip and select Convert To Arc from the multifunction grip menu that appears (see Figure 7.3).

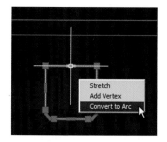

FIGURE 7.3   Converting a straight polyline segment into an arc

9. Move the cursor upward, type 3 (or 7 for metric), press Enter, and then press Esc to clear the selection. You've created the curve of the backrest.

10. Click the Explode tool on the Modify panel, press Enter, select the chair, and press Enter again. The polyline is converted into three lines and three arcs.

11. Click the Offset tool in the Modify panel, type 2 (or 5 for metric), and press Enter. Select the arc you created in step 8 and then click a point above it on the drawing canvas to offset a new arc 2" (or 5 cm) above. Press Enter to exit the OFFSET command.

12. Type **BLEND**, press Enter, and select the two arcs making up the backrest near their left endpoints. A spline object smoothly joins the arcs.

13. Press Enter to repeat the BLEND command, and select the two arcs near the right endpoints; another spline object is created (see Figure 7.4).

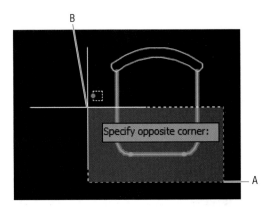

FIGURE 7.4 Blending between concentric arcs

14. Click the Stretch tool in the Modify panel, click points A and B shown in Figure 7.4 to create a crossing window, and press Enter. Click an arbitrary point on the drawing canvas as the first point of the Stretch operation. Move the cursor upward on the drawing canvas, type 3 (or 7 for metric), and press Enter. The seat depth is reduced.

15. Select the entire chair with an implied window. Click the Create tool in the Block panel on the ribbon's Home tab, and the Block Definition dialog box appears. Type **Chair** in the Name field. Every block must have a name.

16. Every block has a *base point*, which should be related to its geometry. Click the Pick Point button in the Base Point section; the Block Definition dialog box disappears. Hold Shift and right-click to open the context menu; select Midpoint. Click the midpoint of the chair's front edge. The Block Definition dialog box reappears, showing the coordinates of the point to which you snapped (see Figure 7.5).

A preview image of the chair appears to the right of the Name field because you selected its constituent objects prior to opening the Block Definition dialog box.

Certification Objective

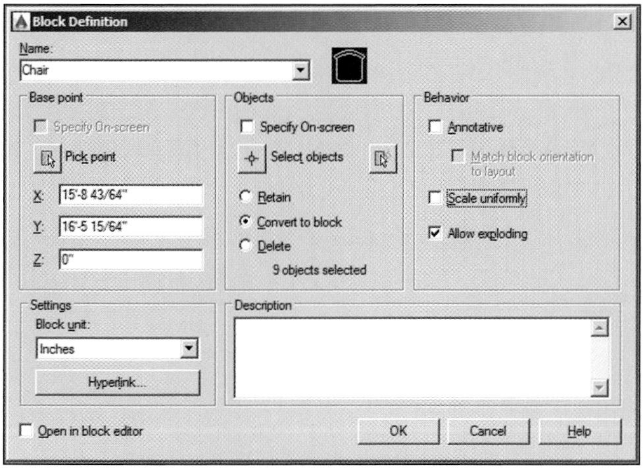

FIGURE 7.5 Defining a chair block

17. Choose the Delete radio button in the Objects section of the Block Definition dialog box. Select Scale Uniformly and Allow Exploding. Deselect Annotative and Open In Block Editor. Set the Block Unit drop-down to Inches (or Centimeters for metric) and click OK. The chair disappears; don't worry, you will insert it later.

Your model should now resemble Ex07.1-end.dwg, which is available among this chapter's companion files.

UNDERSTANDING THE BLOCK TABLE

When the chair disappeared from the drawing canvas, it was defined in the drawing's *block table*. Although every drawing has a block table, you can't see it. Blocks defined there can be inserted into the drawing as block references. Changes made to block definitions (stored in the block table) affect all block references in the drawing.

Exercise 7.2: Draw a Door and Define It as a Block

In the following steps, you will draw a door and the representation of its swing (an arc) and define it as a block. To begin, open the file Ex07.2-start.dwg from the Chapter 7 companion files.

1. Pan over to the middle room. Zoom into the door opening along the bottom edge of this room.

2. Toggle on Running Object Snap mode on the status bar. Right-click this button and turn on Endpoint snap if it's not already highlighted in the context menu.

3. Click the Rectangle tool in the Draw panel. Snap the first corner at point A, shown in Figure 7.6. Type @1.5,2'6 (or @4,75 for metric) and press Enter to complete the door.

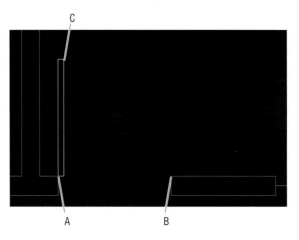

FIGURE 7.6 Drawing a door

4. Click to open the Arc pull-down menu on the Draw panel, and select the Center, Start, End tool. Click points A, B, and C, as shown in Figure 7.6, to create the swing.

5. Type **B** (for Block) and press Enter. The Block Definition dialog box appears.

6. Type **Door** in the Name field and click the Select Objects button. Select the rectangle and the arc and press Enter. Select the Pick Point button and click the door hinge. Select the Convert To Block radio button and click OK.

> The Convert To Block option both creates a block definition and inserts it into the drawing as a block reference.

7. Select the door, and observe that it has only one grip because it is now a block reference (see Figure 7.7). Press Esc to deselect.

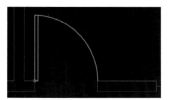

FIGURE 7.7 The door has only one grip because it is a block reference.

Your model should now resemble Ex07.2-end.dwg, which is available among this chapter's companion files.

Insert Blocks

After you create a block definition, you can insert *local block references* (from the current drawing's block table) into the drawing. In Chapter 9, "Working with Blocks and Xrefs," you will learn how to create and insert *global blocks*, which are blocks that exist outside the current drawing file.

Exercise 7.3: Use Blocks

In this section, you will focus on inserting local chair and door blocks. To begin, open the file Ex07.3-start.dwg from this chapter's companion files.

1. Type **UN** (for Units) and press Enter. Open the Insertion Scale drop-down menu and select Inches (or Centimeters for metric) if it is not already selected (see Figure 7.8). Click OK to close the Drawing Units dialog box.

The units you use in the Block Definition dialog box should match the Insertion Scale units; otherwise, AutoCAD will scale blocks when you insert them into the drawing.

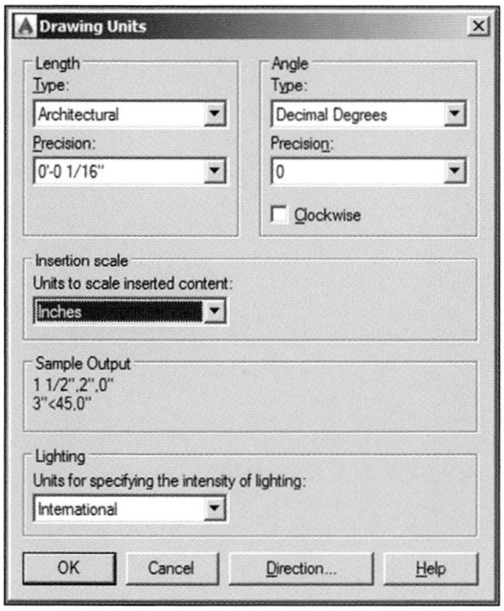

FIGURE 7.8 Setting Insertion Scale in the Drawing Units dialog box

2. Pan over to the room on the left with the table.

3. Right-click Running Object Snap on the status bar, and turn on Midpoint snap if it's not already highlighted in the context menu.

4. Click the Insert tool on the Block panel on the ribbon's Home tab. This opens the block gallery, a graphic menu of block thumbnails defined in this drawing. If you don't see the block gallery, set the GALLERYVIEW system variable to 1. Select the chair icon to insert this block (see Figure 7.9).

F I G U R E 7 . 9   Selecting the Chair block definition in the Insert dialog box

5. Hold Shift, right-click, and choose From in the context menu. Click the centroid marker at the center of the desk, type @0,1'6 (or @0,45 for metric), and press Enter. The Chair block reference appears slightly up from the edge of the desk on its centerline (see Figure 7.10).

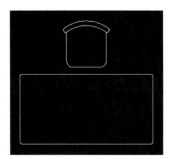

F I G U R E 7 . 1 0   Chair block inserted above the desk

6. Click the Move tool in the Modify panel, select the Chair block, and press Enter. Click an arbitrary point on the drawing canvas, type @1'3<180 (or @40<180 for metric), and press Enter to move the chair to the left.

7. Click the Copy tool in the Modify panel, type **L** (for Last), and press Enter twice. Click an arbitrary point on the drawing canvas, type @2'6<0 (or @80<0 for metric), and press Enter to copy a chair to the right (see Figure 7.11). Press Esc to end the COPY command.

FIGURE 7.11 Copying a block reference

8. Type **I** (for Insert) and press Enter. Type **180** in the Angle text box in the Rotation section of the Insert dialog box and click OK.

9. Hold Shift, right-click, and choose From in the context menu. Click the midpoint of the lower desk edge, type @0,-3" (or @0,-7 for metric), and press Enter. The Chair block reference appears 3" (or 7 cm) down from the center of the desk.

10. Press Enter to repeat the last command (INSERT) and select Door from the Name drop-down list in the Insert dialog box. Select Specify On-Screen in the Rotation section and click OK.

11. Click point A in the leftmost room, shown in Figure 7.12. Verify that Ortho mode is on in the status bar; if not, toggle it on. Move the cursor to the left to rotate the door into the proper orientation (see Figure 7.12). Click the canvas approximately at point B to insert the door.

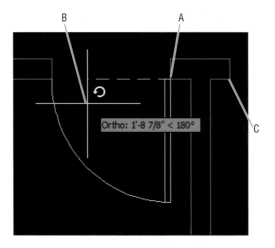

FIGURE 7.12 Inserting a door and rotating it onscreen

12. Press the spacebar to repeat the INSERT command. Select Specify On-Screen in the Scale section of the Insert dialog box (see Figure 7.13) and click OK.

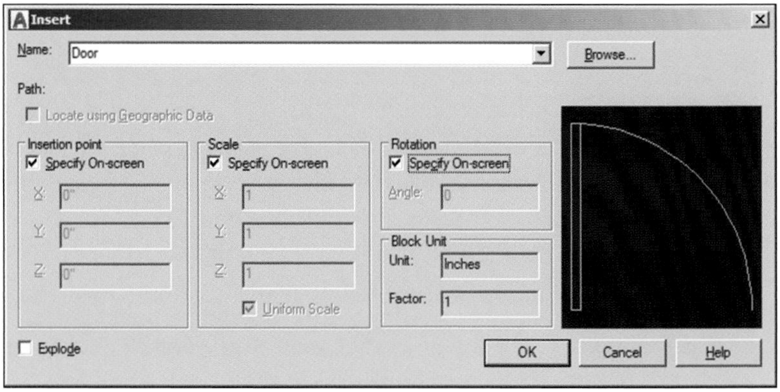

FIGURE 7.13 Specifying everything onscreen when inserting a block

13. Click point C shown in Figure 7.12. The command prompt reads as follows:

```
INSERT Specify insertion point or [Basepoint Scale
Rotate]:
Specify scale factor <1>:
```

Type –1 and press Enter.

14. The command prompt now says the following:

```
Specify rotation angle <0>: 180
```

Type **180** and press Enter.

15. Click the Copy tool in the Modify panel, select the door at the bottom of the middle room, and press Enter. Click points A and B shown in Figure 7.14 to copy a door block into the room on the right. Press Esc to end the COPY command.

Copying a block has the same effect as inserting a block: a new block reference is added to the drawing.

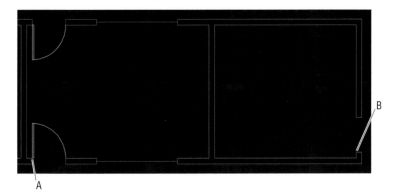

FIGURE 7.14 Copying a block

16. Select the new door in the rightmost room. Click its single blue grip to activate Grip Editing mode. Press the spacebar twice so that the command prompt reads as follows:

```
** ROTATE **
Specify rotation angle or
[Base point Copy Undo Reference eXit]:
```

Type **90** and press Enter to rotate the door block around its base point. Press Esc to deactivate grip editing mode.

Your model should now resemble Ex07.3-end.dwg, which is available among this chapter's companion files.

Edit Blocks

You can edit blocks after they have been defined and inserted into the drawing as block references. In addition to editing geometry, you can assign floating properties to control property inheritance, nest blocks within blocks, or explode blocks entirely.

Exercise 7.4: Edit Block Definitions

Block definitions are not set in stone; you can redraw them after block references have been inserted multiple times in a drawing. In fact, this is one of the reasons to use blocks: efficient control over multiple objects from a single editable definition. In the following steps, you will alter the door block and see all its references update automatically.

To begin, open the file Ex07.4-start.dwg from this chapter's companion files.

1. Zoom in on the lower door in the middle room.

2. Select the door, right-click, and choose Edit Block In-Place from the context menu. Click OK in the Reference Edit dialog box that appears (see Figure 7.15).

F I G U R E 7 . 1 5   Editing a block reference in place

3. Click the Rotate tool on the Modify panel, select the door itself (the rectangle rather than the arc), and press Enter. Click the hinge point, and the command prompt reads as follows:

        Specify rotation angle or [Copy Reference] <0>:

    Type −45 and press Enter.

4. Click the Trim tool in the Modify panel and press Enter. Click the portion of the wing that extends beyond the door to trim it off, and press Esc to end the TRIM command.

5. Click the Save Changes button in the temporary Edit Reference panel on the Home tab of the ribbon. Click OK in the AutoCAD warning dialog box that appears, which says, "All reference edits will be saved."

Figure 7.16 shows the result: all door references have been automatically updated with the new door geometry.

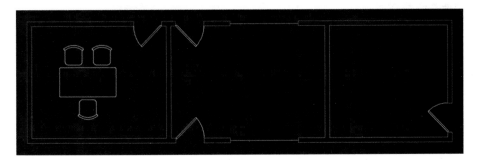

F I G U R E   7 . 1 6 All doors have been updated by editing the door block in place.

Your model should now resemble Ex07.4-end.dwg, which is available among this chapter's companion files.

Exercise 7.5: Assign Floating Properties

When you set an object's color, linetype, or lineweight to specific values such as Red, Hidden, or 0.5 mm, you are setting those properties explicitly. Explicit object properties assigned to objects in block definitions are retained when those blocks are inserted onto different layers in the drawing.

It is often advantageous to assign floating properties—either *ByLayer* or *ByBlock*—to the objects in block definitions. Floating properties allow block references to inherit properties from the layer on which they are inserted. Alternatively, you can override these inherited properties with explicit properties by assigning them to the block reference.

The Furniture layer has been current throughout this chapter, so the objects you drew to define the chair and door blocks reside on this layer. In the following steps, you will assign floating properties to the chair and door blocks.

To begin, open the file Ex07.5-start.dwg from this chapter's companion files.

1. Click each of the four door block references to select them. Type **qp** (for Quick Properties) and press Enter. Select Door from the Layer drop-down menu (see Figure 7.17). Notice that the doors are still yellow even though the Door layer is green. Click the Close box in the upper-right corner to close the Quick Properties palette and press Esc to deselect.

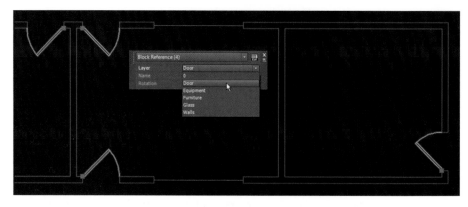

F I G U R E   7 . 1 7   Assigning the Door layer to the door block references

[Edit Block In-place] **2.** Select one of the doors (it doesn't matter which one), right-click, and choose Edit Block In-Place from the context menu. Click OK in the Reference Edit dialog box that appears.

3. Select the rectangle and arc making up the door.

4. Type **qp** (again, for Quick Properties) and press Enter. Open the Color drop-down menu and select ByBlock. Press Esc to deselect.

[Save Changes] **5.** Click the Save Changes button in the Edit References panel. Click OK in the AutoCAD warning dialog box. The doors turn green because the ByBlock floating property allows them to inherit the Door layer's green color.

6. Select the lower chair by clicking it. Open the Color drop-down menu in the Properties panel, select Magenta, and press Esc. The chair turns magenta because ByBlock allows explicit properties assigned to the block reference to override inherited layer properties.

The table, chairs, and doors disappear because the objects in the chair and door block definitions are on the Furniture layer.
▶

7. Open the Layer drop-down menu in the Layers panel and set layer 0 as the current layer.

8. Open the Layer drop-down menu again and toggle off the Furniture layer.

9. Toggle on the Furniture layer and click outside the Layer drop-down menu to close it.

[Edit Block In-place] **10.** Select a door, right-click, and choose Edit Block In-Place from the context menu. Click OK in the Reference Edit dialog box that appears.

11. Create a crossing window to select both the rectangle and arc making up the door.

12. Open the Layer drop-down menu, and select layer 0 to assign this layer to the selection. Press Esc to deselect the layer.

13. Click the Save Changes button in the Edit References panel. Click OK in the AutoCAD warning dialog box.

14. Open the Layer drop-down menu in the Layers panel and toggle off the Furniture layer.

BLOCKS AND LAYER 0

You should always draw objects within block definitions on layer 0 so that block references will inherit the layer on which they are inserted. Layer 0 is the only layer that works like this for block definitions. In addition, you should assign floating properties for the color, linetype, and/or lineweight of the objects in the block definition.

15. Toggle on the Furniture layer.

Your model should now resemble Ex07.5-end.dwg, which is available among this chapter's companion files.

Exercise 7.6: Nest Blocks

You can *nest* blocks within other blocks to simplify complex block definitions. However, you can't create circular references where blocks reference themselves, or you'd create an infinite loop. In the following steps, you'll nest a phone block reference inside the desk block definition so that every desk you insert will have a phone on it.

To begin, open the file Ex07.6-start.dwg from this chapter's companion files.

1. Type **BEDIT** (for Block Editor) and press Enter. Select Desk in the Edit Block Definition dialog box that appears (see Figure 7.18). Click OK.

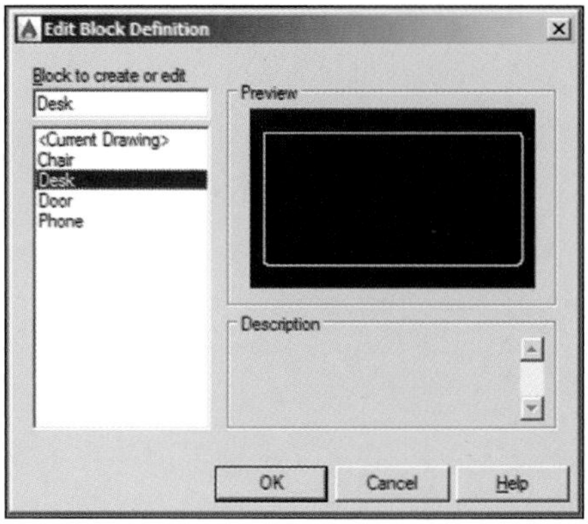

FIGURE 7.18 Selecting a block definition to edit

2. A temporary tab called Block Editor appears on the ribbon, and the selected block (desk) fills the drawing canvas. Click the Authoring Palettes button on the Manage panel to toggle them off because they are not needed for this exercise.

3. Type **I** (for Insert) and press Enter. Select Phone in the Name drop-down list. Deselect Specify On-Screen in the Scale and Rotation sections of the Insert dialog box and click OK (see Figure 7.19).

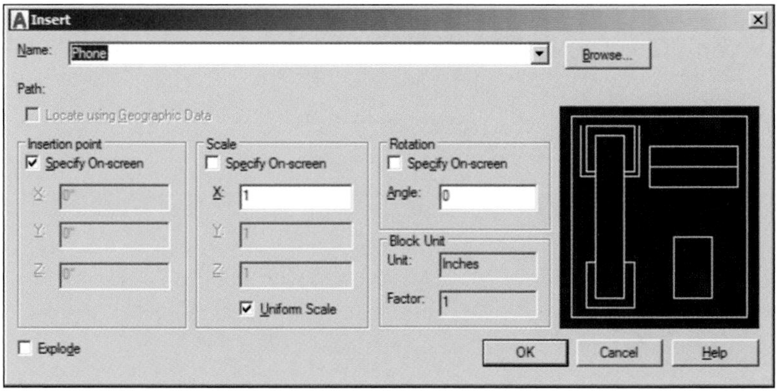

FIGURE 7.19 Inserting a phone block

The phone is magenta because the objects in the phone block definition have floating properties that allow the Equipment layer's magenta color to be inherited.

4. Click an arbitrary point on the right side of the desk and press Enter to insert the phone block reference there.

5. Select the phone block, type **qp** (for Quick Properties), and press Enter. Change Layer Assignment to Equipment, and press Esc to deselect.

6. Click the Close Block Editor button on the Close panel. Click Save The Changes To Desk in the dialog box that appears. Figure 7.20 shows the result.

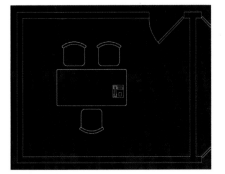

F I G U R E 7 . 2 0 A phone nested within the desk block and surrounding chair blocks

Your model should now resemble Ex07.6-end.dwg, which is available among this chapter's companion files.

Exercise 7.7: Explode Blocks

There are two commands that blow away blocks, leaving you with only their defining geometry: EXPLODE and XPLODE. The former has no options whatsoever; the latter offers many options dealing with what happens to object properties after the block is disassembled.

To begin, open the file Ex07.7-start.dwg from this chapter's companion files.

1. Click the Explode button on the Modify panel. Select the chair at the bottom of the desk and the door at the bottom of the middle room and press Enter.

2. Select the parts of the door, and observe in the Layers panel that the objects are on layer 0 and in the Properties panel that their color is set to ByBlock. Press Esc to deselect.

3. Click the Undo button on the Quick Access toolbar. The block is re-created.

Use the PURGE command to delete unused block definitions to make the drawing file smaller.

4. Type **xp** (for Xplode) and press Enter. Select the same green door and press Enter. The command prompt reads as follows:

```
[All Color LAyer LType LWeigh
Inherit from parent block Explode]
<Explode>:
```

Select Inherit From Parent Block in the Dynamic Input display.

5. Select the parts of the door and observe that the objects are on the green Door layer and their color is ByLayer. This time the disassembled objects received the layer assignment and object properties of the block reference.

Your model should now resemble Ex07.7-end.dwg, which is available among this chapter's companion files.

Redefine Blocks

You already know that block definitions have names and that blocks are inserted by name. So, what do you suppose happens if you define a new block using a name that has already been used in the drawing?

Exercise 7.8: Redefine Block Definitions

In the following steps, you are presented with just such a situation; you will have the opportunity to redefine a block definition. Any block references in the drawing will be automatically updated with the new definition.

To begin, open the file Ex07.8-start.dwg from this chapter's companion files.

1. Zoom into the chair at the bottom of the desk.

 2. Click the Rectangle tool on the Draw panel. The command prompt reads as follows:

```
RECTANG Specify first corner point or [Chamfer Elevation
Fillet Thickness Width]:
```

Click Fillet on the command line. The prompt now says the following:

```
Specify fillet radius for rectangles <0'-0">:
```

Type **1** (or 3 for metric) and press Enter.

3. For the first corner, click point A shown in Figure 7.21. Then type @3,-10 (or @7,-25 for metric) and press Enter to complete the RECTANGLE command.

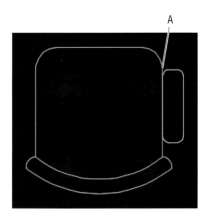

A

FIGURE 7.21 Drawing an armrest

4. Click the Mirror tool in the Modify panel. Type **L** (for Last) and press Enter twice. The command prompt reads as follows:

   MIRROR Specify first point of mirror line:

   Snap to the midpoint of the chair's front edge, toggle on Ortho on the status bar if it is not on already, move the cursor downward, and click the drawing canvas to specify the second point of the mirror line. Press Enter to complete the MIRROR command.

5. Select all objects in the chair and its armrests with a crossing window. Open the Layer drop-down menu and select layer 0 to change the assignment of the selected objects.

6. Type **B** (for Block) and press Enter. Type **Chair** in the Name field in the Block Definition dialog box. Click the Pick Point button and then snap to the midpoint of the chair's front edge.

7. Select the Convert To Block radio button in the Objects section of the Block Definition dialog box and click OK. Click Redefine Block in the Block – Redefine Block dialog box that appears. Figure 7.22 shows the result: All three chair block references are updated.

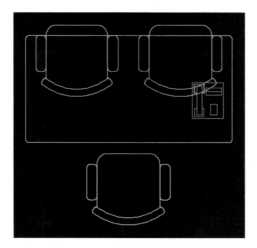

FIGURE 7.22 Redefining the chair block causes the chairs to lose their original orientation.

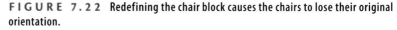 **8.** Click the Mirror tool on the Modify panel, select the top two chairs, and press Enter. Snap to the front edge of one of the seats, move the cursor to the right, and click the drawing canvas. The command prompt reads as follows:

```
Erase source objects? [Yes No] <N>:
```

Type **Y** (for Yes) and press Enter. The chairs are now oriented correctly (see Figure 7.23).

> The redefined chair block references didn't preserve their original orientations because the original chair block was defined in the opposite orientation.

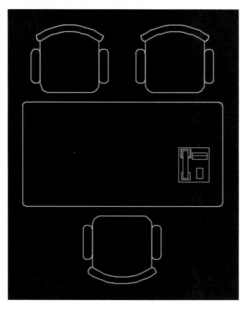

FIGURE 7.23 Mirroring two chair blocks

9. Select the lower chair, open the Layer drop-down menu in the Layers panel, and select Furniture. Press Esc to deselect.

Your model should now resemble Ex07.8-end.dwg, which is available among this chapter's companion files.

Work with Groups

Groups are a means of organizing objects in a way that is less formal than blocks. Groups don't need to be named, nor do they require base points like blocks do. You can toggle group selection on and off so that you can manipulate the entire group as a unit or access individual members of the group at will. You can't redefine the many with the few like you can with blocks, however. That said, it's certainly convenient to be able to manipulate many blocks with a few groups.

Exercise 7.9: Create Groups

In the following steps, you will group the desk and chairs, copy this group into adjacent rooms, and make adjustments to various blocks within the groups.

To begin, open the file Ex07.9-start.dwg from this chapter's companion files.

1. Click the Group tool on the Groups panel on the ribbon's Home tab. Select the desk and the three chairs surrounding it and then press Enter.

2. Click the Copy tool on the Modify panel, click the group to select it, and press Enter. Click an arbitrary point inside the desk and then click in the middle and right rooms to copy the group twice. Press Esc to end the COPY command.

3. Click the Rotate tool on the Modify panel, select the group in the room on the right, and press Enter. Click an arbitrary point inside the desk, type –90, and press Enter (see Figure 7.24).

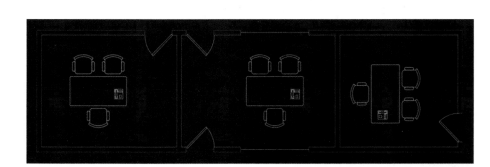

FIGURE 7.24 Copying and rotating groups in rooms

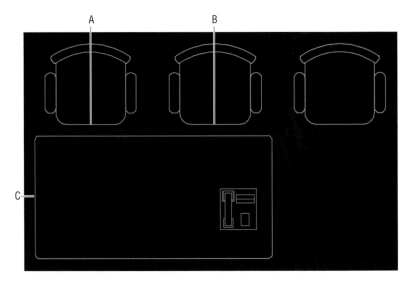

4. Click the Group Selection On/Off toggle in the Groups panel (turning it off).

5. Select the lower chair in the middle room and press the Delete key.

6. Click the Copy tool on the Modify panel, select the chair on the right in the middle room, and press Enter. Snap to the midpoints at points A and B shown in Figure 7.25 and press Enter. A third chair is copied so that all three are equidistant.

FIGURE 7.25 Copying a chair

7. Click the Mirror tool on the Modify panel, select the three chairs in the middle room, and press Enter. Click point C shown in Figure 7.25, move the cursor to the right, and, with Ortho selected, click in the drawing canvas to complete the mirror line. Press Enter to mirror three more chairs on the opposite side of the desk.

8. Type **xp** (for Xplode) and press Enter. Select the desk and press Enter. Click Inherit From Parent Block in the Dynamic Input display.

9. Click the Stretch tool on the Modify panel; select the right edge of the desk with a crossing window so that the top, bottom, and right edges are selected, and press Enter. Click an arbitrary point inside the desk, move the cursor to the right, type **2'6** (or **80** for metric), and press Enter. The desk is enlarged to accommodate the extra chairs.

10. Select the phone block on the desk, and press the Delete key.

11. Click the Group Edit tool on the Groups panel, select the upper-left chair in the middle room, and press Enter. The command prompt reads as follows:

    ```
    GROUPEDIT Enter an option [Add objects Remove objects
    REName]:
    ```

    Click Add Objects in the Dynamic Input display. Select all six chairs and the desk and then press Enter.

12. Click the Group Selection On/Off toggle in the Groups panel (turning it on). Hover the cursor over the desk and observe that the entire group is highlighted (see Figure 7.26).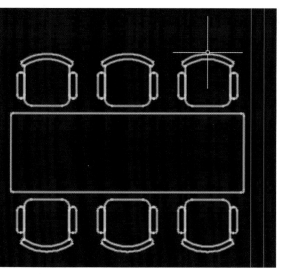

FIGURE 7.26 Reconstituted group after its constituent objects have been deleted, added, and stretched

Your model should now resemble Ex07.9-end.dwg, which is available among this chapter's companion files.

Now You Know

In this chapter, you learned how to define, insert, edit, and redefine blocks. You also learned how to group objects and blocks, how to toggle group selection so that you can manipulate the contents of a group, and how to add objects to a group. In short, you now know how to structure data to work efficiently.

CHAPTER 8

Hatching and Gradients

The term hatching *refers* to filling bounded areas with solids, patterns, and/or gradients. You create hatching in the AutoCAD® program to indicate transitions between materials and to improve the readability of drawings in general. Hatching with solid fill, patterns, and/or tonal gradients can transform staid line drawings into attractive illustrations. This chapter covers the basics of hatching so that you can use it in your own drawings. In AutoCAD 2018, hatch display and performance are enhanced.

In this chapter, you'll learn to do the following:

▶ **Specify hatch areas**

▶ **Associate hatches with boundaries**

▶ **Hatch with patterns**

▶ **Hatch with gradients**

Specify Hatch Areas

Every hatch area is defined by a boundary containing the solid fill, pattern, or gradient. You can determine the boundary either by picking a point on the drawing canvas or by selecting an object or set of objects.

Exercise 8.1: Pick Points to Determine Boundaries

When a boundary is picked, AutoCAD uses a raycasting algorithm to determine the precise extents of the area bounded by the objects onscreen. In the following steps, you will pick points to determine the boundaries of multiple hatch objects.

To begin, open the file Ex08.1-start.dwg, which is available for download from the book's web page at www.sybex.com/go/autocad2018essentials. The drawing is based on a 100-year-old patent for fluid propulsion (CA 135174) by Nikola Tesla (see Figure 8.1). Tesla is best known for inventing the alternating electrical current that powers the modern age.

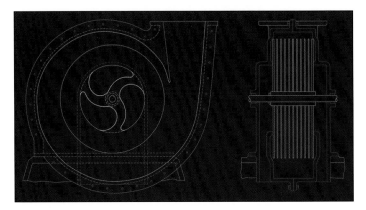

FIGURE 8.1   Initial line drawing based on Tesla's patent for fluid propulsion

1. Zoom into the center of the rotor in the drawing on the left.

Certification
Objective

2. Click the Hatch tool in the Draw panel on the ribbon's Home tab. Click point A in Figure 8.2.

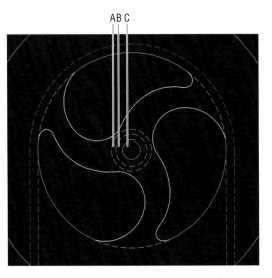

FIGURE 8.2   Picking a point to detect a boundary

3. A temporary tab called Hatch Creation appears on the ribbon. This tab will remain active while you configure the hatch object you are creating. Click Solid in the Pattern panel, and turn off Associative mode if it is on by clicking its button in the Options panel (see Figure 8.3). (You'll learn about associative hatches in the next section.)

FIGURE 8.3 Using ribbon controls when creating a hatch

4. Expand the Options panel, open the Island Detection menu, and select Outer Island Detection.

5. Open the Hatch Color drop-down in the Properties panel, and select light gray with color values of 199, 200, 202 in the red, green, and blue channels, respectively (see Figure 8.4).

The thumbnails indicate different ways of treating nested boundaries, called *islands*. In this case, you want only the outer island filled with a solid hatch.

FIGURE 8.4 Selecting a color override for the hatch object

6. Expand the Properties panel, open the Hatch Layer Override drop-down, and select the Solid layer (see Figure 8.5).

You can override a hatch object's default color, transparency, and layer assignment on the Hatch Creation tab's Properties panel.

FIGURE 8.5 Using Hatch Layer Override

All the settings and overrides in the Hatch Creation tab are "sticky," meaning that they remain the same the next time you create a hatch object.

7. Click the Close Hatch Creation icon in the Close panel at the extreme right edge of the ribbon's Hatch Editor tab. The outer island is filled with a solid hatch object, and the HATCH command ends.

8. Type **H** (for Hatch) and press Enter. Click point B in Figure 8.2.

9. Open the Hatch Color drop-down in the Properties panel and click medium gray: 147, 149, 152.

10. Click the Close Hatch Creation icon in the Close panel.

11. Press the spacebar to repeat the last command. Click point C in Figure 8.2.

12. Open the Hatch Color drop-down in the Properties panel and choose dark gray: 99, 100, 102.

13. Click the Close Hatch Creation icon in the Close panel. The Hatch Editor tab disappears.

14. Click the Isolate tool on the Layers panel of the ribbon's Home tab, drag a crossing selection over the hub, and include the selection of at least one of the dashed yellow lines defining the edge of a spoke. Press Enter, and all the other layers are hidden. Zoom out until you can see the entire rotor.

Use the BOUNDARY command to create a polyline or region object from a picked point. BOUNDARY uses the same ray-casting algorithm used by the HATCH command.

15. Click the Hatch tool on the Draw panel and then click point A in Figure 8.6.

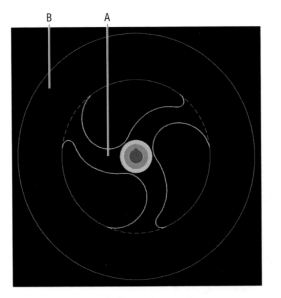

FIGURE 8.6 Picking points on the rotor

16. Choose ANSI31 from the Pattern panel. Click the Close Hatch Creation button in the Close panel. Figure 8.7 shows the result.

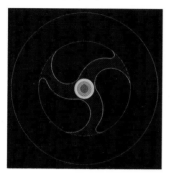

F I G U R E   8 . 7   Hatching the rotor arms

17. Type **H** (for Hatch) and press Enter. Click point B shown in Figure 8.6. The command prompt reads as follows:

```
Analyzing the selected data...
```

AutoCAD can't find this particular area; press Esc before the program crashes.

Your model should now resemble Ex08.1-end.dwg, which is available among this chapter's companion files.

> The raycasting algorithm has a tendency to crash when analyzing complex areas, such as arcs, splines, and a circle forming the boundary of the outer portion of the rotor.

Exercise 8.2: Select Objects to Define Boundaries

In complex drawings, picking points to determine boundaries sometimes doesn't work. Fortunately, you can always define boundaries successfully using closed objects. In the following steps, you will select two closed objects to define a hatch boundary.

Begin by opening the file Ex08.2-start.dwg from this chapter's companion files.

> Don't worry about which layer the circle is on; you will delete the circle later.

1. To simplify the hatch boundary, you will draw a circle. Click the Circle tool on the Draw panel.

2. Shift+right-click and choose Node from the context menu. Click point A, shown in Figure 8.8, as the center point. Type **QUA** (for Quadrant) and press Enter. Click point B, also shown in Figure 8.8, to set the inner circle's radius. The CIRCLE command ends.

> The Hatch tool will prompt you with either Pick Internal Point or Select Objects, according to whichever option you used last to create a hatch object.

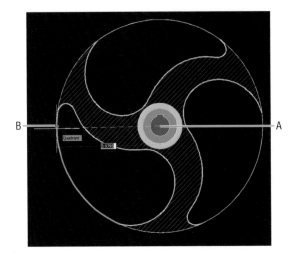
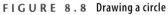

FIGURE 8.8 Drawing a circle

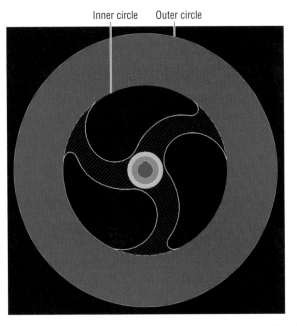

3. Type **H** (for Hatch) and press Enter. Click the Select tool in the Boundaries panel of the ribbon's Hatch Editor tab. Select the circle making up the inner circle of the rotor and then select the single outer circle. Select Solid in the Pattern panel and press Enter. The hatch appears correctly (see Figure 8.9).

FIGURE 8.9 Hatching the outer portion of the rotor by selecting objects

4. Click the Erase tool on the Home tab's Modify panel. Select the inner circle you drew in step 3 and press Enter.

5. Type **REGEN** and press Enter. The dashed arcs are again visible.

Your model should now resemble Ex08.2-end.dwg, which is available among this chapter's companion files.

Associate Hatches with Boundaries

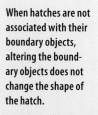

When hatches are not associated with their boundary objects, altering the boundary objects does not change the shape of the hatch.

When hatches are associated with their boundary objects, the boundary objects themselves define the extents of the hatch fill, pattern, or gradient. Altering the shape of any of the boundary objects necessarily changes the extents of an associated hatch object. For example, the rotor needs to have a larger diameter, and by associating the hatch with the outer circle, you will be able to get the hatch to expand to fill the larger rotor simply by changing the diameter of the circle.

Exercise 8.3: Associate Boundaries

In the following steps, you will re-create the boundary objects from the last hatch pattern created in the previous section. Then you will alter the shape of one of the boundary objects to change the extents of the solid hatch.

To begin, open Ex08.3-start.dwg from this chapter's companion files.

The Hatch Edit dialog box has the same functionality as the Hatch Editor tab on the ribbon.

1. Type **HATCHEDIT** and press Enter. Select the solid hatch in the outer portion of the rotor. The Hatch Edit dialog box appears (see Figure 8.10).

2. Click the Recreate Boundary tool on the Boundaries panel. Choose Polyline from the dynamic prompt menu and then click Yes to associate the hatch with the new boundary. Click OK.

3. Toggle on Object Snap on the status bar. Right-click this toggle button and turn on Center, Quadrant, and Endpoint running object snap modes in the context menu if they are not already on.

4. Toggle on Ortho mode on the status bar.

5. Toggle on Object Snap Tracking on the status bar.

6. Click the Scale tool on the Modify panel, select the rotor's outer circle, and press Enter. Select the center of the rotor (point A in Figure 8.11) as the base point. The command prompt reads as follows:

       SCALE Specify scale factor or [Copy Reference]:

   Type **R** (for Reference) and press Enter. Pick the reference length by clicking points A and B, shown in Figure 8.11.

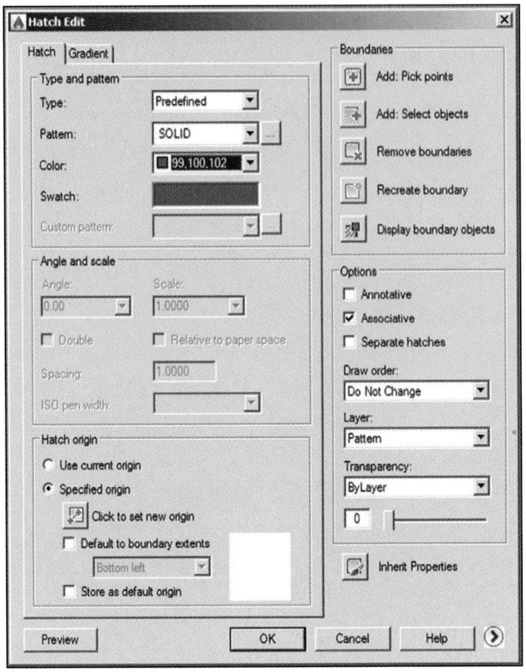

FIGURE 8.10   Hatch Edit dialog box

7. Hover the cursor over point C, shown in Figure 8.11. Then bring the cursor back toward point D. When the tracking X appears on the drawing canvas, click point D. When the SCALE command ends, the rotor matches its depiction in the drawing on the right, and the solid associative hatch fills the new boundary.

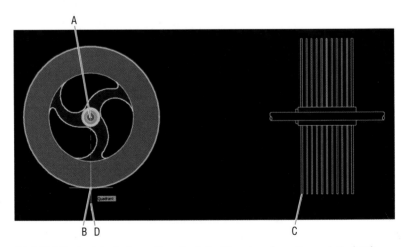

FIGURE 8.11   Scaling up the outer circle of the rotor enlarges its associative hatch.

8. Click the outer portion of the rotor to select the hatch object; the Hatch Editor tab appears on the ribbon.

Certification Objective

9. Convert the object into a nonassociative hatch by clicking to toggle off the Associative button in the Options panel and then click the Close Hatch Editor icon.

10. Click the Erase tool on the Modify panel, select the two re-created boundaries as shown in Figure 8.12, and press Enter.

Delete two circles.

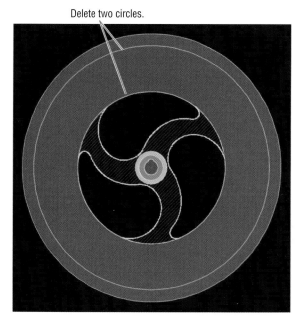

FIGURE 8.12 Deleting the re-created boundary objects

11. Click the Unisolate tool on the Layers panel.

Your model should now resemble Ex08.3-end.dwg, which is available among this chapter's companion files.

Hatch with Patterns

Hatch patterns are repeating arrangements of lines and/or dots used to identify a material or a cutting plane or to highlight an area visually. You'll learn how to specify pattern properties, separate hatch areas, and set the origin point of the pattern.

Exercise 8.4: Specify Properties

Hatch patterns have a few additional properties as compared to solid hatch objects. In the following steps, you will select a pattern, set its scale, and adjust the pattern angle.

To begin, open Ex08.4-start.dwg from this chapter's companion files.

1. Pan over to the drawing on the right.

2. Click the Hatch tool on the Draw panel.

3. Click the Pick Points button in the Boundaries panel.

4. Click points A through F inside the red housing, as shown in Figure 8.13. A hatch appears within the red boundaries.

If AutoCAD says the boundary is not closed, try increasing the Gap Tolerance value in the Options panel. For example, you might try a value of 0.1.

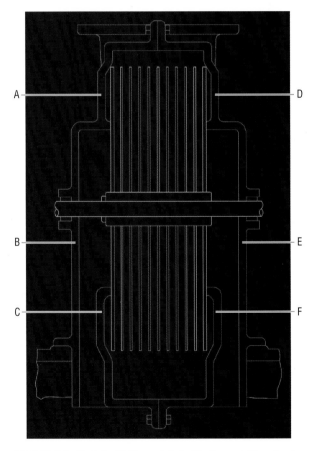

FIGURE 8.13 Picking points inside the metal housing to determine hatch boundaries

5. Select the pattern called ANSI31 in the Pattern panel if it is not already selected. Select index color Red in the Color drop-down in the Properties panel. Select color 99, 100, 102 in the Background Color drop-down. Change the Scale value to 2.0000. Expand the Properties panel, and select Pattern from the Hatch Layer Override drop-down (see Figure 8.14).

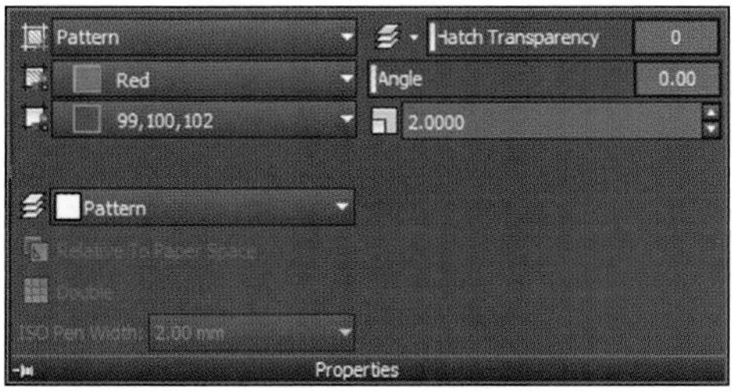

FIGURE 8.14 Configuring hatch properties

6. Click Close Hatch Editor in the Close panel.

7. Type **REGEN** and press Enter.

Your model should now resemble Ex08.4-end.dwg, which is available among this chapter's companion files.

Exercise 8.5: Separate Hatch Areas

When you picked points within multiple boundaries in the previous section, doing so formed a single hatch object. The properties you specified were assigned to this object. However, at this point, you want to rotate the cross-sectional pattern 90° on the right side to illustrate the separate pieces of metal that are bolted together. In the following steps, you will separate the multiple bounded areas of a single object into individual hatch objects and then rotate patterns on half of them.

To begin, open Ex08.5-start.dwg from this chapter's companion files.

1. Type **HATCHEDIT** and press Enter. Select the hatch object inside the red boundaries on the right-hand section drawing.

2. Check Separate Hatches in the Options group of the Hatch Edit dialog box (see Figure 8.15) and click OK.

Exploding hatch patterns removes their associativity (if any). Exploding them again converts the hatch pattern into its constituent lines; background color fill is lost in the process.

FIGURE 8.15 Separating multiple bounded areas into multiple hatch objects

 3. Select the upper-right hatch pattern, type **90** in the Angle text box, and press the Tab key. Click the Set Origin button and then click point A shown in Figure 8.16. Press Esc to exit the ribbon's Hatch Editor tab.

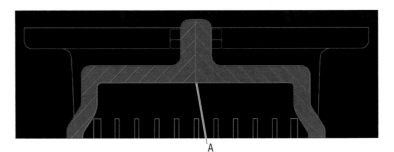

FIGURE 8.16 Changing the angle and setting the origin of an individual hatch pattern object

 4. Select the hatch pattern on the left side, click the Set Origin button, click point A shown in Figure 8.16, and press Esc. The outer patterns on the left and right both meet symmetrically at point A.

5. Select the outer pattern on the lower right, click the Match Properties tool in the Options panel, and select the upper-right pattern. Press Esc to deselect; the lower pattern matches the upper pattern's angle.

The inner patterns on the lower left and lower right both meet symmetrically at point B.

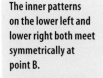

6. Select the inner pattern on the lower right. Click the Match Properties tool in the Options panel and select the outer lower-right pattern.

 7. Click the Set Origin button and click point B in Figure 8.17. Press Esc to deselect.

B

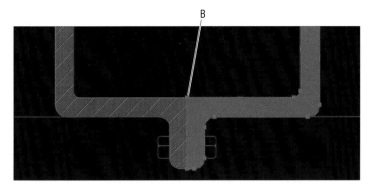
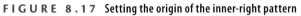

F I G U R E 8 . 1 7 Setting the origin of the inner-right pattern

8. Select the inner pattern on the left. Click the Set Origin button and once again click point B in Figure 8.17. Press Esc to deselect.

9. Type **REGEN** and press Enter. Figure 8.18 shows the result.

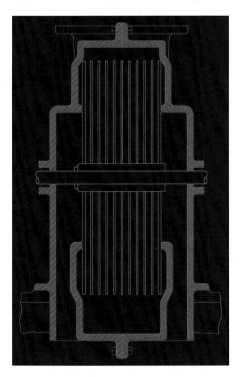

F I G U R E 8 . 1 8 Symmetrical crosshatching highlights separate metal castings.

Your model should now resemble Ex08.5-end.dwg, which is available among this chapter's companion files.

Hatch with Gradients

In addition to hatching with solid fill and line patterns, you can hatch with one- and two-color *gradients* to vary tonality in a smooth fashion. Gradients can subtly hint at an extra dimension that helps make drawings more readable. In the following steps, you will create gradient hatches that give depth to metal parts in the drawings.

Exercise 8.6: Create Gradients

To begin, open Ex08.6-start.dwg from this chapter's companion files.

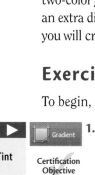

Click the Gradient Tint and Shade button to toggle between one- and two-color gradients. You can select both colors in two-color gradients, whereas one-color gradients fade to white.

Certification Objective

1. Open the flyout next to the Hatch tool on the Draw panel and select Gradient from the menu. Click the Pick Points button in the Boundaries panel and then click points A through F shown in Figure 8.19.

FIGURE 8.19 Picking points to determine boundaries for gradient hatch

2. Scroll down in the Pattern panel and select the GR_HEMISP gradient. In the Properties panel, select 99, 100, 102 (see Figure 8.20) in the Gradient Color 1 drop-down. In the right column, click the Gradient Tint and Shade button to create a one-color gradient. Expand the Properties panel and select Gradient in the Hatch Layer Override drop-down. Press Esc.

Use the DRAWORDER command to change the display behavior of individual overlapping objects.

Gradient Tint and Shade

FIGURE 8.20 Configuring a gradient hatch

3. Objects typically overlap other objects that were drawn earlier. Type **HATCHTOBACK** and press Enter. All hatch objects (solid fills, patterns, and/or gradients) are sent to the back of the *draw order* stack so that they don't overlap any of the other objects in the drawing.

Your model should now resemble Ex08.6-end.dwg, which is available among this chapter's companion files.

Now You Know

In this chapter, you learned how to specify hatch areas and fill them with patterns and gradients. You also learned how to associate a boundary with hatches and gradients so that changes to the boundary automatically cause the fill to update. You can now use hatches and gradients to create attractive illustrations that add another layer of visual information to line drawings.

CHAPTER 9

Working with Blocks and Xrefs

In Chapter 7, "Organizing Objects," you learned how to define and reference blocks within a single drawing in the AutoCAD® program. In this chapter, you will create and insert *global blocks* from outside the current drawing. Harnessing the power of a search engine, you'll cast a net across multiple drawings to locate specific blocks and a variety of other content. Once key content is found, you will place it on tool palettes for quick access in the future. In addition, you will make external references (Xrefs) to drawings outside the current file.

In this chapter, you'll learn to do the following:

▶ **Work with global blocks**

▶ **Access content globally**

▶ **Store content on tool palettes**

▶ **Reference external drawings and images**

Work with Global Blocks

Global blocks are drawing files that you will later insert as blocks into another drawing. In this section, you will learn how to write local blocks to files, insert a drawing file as a local block, and redefine local blocks with global blocks.

Exercise 9.1: Write a Local Block Definition to a File

Certification
Objective

In the following steps, you will export one of the current drawing's block definitions to an individual drawing file. In addition, you will open the newly created file and alter its contents.

Begin by opening the file Ex09.1-start.dwg, which is among the companion files available for download from the book's web page, www.sybex.com/go/autocad2018essentials.

1. Type **W** (for Write block) and press Enter. Select the Block radio button in the Source area of the Write Block dialog box. Select Sofa from the Block drop-down. Select Inches (or Centimeters for metric) from the Insert Units drop-down in the Destination area (see Figure 9.1). Click OK, and the geometry within the Sofa block definition is written to Sofa.dwg.

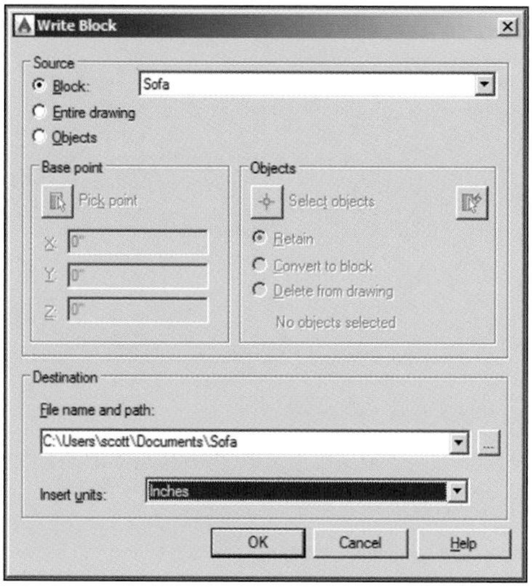

FIGURE 9.1 Writing a block to a file

2. Click the Open tool on the Quick Access toolbar. Browse to the folder where you wrote the file in the previous step.

   C:\Users\<your user name>\My Documents

   Open Sofa.dwg (see Figure 9.2).

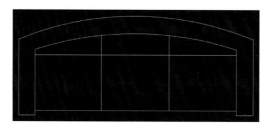

FIGURE 9.2 Open the Sofa.dwg file.

3. Click Zoom Extents on the Navigation bar.

4. Click the Erase tool on the Modify panel, select the two arcs in the sofa's backrest, and press Enter.

5. Toggle on Ortho mode on the status bar.

6. Toggle on Object Snap on the status bar. Right-click the Object Snap toggle and select Endpoint if it is not already selected.

7. Click the Line tool on the Draw panel. Snap the first point of the line to the endpoint shown in Figure 9.3. Move the cursor to the right and click an arbitrary second point. Press Esc to end the LINE command.

Snap the first point to this endpoint.

FIGURE 9.3 Drawing a straight-backed sofa

8. Click the Fillet tool on the Modify panel. Verify that the command prompt says the following:

```
Current settings: Mode = TRIM, Radius = 0'-0"
```

If the radius is not 0, type **R** (for Radius), press Enter, type **0**, and press Enter again. Select the line you just drew and then click the inner line on the right arm of the sofa.

9. Press the spacebar to repeat the FILLET command. Click the inner line on the left arm of the sofa and then click the back line. Figure 9.4 shows the result.

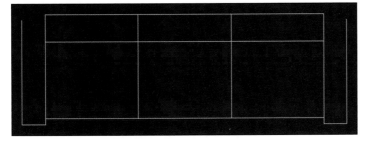

FIGURE 9.4 Filleting lines to meet at sharp corners

10. Click the Offset tool on the Modify panel. Click points A and B in Figure 9.5 to set the offset distance. Select the back line of the sofa and then click above it to offset another line.

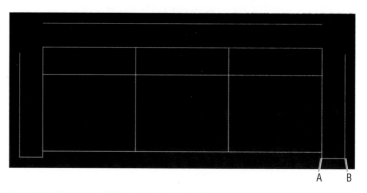

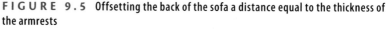

FIGURE 9.5 Offsetting the back of the sofa a distance equal to the thickness of the armrests

 11. Click the Fillet tool on the Modify panel. Select the line you just offset and then click the outer line on the right arm of the sofa.

12. Press the spacebar to repeat the FILLET command. Click the outer line on the left arm of the sofa and then click the top back line. The sofa redesign is complete (see Figure 9.6).

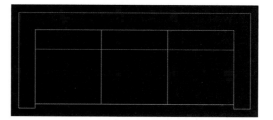

FIGURE 9.6 Redesigned sofa drawing

13. Click the Save As tool on the Quick Access toolbar. Type **Sofa2.dwg** in the File Name text box and then click the Save button.

14. Type **CLOSE** and press Enter to close the file you just saved.

Your model should now resemble Ex09.1-end.dwg, which is available among this chapter's companion files.

Exercise 9.2: Insert a Drawing as a Local Block

When you insert into the current drawing a DWG file that has global scope, it comes in as a block. In the following steps, you will insert the new sofa block twice into the same file in which you started this chapter.

Certification Objective (margin note)

To begin, open the file Ex09.2-start.dwg from the Chapter 9 companion files.

1. Zoom into the upper-right building quadrant, select the two arm-chairs and round side table, and press the Delete key (see Figure 9.7).

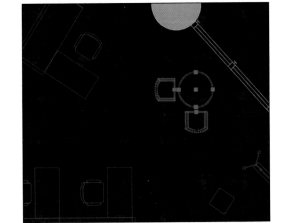

FIGURE 9.7 Deleting two armchairs and a side table to make way for a new sofa

2. Toggle off Object Snap on the status bar.

3. Click the Make Object's Layer Current tool in the Layers panel. Click the Manager's chair, and A-furn becomes the current layer.

4. Click the Insert tool on the Block panel. The Sofa2 block is not yet defined in this drawing's block table, so you won't find it in the Name drop-down. Click the Browse button and locate the Sofa2.dwg file you saved in the previous exercise, or use the Sofa2.dwg file provided in the Samples folder for Chapter 9. Select Specify On-screen for both Insertion Point and Rotation in the Insert dialog box (see Figure 9.8) and click OK.

5. Click approximately where you deleted the armchairs and side table to insert a Sofa2 block reference in the drawing and estimate the rotation angle so that the sofa is parallel to the exterior wall (see Figure 9.9).

The path identifies this as a global block.

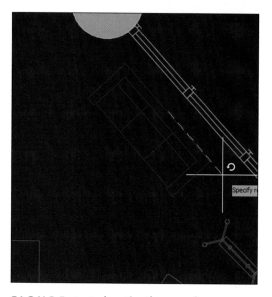

FIGURE 9.8 Configuring a global block in the Insert dialog box

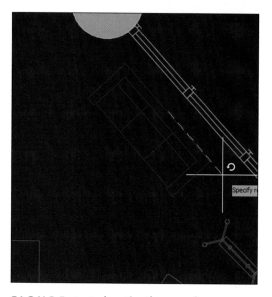

FIGURE 9.9 Inserting the new sofa

6. Pan down to the lower-right building quadrant. Delete the two armchairs and side table there.

7. Type **I** (for Insert) and press Enter. Sofa2 is already selected in the Name drop-down. No path is listed in the Insert dialog box this time because Sofa2 was defined as a local block when you inserted it in step 4. Click OK.

8. Click approximately where you deleted the armchairs and side table to insert a Sofa2 block reference in the drawing and rotate it so that the sofa is again parallel to the exterior wall (see Figure 9.10).

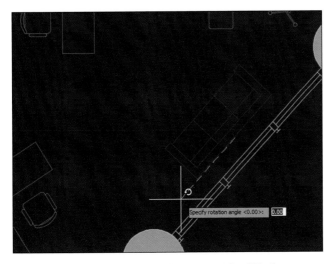

FIGURE 9.10 Inserting Sofa2 again as a local block

9. Save your work.

Your model should now resemble Ex09.2-end.dwg, which is available among this chapter's companion files.

Exercise 9.3: Redefine Local Blocks with Global Blocks

When you insert a global block with the same name as a local block, the local block is redefined. In the following steps, you will redefine the original sofa block with the new sofa design.

Certification Objective

1. If you are continuing from the previous exercise, click the Open tool on the Quick Access toolbar. Browse to the following folder:

    C:\Users\<your user name>\My Documents

    Open Sofa2.dwg (see Figure 9.6).

2. Click the Save As tool on the Quick Access toolbar. Save the file as Sofa.dwg and click Yes when prompted to replace the file.

3. Click the close box on the Sofa.dwg file tab.

4. From among the Chapter 9 companion files, open Ex09.3-start.dwg. Pan over to Reception.

5. Click the Insert tool in the Block panel. Open the Name drop-down and select Sofa in the list. The preview image in the upper right shows that the local block definition is based on the curved-back design (see Figure 9.11).

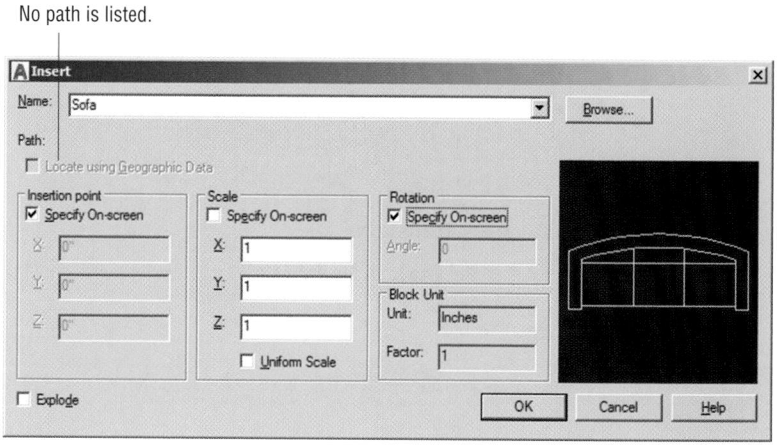

No path is listed.

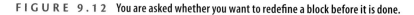

FIGURE 9.11 Examining the preview of the local block definition in the Insert dialog box

6. Click the Browse button in the Insert dialog box. Select the Sofa.dwg file you saved in step 2. Click OK in the Insert dialog box, and the Block – Redefine Block dialog box appears (see Figure 9.12). Notice that it says that there are two Sofa block references in the drawing. These are two sofas in Reception. Click Redefine Block.

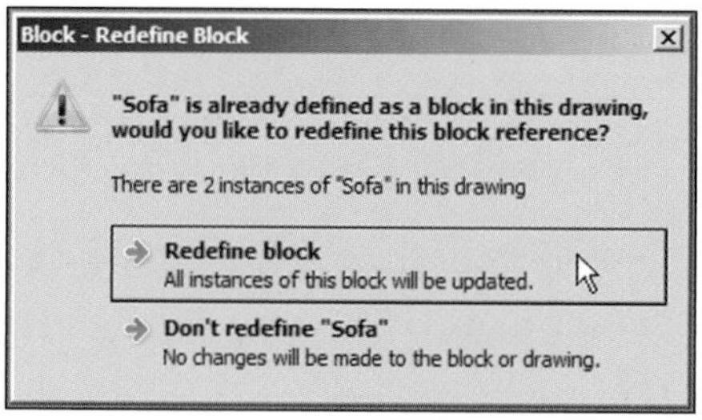

FIGURE 9.12 You are asked whether you want to redefine a block before it is done.

7. The two sofas in Reception are redefined with the straight-back design (see Figure 9.13). Press Esc to cancel the INSERT command; you do not need to insert a new block reference.

FIGURE 9.13   Two local block references redefined with a global block

8. Save your work.

Your model should now resemble Ex09.3-end.dwg, which is available among this chapter's companion files.

Access Content Globally

The DesignCenter™ allows you to search for—and insert—content from *within* other drawings on your local area network (LAN). Using the DesignCenter to locate and insert blocks is much more efficient than writing blocks to files and then inserting the resulting files into drawings, as you learned in the previous section.

Exercise 9.4: Access Global Content

In the following steps, you will use the DesignCenter to search for blocks and other types of content. To begin, open the file Ex09.4-start.dwg from the Chapter 9 companion files.

1. Type **ADC** and press Enter to launch Autodesk's DesignCenter, an older interface for accessing global blocks.

2. Navigate to the folder shown at the bottom of Figure 9.14 and expand the Home - Space Planner.dwg sample file.

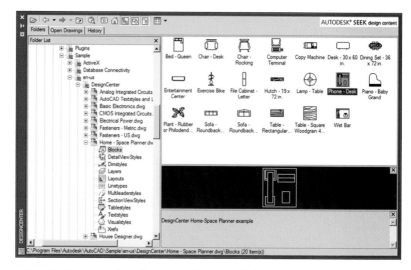

FIGURE 9.14 Inserting content from Autodesk DesignCenter into a drawing

3. Select the Blocks node in the folder tree to display this drawing's block files.

4. Drag and drop the Phone–Desk global block from this drawing into the current drawing and then move it onto the Receptionist's desk.

5. Save your work.

Your model should now resemble Ex09.4-end.dwg, which is available among this chapter's companion files.

Store Content on Tool Palettes

Tool palettes are used for storing just about any type of content for quick reuse. You create tools on a palette by dragging objects—including blocks, hatches, images, dimensions, tables, lights, cameras, materials, visual styles, and Xrefs—onto the palette from any saved drawing.

Exercise 9.5: Add to the Tool Palettes

In the following steps, you'll create a new palette, drag a sofa onto it, and then use the tool to add another sofa. To begin, open the file Ex09.5-start.dwg from this chapter's companion files.

1. Select the ribbon's View tab and click the Tool Palettes button on the Palettes panel.

2. Right-click the Palette menu bar and select New Palette. Type **Furniture** and press Enter (see Figure 9.15).

Blocks dragged to tool palettes are global blocks that can be inserted into any drawing.

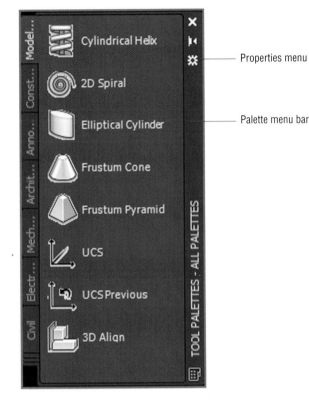

Properties menu

Palette menu bar

FIGURE 9.15   Tool palettes

3. Select the Receptionist's chair. Drag this chair (not using a grip) onto the Furniture palette. TaskChair appears with a preview icon (see Figure 9.16).

4. Right-click the TaskChair tool in the Furniture palette and choose Properties from the context menu. Change Prompt For Rotation to Yes in the Tool Properties dialog box that appears (see Figure 9.17). Click OK.

Use the Lock UI control in the status bar to lock toolbars, panels, and/or windows. Tool palettes are considered windows in this feature.

5. Select the Manager's offices on the other side of the wall behind the Receptionist's chair. Type **UNGROUP** and press Enter. Erase the Manager's chair immediately behind the Receptionist's chair.

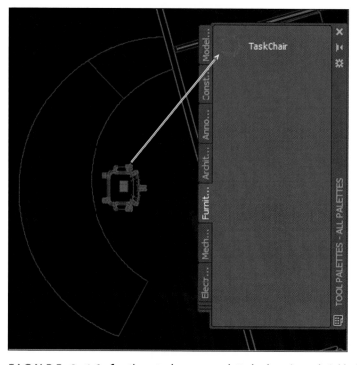

FIGURE 9.16 Creating a tool on a new palette by dragging a chair block onto it

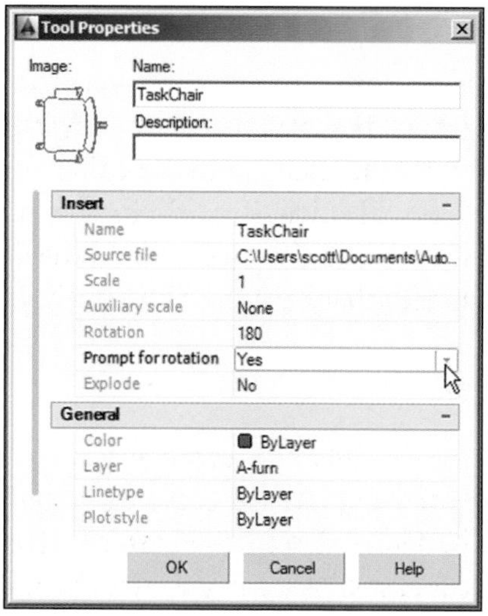

FIGURE 9.17 Adjusting tool properties to prompt for rotation

6. Click the TaskChair tool on the Furniture tool palette. Click the place where the Manager's chair used to be and then specify the rotation by clicking a second time. Click OK or Cancel to close the Edit Attributes dialog box that appears. Figure 9.18 shows the result.

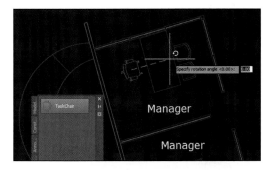

FIGURE 9.18 Inserting a chair from the tool palette

7. Save your work.

Your model should now resemble Ex09.5-end.dwg, which is available among this chapter's companion files.

Reference External Drawings and Images

External references (called *Xrefs*) are a more dynamic alternative to blocks. Xrefs linked to the current drawing are automatically updated every time the current drawing is opened. Blocks, on the other hand, must be edited in place or redefined when they are changed. The real efficiency with Xrefs comes when you link one file to multiple drawing files because changes made to the linked file are automatically reloaded in all the files that have the Xref attached.

Exercise 9.6: Use Xrefs

In the following steps, you will externally reference a *core* (elevators, stairs, shafts) and *shell* (exterior envelope) drawing into the drawing containing items owned by the building tenant (walls, doors, furniture, and so on). The advantage of working this way is that the core and shell generally do not change from floor to floor, whereas the tenant improvement drawings are typically unique to each floor. Changes to the core and/or shell can be made in separate drawings that are linked to all the individual tenant drawings.

This is just one example of using Xrefs in the case of a high-rise building. Xrefs can be used in every discipline whenever you want the advantages they provide.

To begin, open the file Ex09.6-CoreShell.dwg from the Chapter 9 companion files.

1. Return to the book's web page, browse to Chapter 9, get the files Ex09-CoreShell.dwg and Ex09-Tenant.dwg, and open them. Figure 9.19 shows the building core and shell. Figure 9.20 shows the objects owned by the tenant.

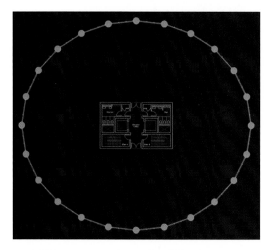

FIGURE 9.19 Core and shell drawing

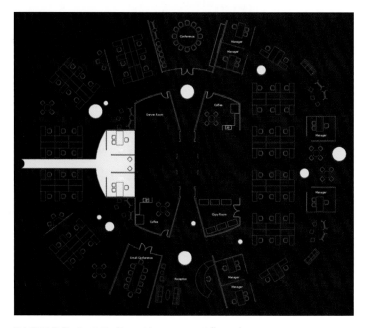

FIGURE 9.20 Tenant improvement floor plan

2. Select the file tab of Ex09-Tenant.dwg. Then select the ribbon's View tab and click the External References Palette button in the Palettes panel. Open the Attach menu, as shown in Figure 9.21.

FIGURE 9.21 Attaching a DWG file in the External References palette

3. Select Attach DWG from the menu. Select the file Ex09-CoreShell .dwg and click Open in the Select Reference File dialog box.

4. In the Attach External Reference dialog box that appears, deselect Specify On-Screen in the Insertion Point area (see Figure 9.22). Click OK.

5. The core and shell appear faded with respect to the tenant drawing. Select the core or shell to select the single Xref object (see Figure 9.23).

6. Click the Open Reference tool on the Edit panel of the External Reference tab that appears on the ribbon.

You can externally reference DWG, DWF, DGN, PDF, NWD, NWC, point cloud data, and a variety of image file formats.

In AutoCAD 2018, the default Xref path type is set to Relative. You can now attach relative-pathed Xrefs without previously saving the host drawing.

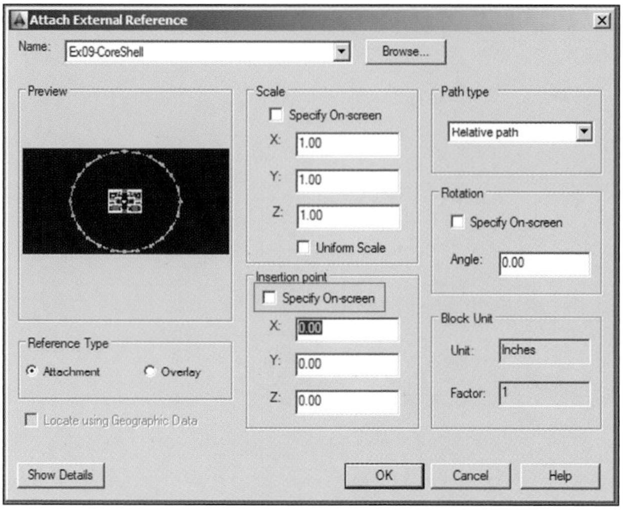

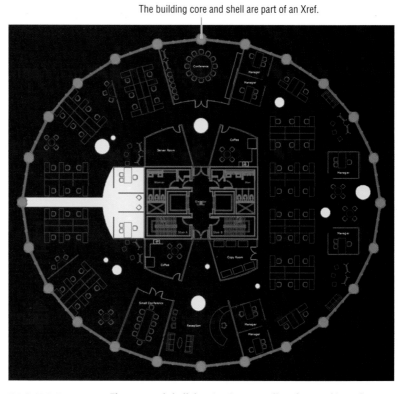

FIGURE 9.22   Attaching an external reference

The building core and shell are part of an Xref.

FIGURE 9.23   The core and shell drawing is externally referenced into the tenant drawing.

7. Redesign the women's washroom so that it has three sinks, as shown in Figure 9.24.

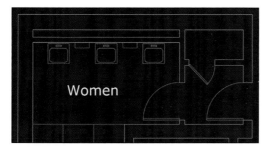

FIGURE 9.24 Redesigning the women's washroom for three sinks

8. Type **CLOSE** and press Enter twice to close and save Ex09-CoreShell.dwg.

9. A balloon appears in the drawing status bar informing you that an external reference has changed (see Figure 9.25). If no notification balloon appears, right-click the Xref that needs to be reloaded in the External References palette and choose Reload. Click the hyperlinked blue text in the balloon to reload the Ex09-CoreShell Xref. The changes made to the women's washroom are now visible in the tenant drawing.

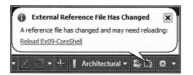

FIGURE 9.25 Balloon notification that an Xref has changed

10. Save your work.

Your model should now resemble Ex09.6-end.dwg, which is available among this chapter's companion files.

Setting the system variable XREFOVERRIDE to 1 overrides object properties so that all objects inherit their properties by layer.

EXTERNALLY REFERENCING OR IMPORTING PDFs

Xrefing a PDF works identically to Xrefing an image in that either type of data can be attached to your drawings but not edited. Use `IMPORT` to edit PDF geometry in AutoCAD. Any images that are part of an imported PDF file are attached to the drawing as Xrefs.

NOW YOU KNOW

In this chapter, you learned how to work with global blocks, access content globally, store content on tool palettes, and reference external drawings and images.

CHAPTER 10

Creating and Editing Text

Text is an essential part of every drawing. You use the written word to clarify graphical depictions and delineate your design intent with specific language. It's good to remember that drawings can be used as part of legal construction documents, and you typically need to clarify your design intent with text that appears on the drawings themselves. In this chapter, you'll learn how to style text, how to write both lines and paragraphs of text using specialized commands, and how to edit existing text.

In this chapter, you'll learn to do the following:

▶ **Style text**

▶ **Write lines of text**

▶ **Write and format paragraphs using** MTEXT

▶ **Edit text**

▶ **Recognize and combine text**

Style Text

The AutoCAD® software can't help you with your grammar or linguistic style, but it can style the appearance of text. Text styles associate specific fonts, optional text heights, and special effects with text objects.

Exercise 10.1: Create Text Styles

In the following steps, you will create the text styles that you will use in the next section when creating text objects. Begin by opening the file Ex10.1-start.dwg, which is among the companion files available for download from this book's web page, www.sybex.com/go/autocad2018essentials.

1. On the ribbon's Annotate tab, open the first drop-down menu (for text styles). Every drawing has both an Annotative and Standard style by default. Select Manage Text Styles at the bottom of the panel (see Figure 10.1).

FIGURE 10.1 Managing text styles

2. Click the New button in the Text Style dialog box that appears. Type **Title** in the New Style dialog box and click OK.

3. Open the Font Name drop-down and select Garamond. The symbol next to the font name indicates this is a TrueType font. Set Font Style to Bold, and deselect Annotative if it is checked (see Figure 10.2). Click the Apply button.

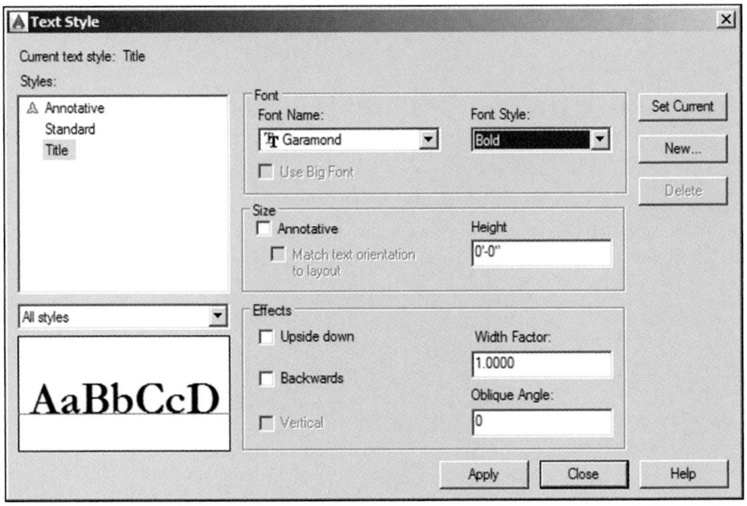

AutoCAD SHX fonts were designed to optimize motion in pen plotters (now obsolete) but are still commonly used today as simple fonts suitable for architectural and engineering lettering.

FIGURE 10.2 Configuring the Title style

4. Select Standard in the Styles list on the left side of the Text Style dialog box. Open the Font Name drop-down and select `simplex.shx`.

The symbol next to the font name indicates this is a shape-based font that is specific to AutoCAD. Type 1' (or 30 for metric) in the Height text box and press the Tab key. Type 0.8 as the Width Factor value in the Effects area and press Tab. Click the Apply, Set Current, and Close buttons (in that order).

5. Save your work.

Your model should now resemble Ex10.1-end.dwg, which is available among this chapter's companion files.

The styles you created are saved within the drawing even though you can't see them on the drawing canvas.

Write Lines of Text

You will use the TEXT command when you want to create a single line of text. TEXT creates independent objects on every line so that these objects are suitable for use in symbols or labels on drawings. You will learn how to create text that fits within a rectangle or circle, for example. In addition, you will justify text so that it can be easily reused and its content changed without having to reposition the text every time to maintain alignment with surrounding geometry. You will also discover that text objects can be manipulated and duplicated using many of the commands you already know.

Exercise 10.2: Create Text to Fit

There are many situations where you will want to fit text within geometric objects. For example, you might employ a rectangular symbol in which a number of room names might be displayed in each case where the symbol is to be used. If a text object were always to fit perfectly within the given rectangle, it would simplify having to create rectangles of different widths for each room in which the symbol is to be used. In the following steps, you will create single-line text, justified to fit within just such a rectangular symbol.

To begin, open the file Ex10.2-start.dwg from this chapter's companion files.

1. Zoom in on the small rectangle in the upper-left corner of the drawing canvas.

2. Click the Offset tool in the Modify panel, type 4 (or 10 for metric) to set the offset distance, and press Enter. Select the small rectangle

and then click a point inside the rectangle to offset another smaller rectangle inside. Press the Esc key.

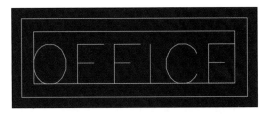

3. Toggle on Object Snap on the status bar. Right-click the same button and select both Endpoint and Center running object snap modes if they are not already selected.

4. Open the menu under the Multiline Text tool on the Annotation panel and select Single Line from the menu. The command prompt reads as follows:

```
Current text style: "Standard"
Text height: 1'-0" Annotative: No Justify: Left
TEXT Specify first endpoint of text baseline or
[Justify Style]:
```

Click Justify on the command line.

5. The command prompt now reads as follows:

```
TEXT Enter an option [Align Fit Center Middle Right
TL TC TR ML MC MR BL BC BR]:
```

Click Fit on the command line.

6. Click points A and B in Figure 10.3. A blinking cursor appears.

A   B

FIGURE 10.3 Specifying the ends of a fit baseline

7. Type **OFFICE** and press Enter twice. The TEXT command ends, and the single line of text appears on the drawing canvas (see Figure 10.4).

FIGURE 10.4 Making single-line text fit within a predefined space

8. Select the inner rectangle and press the Delete key.

9. Toggle on Ortho mode on the status bar.

10. Click the Move tool on the Modify panel, select the Office text object, and press Enter. Click an arbitrary point on the drawing canvas, move the cursor upward from that point, type **2** (or **5** for metric), and press Enter. The text moves up so that the word *OFFICE* is centered within the rectangle (see Figure 10.5).

FIGURE 10.5 Centering the text within the rectangle by moving it upward

11. Save your work.

Your model should now resemble Ex10.2-end.dwg, which is available among this chapter's companion files.

Exercise 10.3: Justify Text

AutoCAD has numerous options that let you justify text to suit almost any conceivable geometric situation. In the following steps, you will align text so that it appears centered within a *callout symbol* indicating the drawing and sheet number.

To begin, open the file Ex10.3-start.dwg from this chapter's companion files.

1. Click the Pan tool in the Navigation bar and drag from right to left to reveal the circle with a line running through it. Press Esc to exit the Pan tool.

2. Type **TEXT** and press Enter. The command prompt reads as follows:

   TEXT Specify first endpoint of text baseline or [Justify Style]:

   Type **J** (for Justify) and press Enter.

3. The command prompt now reads as follows:

   TEXT Enter an option [Align Fit Center Middle Right TL TC TR ML MC MR BL BC BR]:

If you press Enter when the command prompt says Specify start point of text or [Justify Style]:, the new text object will appear directly below the previous text object on the next line. Be aware that each text line is a separate object, however.

Type **MC** (for Middle Center) and press Enter. Type **CEN** (for Center) and click the circle to make the center of the circle the insertion point of the text. Press Enter to accept 0 as the default rotation angle. Type **3** and press Enter twice.

4. Click the Move tool on the Modify panel, type **L** (for Last), and press Enter twice. Click an arbitrary point on the drawing canvas, move the cursor upward from that point, type **18** (or **40** for metric), and press Enter. The text is centered within the upper semicircle.

5. Save your work.

Your model should now resemble Ex10.3-end.dwg, which is available among this chapter's companion files.

Exercise 10.4: Transform and Create Text

Text objects can be transformed with the same commands you might use on other types of objects—commands such as MOVE, COPY, ROTATE, SCALE, and MIRROR. In the following steps, you will mirror and copy existing text to create new text objects that you will alter later, in the "Edit Text" section. In addition, you will create new text in a different style.

To begin, open the file Ex10.4-start.dwg from this chapter's companion files.

1. Click the Mirror tool on the Modify panel, select the text object (3), and press Enter. Click the start point at A and the endpoint at B in Figure 10.6 to define the mirror. The command line reads as follows:

```
MIRROR Erase source objects? [Yes No] <N>:
```

> Transforming and editing existing text is an alternative to creating new text objects from scratch.
>
>

2. Press Enter to accept the default, No, and the MIRROR command is done.

3. Click the Copy tool on the Modify panel, type **L** (for Last), and press Enter twice. Click an arbitrary point on the drawing canvas, move the cursor to the right from this point, type **4'** (or **140** for metric), and press Enter twice. A new text object is created to the right of the text you mirrored in the previous step.

4. Select the Annotate tab on the ribbon and select the Single Line text tool in the Text panel. The command prompt reads as follows:

```
Current text style: "Standard" Text height: "1'-0"
Annotative: No Justify: MC
TEXT Specify middle point of text or [Justify Style]:
```

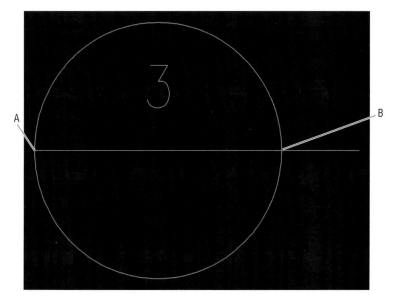

FIGURE 10.6 Mirroring text to create a duplicate text object

5. Type **S** (for Style) and press Enter. Type **Title** (the name of one of the styles you created in Exercise 10.1) and press Enter. Title is now the current style.

6. Type **J** (for Justify) and press Enter. Type **BL** (for Bottom Left) and press Enter.

7. Type **NEA** (for Nearest) and press Enter. Click point A in Figure 10.7 as the start point of the text. The command prompt now reads as follows:

```
TEXT Specify height <6">:
```

The justification option stays the same until you change it.

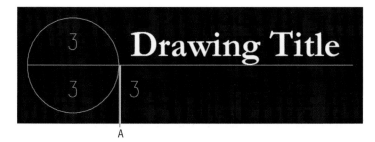

FIGURE 10.7 Creating Title text

Mirroring Text and Monitoring System Variables

Set the MIRRTEXT system variable to 1 to mirror text as well as objects with the MIRROR command. Text mirrored with MIRRTEXT set to 1 appears backward or upside down.

The System Variable Monitor (SYSVARMONITOR command) notifies you when any system variables you put into a list are changed by yourself or others. For example, by default whenever MIRRTEXT is changed from the preferred value of 0, you will be notified on the command line so you can decide whether you really want to mirror text backward or upside down.

System Variable Monitor dialog box:

☑ Notify when these system variables change
☐ Enable balloon notification

Status	System Variable	Preferred	Current	Help
✗	MIRRTEXT	0	1	?
	CMDDIA	1		?
	FILEDIA	1		?
	HIGHLIGHT	1		?
	PICKADD	2		?
	PICKAUTO	5		?
	PICKFIRST	1		?
	SDI	0		?
	SELECTIONPREVIEW	3		?

Reset All

Edit List ...

OK   Cancel   Help

In AutoCAD 2018, you can right-click the System Variable icon in the status bar to reset to preferred values without having to open the System Variable Monitor dialog box.

You are only prompted to enter a text height in text objects whose style's text height is set to 0.

8. Type **1'-6** (or **45** for metric) to specify the text height and press Enter. Press Enter again to accept a default rotation of 0 degrees (horizontal). Type **Drawing Title** (see Figure 10.7) and press Enter twice to end the TEXT command.

9. Save your work.

Your model should now resemble Ex10.4end.dwg, which is available among this chapter's companion files.

Write and Format Paragraphs Using *MTEXT*

The MTEXT command is a word processing program within AutoCAD that treats all the lines and paragraphs you write as a single object. The powerful MTEXT command gives you word wrap, per-letter style overrides, tabs, inline spell checking, control over line spacing, bulleted and numbered lists, column formatting, and many other features.

MTEXT is ideally suited to writing general notes on drawings and other lengthy blocks of text. In the following steps, you will create and format some unusual general notes. Instead of typing multiple paragraphs, you'll import one of the most famous monologues in the English language and turn it into a series of hypothetical steps.

Exercise 10.5: Write and Format with *MTEXT*

To begin, open the file Ex10.5-start.dwg from this chapter's companion files. In addition, get the file Hamlet.txt and double-click the file to open it in Notepad on the PC or TextEdit on the Mac. Select Format ➢ Word Wrap to see the text wrap onto multiple lines.

1. Press Alt+Tab to switch back to AutoCAD. Pan to the large rectangle in Ex10.5-start.dwg.

2. Type **ST** (for Style) and press Enter. Double-click Standard in the Styles list on the left side of the Text Style dialog box. Standard is now the current style. Click the Close button.

3. Select the Annotate tab on the ribbon and select the Multiline Text tool from the drop-down menu in the Text panel. Click points A and B shown in Figure 10.8.

Certification
Objective

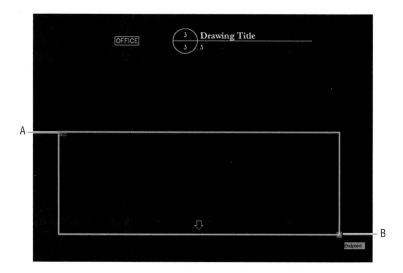

FIGURE 10.8 Specifying the opposite corners of a block of multiline text

Import Text **4.** The Text Editor tab appears on the ribbon. Expand its Tools panel
and click the Import Text button.

If you exit the text
editor, reactivate it by
double-clicking the
text block. Click within
a block of text you are
creating or editing to
place the cursor at that
location. Double-click to
select an entire word.
Triple-click to select an
entire paragraph.

CONTEXT TAB OR IN-PLACE EDITOR

If you are in a workspace that doesn't support the ribbon, then the Text Editor
tab cannot appear. Instead, you will see the In-Place Editor, which has most of
the same functionality.

5. Click Hamlet.txt in the Select File dialog box that appears. Click
Open, and text appears within the large rectangle (see Figure 10.9).
The built-in spell checker identifies misspelled words by underlining
them in red. Perhaps this is not surprising for English written 400
years ago, but in your own projects, right-click any underlined word
that seems incorrect (which most likely wouldn't include company
or product names or technical jargon) to see some correctly spelled
suggestions.

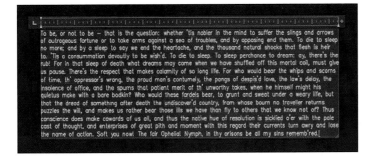

FIGURE 10.9 Importing text with the MTEXT command

6. Drag the cursor from the end to the beginning of the block of text and highlight all the text. Open the Bullets And Numbering menu in the Paragraph panel and choose Numbered from the list. The number 1 appears at the start of the text. Click strategic points in the text and press Enter to separate the paragraph into the numbered notes shown in Figure 10.10. Don't worry if the text extends below the lower edge of the rectangle (it should).

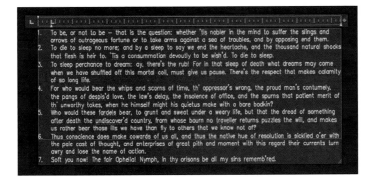

FIGURE 10.10 Turning a block of text into a series of numbered notes

7. Click within the block of text to deselect all text. Drag out a selection that includes the phrase "To be or not to be—that is the question." Open the Text Editor Color Gallery drop-down in the Formatting panel and select Red. Click the Uppercase button in the same panel (see Figure 10.11).

Choose uppercase from the flyout menu.

F I G U R E   1 0 . 1 1   **Formatting selected text**

8. Click anywhere outside the block of text on the drawing canvas to end the MTEXT command.

TEXT FRAME PROPERTY

If you use the Properties panel to change the Text Frame property to Yes, a rectangular border will appear around the text. Editing the text automatically resizes the rectangular border. Only MTEXT entities have the Text Frame property.

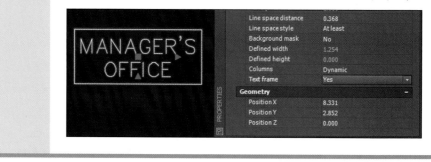

---

9. Save your work.

Your model should now resemble Ex10.5-end.dwg, which is available among this chapter's companion files.

Edit Text

Editing text can mean many different things, from changing content (the words) and text object properties to creating multiple columns of text. You would be frustrated indeed if you couldn't correct typographical errors, because everyone seems to make them. Fortunately, editing text is as simple as double-clicking, highlighting the text in question, and retyping. It is also easy to create multiple columns in AutoCAD by dragging a grip. Creating columns of text can help you fit the required words into the space available on your drawings.

Exercise 10.6: Edit Content and Properties

Editing text content is as simple as double-clicking existing text and typing something new. Editing text properties requires you to use the Quick Properties palette or the Properties panel. In the following steps, you will edit both content and properties.

To begin, open the file Ex10.6-start.dwg from this chapter's companion files.

1. Double-click the text in the lower semicircle of the callout symbol to invoke the TEXTEDIT command. The number 3 is highlighted. Type A-4, click outside the editing window on the drawing canvas, and press Esc to stop editing. The bubble now references the hypothetical drawing 3 on sheet A-4 (see Figure 10.12).

Certification Objective

◄

The last justification setting used for single-line text is maintained as the default for the creation of new text.

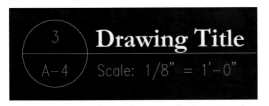

FIGURE 10.12 Edited text

2. Select the 3 under the text "Drawing Title," type **QP** (for Quick Properties), and press Enter. In the Quick Properties window that appears, change Justify to Middle Left and type **Scale: 1/8" = 1'-0"** (or **Scale: 1:20** for metric) in the Contents text box.

3. Press Enter to update the selected object. Press Esc to deselect. Figure 10.13 shows the result.

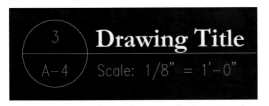

FIGURE 10.13 Edited text content and properties

4. Save your work.

Your model should now resemble Ex10.6-end.dwg, which is available among this chapter's companion download files.

Exercise 10.7: Work with Columns

You can create multiple columns easily with any multiline text object. This feature is perfect if the text you have written doesn't fit into the space between the drawing and its title block on a typical drawing. Creating multiple columns gives you more layout options, allowing you to find the best fit for paragraphs of text within the space available. In the following steps, you will move object grips to create and size two columns.

To begin, open the file Ex10.7-start.dwg from this chapter's companion files.

1. Click the numbered Hamlet text once to select it and reveal its grips. Toggle off Object Snap. Click the Column Height (bottom) grip, move it upward, and click again, automatically creating two columns, as shown in Figure 10.14.

MText Location grip   Column Width grip   MText Width grip

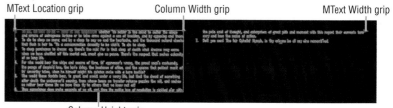

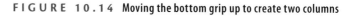

Column Height grip

FIGURE 10.14 Moving the bottom grip up to create two columns

2. Click the Column Width (middle) grip and move it to the left to reduce the size of both columns simultaneously. Click to set its new position. Click and move the right grip until it reaches the right edge of the rectangle and then click to set its new position (see Figure 10.15).

3. The left column is too short compared to the right column. Move the Column Height (bottom) grip down until the text in both columns is roughly equalized. Press Esc to deselect the text. Select the rectangle, and press the Delete key. Figure 10.16 shows the result.

4. Save your work.

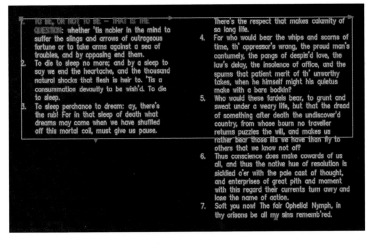

FIGURE 10.15 Moving the middle grip to the left to resize columns

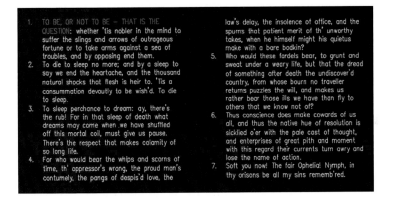

FIGURE 10.16 The result after resizing the column length and deleting the rectangle

Your model should now resemble Ex10.7-end.dwg, which is available among this chapter's companion files.

Recognize and Combine Text

Unfortunately, it is impossible to store AutoCAD's native SHX fonts as text in Adobe PDF files. Instead, AutoCAD's SHX text that is exported to PDF is stored as geometry. The text geometry looks and prints exactly the same from the PDF as it would from AutoCAD. However, if the exported PDF file is later imported back into AutoCAD, its geometric text is not editable as text.

PDF is the most popular format for exchanging data with consultants who don't use AutoCAD, so round-trip exports and imports of PDF files with AutoCAD are common. AutoCAD 2018 has a new Recognize SHX Text tool (PDFSHXTEXT command) that allows text that is imported as geometry to be later converted back into editable SHX text.

The Recognize SHX Text tool outputs single lines of MTEXT. AutoCAD 2018 has another new tool, Combine Text (TXT2MTEXT command), that allows you to combine multiple text entities into a single MTEXT entity. Using the two new tools together allows you to export SHX text written in AutoCAD to the PDF format and import it back again into AutoCAD, maintaining it as multiline text.

Exercise 10.8: Import, Recognize, and Combine Text from PDF

The optimal process for importing text from Adobe PDF files involves three separate commands: PDFIMPORT, PDFSHXTEXT, and TXT2MTXT, optimally used in that order. In the following steps, you will import and recognize SHX text and then combine its output into a single multiline text entity. To begin, start a new drawing.

1. On the Insert tab, click the PDF Import tool and select Ex10.8.pdf. This is the text block from the previous exercise exported to PDF.

2. Click OK to accept the default settings in the Import PDF dialog box (see Figure 10.17).

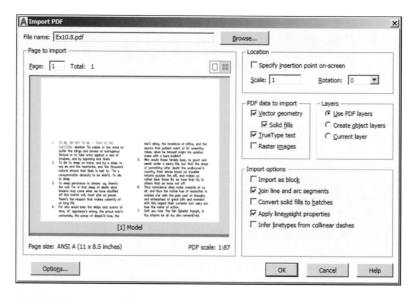

FIGURE 10.17   There is no SHX Text check box in the Import PDF dialog because Autodesk text is not supported in Adobe PDF files.

3. Select some of the text, and you will see that it was imported as geometry. The "text" is composed of numerous small line segments, making it difficult to manage in AutoCAD.

4. Select Recognition Settings on the Insert tab's Import group. Select Simplex because this was the font used to generate the text that was exported as geometry to the PDF file (see Figure 10.18). Click OK. Type C and press Enter to specify a crossing selection window. Make a crossing window from the lower right to the upper left to encompass all the geometric text, including the paragraph numbers, and press Enter. Figure 10.19 shows the resulting message.

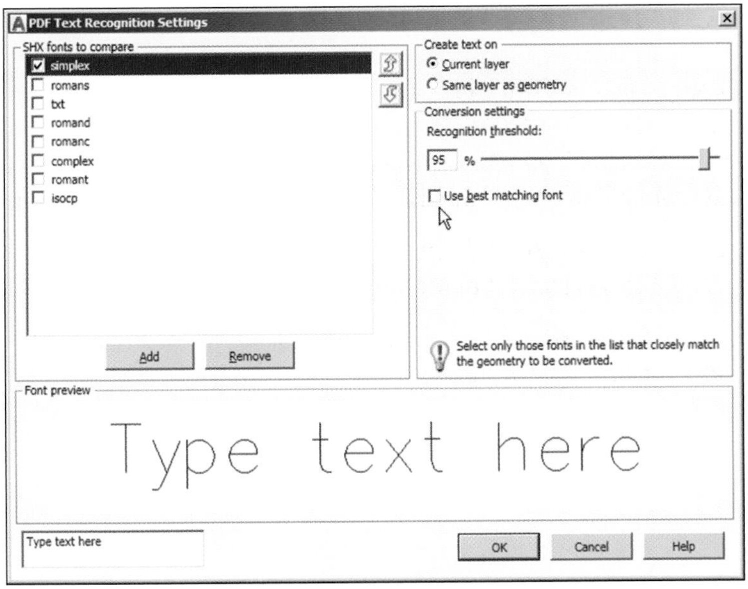

FIGURE 10.18 You can either select the specific font(s) to compare with the geometry if you know which was used or select Use Best Matching Font if you aren't sure.

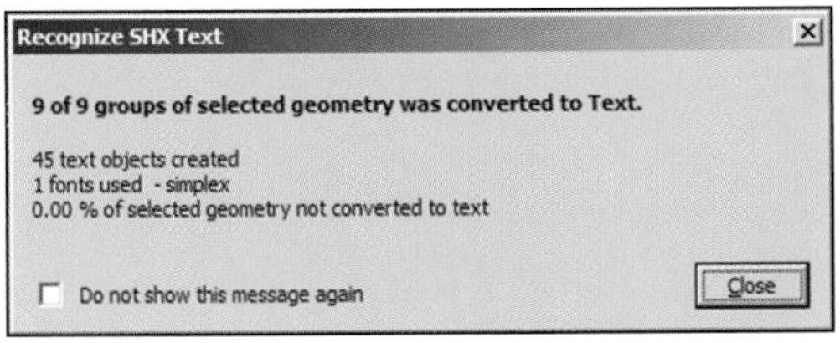

FIGURE 10.19 The number of text objects created and the font used is reported in the Recognize SHX Text dialog box.

5. Select some of the text objects, and you will see that each line is a separate text entity, making editing difficult. Select the Combine Text tool, select only the MTEXT objects in the left column, and press Enter. The line breaks are lost but now the left column is all a single MTEXT entity (see Figure 10.20).

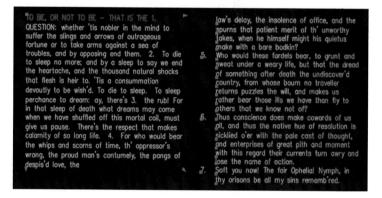

FIGURE 10.20 After combining MTEXT entities in the left column, it is now a single object, while the right column remains a collection of MTEXT entities. Additional formatting is required to restore the look and editability of the SHX text.

6. Press Esc to deselect. Double-click the text column on the left. Remove the numerals and extra spaces, and add returns where needed. Select the paragraphs, choose Bullets And Numbering, and select Numbered. Figure 10.21 shows the desired result. Close the text editor.

FIGURE 10.21 Additional formatting within the MTEXT editor is usually required after combining text entities.

Your model should now resemble Ex10.8-end.dwg, which is available among this chapter's companion files.

Now You Know

In this chapter, you learned how to create text styles, write lines of text, write and format paragraphs, and edit any text object. In short, you know what it takes to document and design with text in AutoCAD.

CHAPTER 11

Dimensioning

Dimensioning is the art of annotating drawings with precise numerical measurements. The process is generally straightforward in the AutoCAD® program because everything is typically drawn in real-world scale. Dimensions will automatically display the correct measurements as long as the geometric objects to which they refer are drawn to actual size.

In this chapter, you'll learn the mechanics of dimensioning in model space. Dimensioning in paper space and in viewports is covered in Chapter 13, "Working with Layouts and Annotative Objects."

In this chapter, you'll learn to do the following:

▶ **Style dimensions**

▶ **Add dimensions**

▶ **Edit dimensions**

Style Dimensions

The appearance of dimensions (the size of text and arrows, the length of extension lines, and so on) is controlled by dimension styles. Every drawing comes with a Standard dimension style, which of course is the current style because there is only one by default. When you create more than one dimension style, you must choose which one is current. New dimension objects are assigned the current dimension style in much the same way that objects and layers or text and text styles work.

You can customize dimension styles and even create substyles to control the way different types of dimensions appear according to your personal preferences or to adhere to a corporate or industry standard established for dimensions. For example, if you want to use architectural tick marks rather than arrowheads for linear and aligned dimensions but want to use arrowheads for radius, diameter, and angular dimensions, you can encode these preferences in a dimension style and a series of substyles.

Exercise 11.1: Create Dimension Styles

In the following steps, you will modify the Standard dimension style and create a few substyles for specific types of dimensions in preparation for adding dimension objects in the next section.

Begin by opening the file Ex11.1-start.dwg (see Figure 11.1), which is among the companion files available for download from the book's web page, www.sybex.com/go/autocad2018essentials.

FIGURE 11.1 The geometric drawing you will dimension

Certification
Objective

You will learn about
Annotative styles in
Chapter 13.

1. Select the Home tab on the ribbon if it is not already selected. Expand the Annotation panel and click the Dimension Style button (see Figure 11.2).

FIGURE 11.2 Accessing the Dimension Style Manager on the ribbon

2. As you can see in the Dimension Style Manager (Figure 11.3), every drawing has Annotative and Standard dimension styles by default. The Standard style is selected by default. Click the Modify button to alter the Standard style.

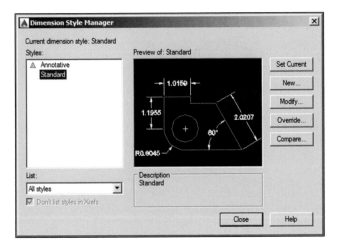

FIGURE 11.3 Dimension Style Manager

STYLING DIMENSIONS IN MULTIPLE DRAWINGS

Modifying dimension styles in a particular drawing in no way affects the dimensions or styles in other drawings. If you want to use the same dimension styles in future drawings, customize the dimension styles in your drawing template.

3. Select the Primary Units tab in the Modify Dimension Style: Standard dialog box (Figure 11.4). Set Precision to 0.000 in the Linear Dimensions section. (If you are in a country that uses a comma instead of a period as a decimal separator, select a comma [,] in the Decimal Separator drop-down menu.) Select Trailing in the Zero Suppression section (see Figure 11.4).

4. Select the Symbols And Arrows tab. In the Arrowheads section, choose Open 30 from the First drop-down (see Figure 11.5). The Second drop-down automatically matches the first by default, so it now says Open 30 as well.

5. Select the Lines tab. Double-click the Offset From Origin value to select it, type **0.125**, and press Tab (see Figure 11.6). Observe in the preview image how the distance between the object and its extension lines increases. Click OK and Close to save the modifications you've made to the Standard style.

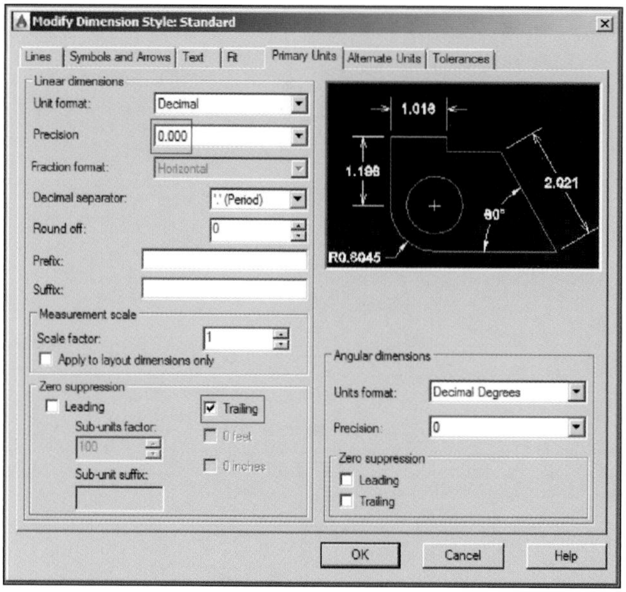

FIGURE 11.4   Configuring dimension style primary units

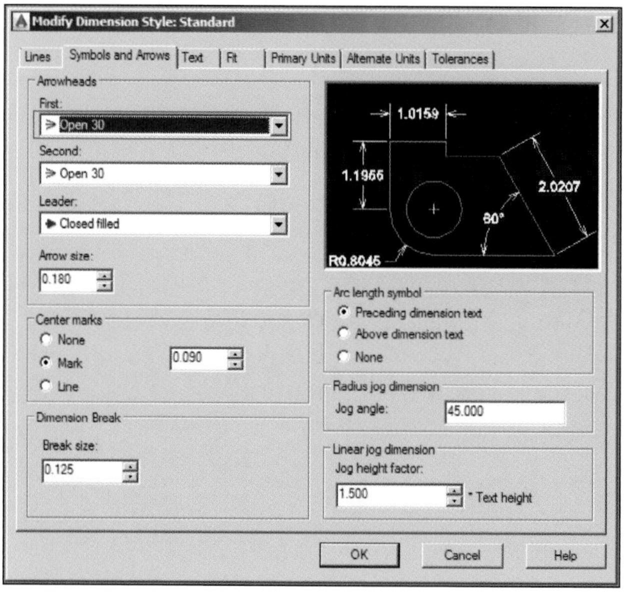

FIGURE 11.5   Changing arrowheads in the Standard dimension style

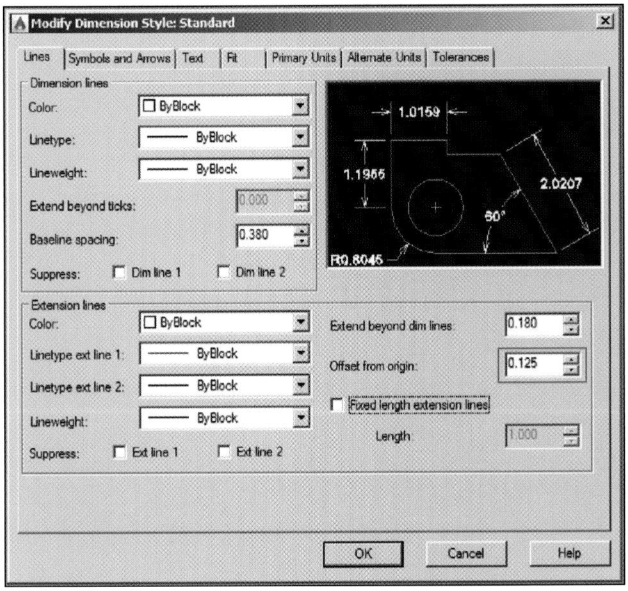

FIGURE 11.6 Increasing the offset from origin distance

UNDERSTANDING DIMENSION STYLES

Changing a dimension style automatically updates all existing dimension objects in the current drawing that have that style assigned.

6. Type **D** (for Dimension Style) and press Enter. The Dimension Style Manager reappears. Click the New button to open the Create New Dimension Style dialog box. Verify that Start With is set to Standard. Choose Angular Dimensions from the Use For drop-down (see Figure 11.7). Click Continue.

7. The New Dimension Style: Standard: Angular dialog box appears. Select the Symbols And Arrows tab. Change the First arrowhead drop-down to Closed Filled. The Second arrowhead automatically changes to Closed Filled as well (see Figure 11.8). The preview image reveals how the angular dimension will appear. Click OK.

Linear dimensions can be either horizontal or vertical. Aligned dimensions measure linear distances at angles other than horizontal or vertical.

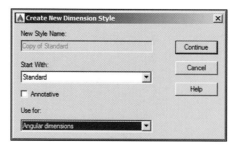

FIGURE 11.7   Creating a dimension substyle for angular dimensions

FIGURE 11.8   Customizing the arrowheads in the Angular substyle

8. Click the New button again in the Dimension Style Manager. Select Radius Dimensions in the Use For drop-down and click Continue. Select Closed Filled in the Second arrowhead on the Symbols And Arrows tab. The preview image again reveals what a radial dimension will look like governed by this substyle; click OK.

9. Select Standard in the styles list in the left pane of the Dimension Style Manager. The preview image now shows the cumulative effect of the style and its substyles: open arrowheads for linear and aligned dimensions and closed filled arrowheads for angular and radial dimensions (see Figure 11.9). Click Close.

Linear dimensions   Aligned dimension

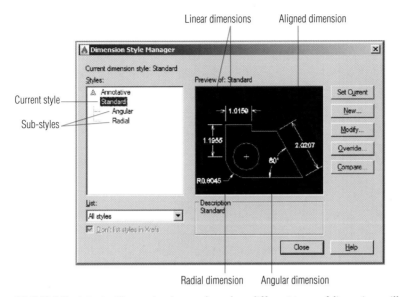

Current style

Sub-styles

Radial dimension   Angular dimension

FIGURE 11.9 The preview image shows how different types of dimensions will appear when they are added to the drawing.

10. Save your work.

Your model should now resemble Ex11.1-end.dwg, which is available among this chapter's companion files.

Add Dimensions

In technical drawings, dimensions are typically measurements for which the designer may be legally responsible. So although it is essential to know how to add specific dimensions to a drawing, it is also useful to use *inquiry commands* that measure linear objects (MEASUREGEOM or DIST) or find areas (AREA) without making specific annotations in the drawing. You will explore how to do so in the following section. In addition, you will add a variety of dimension objects that show specific measurements on the drawing. The section ends with a discussion on how to add a multileader, which is text with an arrow pointing to a specific geometric feature in a drawing.

Exercise 11.2: Use Inquiry Commands

Use inquiry commands when you want to find out (but not document) the length, angle, name, and/or area of a specific feature without annotating the drawing with this information. In the following steps, you'll explore inquiry commands to get these specific types of information from a drawing.

To begin, open the file Ex11.2-start.dwg from this chapter's companion files.

1. Toggle on Object Snap mode on the status bar if it is not already on. Right-click the Object Snap button and turn on Endpoint and Intersection running object snap modes.

2. Click the Distance tool in the Utilities panel of the Home tab on the ribbon. Click points A and B shown in Figure 11.10. The distance 5.000 is shown onscreen, and the command prompt reads as follows:

   ```
   Distance = 5.000, Angle in XY Plane = 26.565,
   Angle from XY Plane = 0.000 Delta X = 4.472,
   Delta Y = 2.236, Delta Z = 0.000
   ```

   Press Esc to end the MEASUREGEOM command.

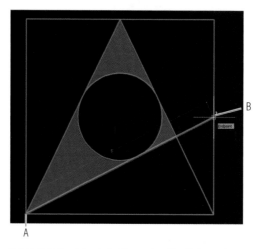

FIGURE 11.10 Measuring the distance between two points

3. Open the Measure menu in the Utilities panel, select the Radius tool, and select the circle. The command prompt reads as follows:

   ```
   Radius = 1.000
   Diameter = 2.000
   ```

4. Select the Angle option in the dynamic prompt. Select lines A and B shown in Figure 11.11. The command prompt now gives the following value:

```
Angle = 36.87°
```

Press Esc to end the MEASUREGEOM command.

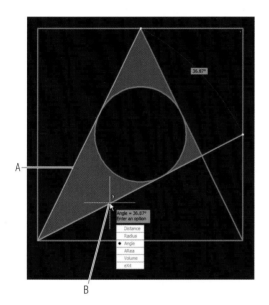

FIGURE 11.11 Measuring the angle between two lines

5. Type **AREA** (for area) and press Enter. The command prompt reads as follows:

```
AREA Specify first corner point or
[Object Add area Subtract area eXit]
<Object>:
```

6. Press Enter to accept the default Object option and select the circle. The command prompt gives these values:

```
Area = 3.142, Circumference = 6.283
```

Press Esc, and the MEASUREGEOM command ends.

7. Save your work.

Your model should now resemble Ex11.2-end.dwg, which is available among this chapter's companion files.

The number of decimal places shown in the inquiry commands is controlled by the Precision drop-down in the Drawing Units dialog box (accessed with the UNITS command).

Exercise 11.3: Add Dimension Objects

In the following steps, you'll add dimension objects one at a time using a variety of specialized tools to produce dimensions that are linear, aligned, angular, radial, and so on.

To begin, open the file Ex11.3-start.dwg from this chapter's companion files.

Use the DIMLAYER command to specify which layer dimension objects go on. By default they will go on the current layer.

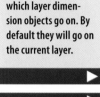

Dimension objects are typically associated with the geometry to which they refer so that when you modify the geometry, the dimensions automatically update with new measurements.

1. Toggle on Object Snap mode on the status bar if it is not already on. Right-click the Object Snap button and turn on Endpoint and Intersection running object snap modes in the shortcut menu that appears if they are not already selected.

2. Click the Dimension tool on the Annotation panel. Click points A and B to specify the first and second extension line origin points, as shown in Figure 11.12. Click point C to specify the dimension line location.

Certification Objective

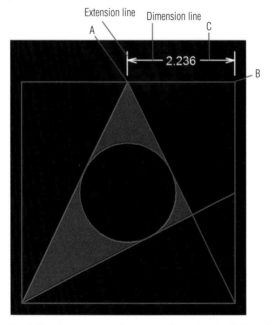

FIGURE 11.12 Creating a dimension by clicking three points

The CENTERLINE command creates an associated centerline between any two existing lines.

3. Click the top red line and then click point A shown in Figure 11.13. Press Enter to end the DIM command.

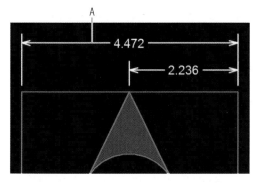

FIGURE 11.13 Creating a linear dimension by selecting an object and its dimension line location

4. Type **CENTERMARK** (for an associated Center Mark) and press Enter. Select the circle, and a crosshair symbol appears at the center of the circle. Press Enter to end the command.

Certification
Objective

5. Type **DIM** and press Enter. Click points A, B, and C shown in Figure 11.14.

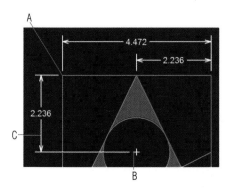

FIGURE 11.14 Creating another linear dimension

6. Type **C** (for the Continue option) and press Enter. Click the last dimension object you created and then click the lower-left corner of the object being dimensioned to add another dimension below the previous one. Press Esc to return to the top level of the DIM command.

7. Click points A, B, and C shown in Figure 11.15. An aligned dimension appears, parallel to the angled line.

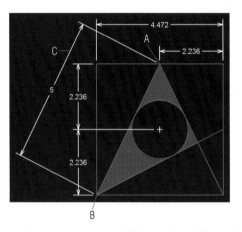

F I G U R E 1 1 . 1 5   Adding an aligned dimension

8. Add the four additional aligned dimensions shown in Figure 11.16, measuring 2, 3, 4, and 5 units.

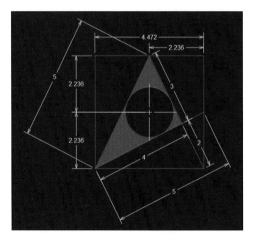

F I G U R E 1 1 . 1 6   Adding additional aligned dimensions

9. Click the Dimension tool in the Annotation panel, select lines 1 and 2 shown in Figure 11.17, and then click point A to create an angular dimension object. Select lines 1 and 3 and then click point B to create a second angular dimension.

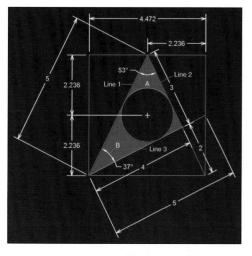

F I G U R E   1 1 . 1 7   Adding angular dimensions

10. Select the circle and then click a point inside the circle to locate the radius value (see Figure 11.18). Press Enter to end the DIM command.

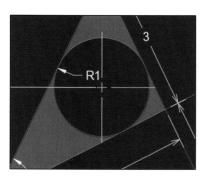

F I G U R E   1 1 . 1 8   Adding a radius dimension

11. Save your work.

Your model should now resemble Ex11.3-end.dwg, which is available among this chapter's companion files.

Exercise 11.4: Add and Style Multileaders

A *multileader* is text with a line tipped by an arrowhead that leads the eye to specific geometric features. Multileader styles control the appearance of leader objects in much the same way that dimension styles control the appearance of dimensions. In the following steps, you will add a leader object and then configure the multileader style.

To begin, open the file Ex11.4-start.dwg from this chapter's companion files.

Certification
Objective

1. Select the Leader tool in the Annotation panel. Click points A and B shown in Figure 11.19, type **Area of circle = 3.142**, and then press Ctrl+Enter.

> You have to use Ctrl in addition to Enter to end the command because Enter by itself advances to the next line.

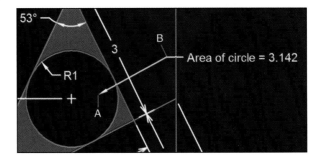

FIGURE 11.19   Adding a leader object

2. Expand the Annotation panel and click the Multileader Style button. Click the Modify button in the Multileader Style Manager dialog box that appears.

3. On the Leader Format tab of the Modify Multileader Style: Standard dialog box, choose Dot from the Symbol drop-down in the Arrowhead section (see Figure 11.20). Click OK and Close, and the leader object automatically has a dot on its end.

4. Save your work.

Your model should now resemble Ex11.4-end.dwg, which is available among this chapter's companion files.

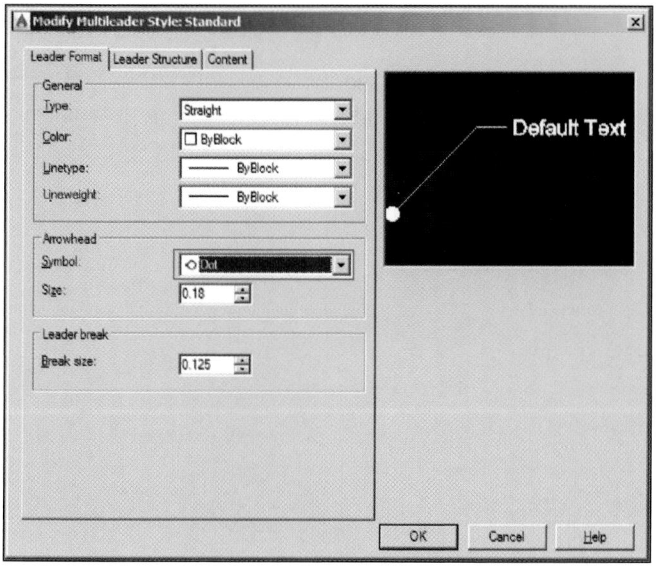

FIGURE 11.20 Editing a multileader style

Edit Dimensions

Dimensions have grips that allow you to reposition extension lines, the dimension line, and the dimension text independently of one another.

Exercise 11.5: Alter Dimension Objects

In the following steps, you will edit the length and location of extension and dimension lines directly with grips, adjust a dimension style to affect the appearance of dimension objects, and use a few specialized dimension-editing commands.

To begin, open the file Ex11.5-start.dwg from this chapter's companion files.

1. Toggle on Object Snap mode on the status bar if it is not already on. Right-click the Object Snap button and turn on Endpoint and Intersection running object snap modes.

2. Click the horizontal linear dimension with a value of 2.236 to select it. Click the lower-left grip to adjust the length of this extension line. Snap the grip to point A in Figure 11.21. Press Esc to deselect.

Certification
Objective

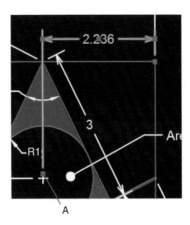

FIGURE 11.21 Grip-editing a dimension object

3. Type **DIMEDIT** (for Dimension Edit) and press Enter. The command prompt reads as follows:

   ```
   DIMEDIT Enter type of dimension editing
   [Home New Rotate Oblique] <Home>:
   ```

4. Type **N** (for New) and press Enter. A text-editing window appears below the last text you entered. Delete the zero by pressing the Delete key.

5. Type **EQ.** (for Equal) and then press Ctrl+Enter to end text-entry mode. Select both vertical linear dimensions having values of 2.236 and press Enter. Figure 11.22 shows the result.

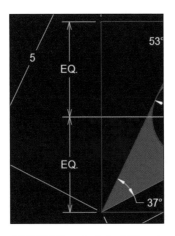

FIGURE 11.22 Editing dimension text content with DIMEDIT

DIMENSION TEXT WRAP

You can wrap text onto multiple lines if there isn't enough space to accommodate all the words in between the extension lines. When editing dimension text, simply drag the arrow icon on the right of the multiline text ruler left or right to resize the column, and the dimension text automatically wraps to fit.

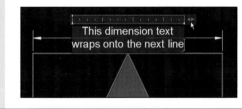

6. Type **DIMTEDIT** (for Dimension Text Edit) and press Enter. Select the aligned dimension with a value of 2 and press Enter. The command prompt reads as follows:

   Certification Objective

   ```
   DIMTEDIT Specify new location for dimension text or
   [Left Right Center Home Angle]:
   ```

7. Type **L** (for Left) and press Enter. The dimension text is now left-justified in relation to the dimension line, so the 2 is more easily read within the space left between the red lines (see Figure 11.23).

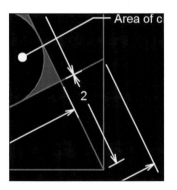

FIGURE 11.23 Changing dimension text justification with DIMTEDIT

8. Select the ribbon's Annotate tab and click the Break tool on the Dimensions panel. The command prompt reads as follows:

   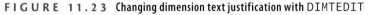

   ```
   DIMBREAK Select dimension to add/remove break or [Multiple]:
   ```

9. Click Multiple on the command line. Select the dimensions with values of 3 and the upper-left dimension with a value of 5 and press Enter. The command prompt reads as follows:

```
Select object to break dimensions or [Auto Remove] <Auto>:
```

10. Press Enter to accept the default Auto option, and the DIMBREAK command ends. Breaks are made in the selected dimensions where they cross other objects (see Figure 11.24).

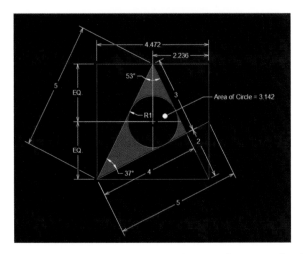

FIGURE 11.24 Using DIMBREAK to clean up overlapping dimension objects

11. Save your work.

Your model should now resemble Ex11.5-end.dwg, which is available among this chapter's companion files.

Now You Know

In this chapter, you learned how to style, add, and edit dimensions. Now you know how to document designs with specific measurements.

CHAPTER 12

Keeping In Control with Constraints

Constraints are specific restrictions applied to objects that allow for design exploration while maintaining object shape and/or size within predefined limits. In this chapter, you will create three types of constraints in the AutoCAD® 2018 program: geometric, dimensional, and user created. Once the design has been sufficiently constrained, you will make a host of geometric and dimensional changes simply by changing a single parameter.

In this chapter, you'll learn to do the following:

▶ **Work with geometric constraints**

▶ **Apply dimensional constraints**

▶ **Constrain objects simultaneously with geometry and dimensions**

▶ **Make parametric changes to constrained objects**

Work with Geometric Constraints

The AutoCAD LT® program cannot create constraints. However, AutoCAD LT 2016 and later users can view and edit constraints that were created in AutoCAD.

Geometric constraints allow you to force specific 2D objects to be coincident, collinear, concentric, parallel, perpendicular, horizontal, vertical, tangent, smooth, and symmetric; to have equal lengths; or to be fixed in world space. In the following exercise, you will assign sufficient geometric constraints to ensure that a rectangle will always remain square even when it is stretched.

Exercise 12.1: Use Geometric Constraints

Begin by opening the file Ex12.1-start.dwg, which is among the companion files available for download from this book's web page, www.sybex.com/go/autocad2018essentials.

1. Select the Rectangle tool on the Draw panel. Click two points on the drawing canvas to create an arbitrarily sized rectangle.

2. Type **CONSTRAINTINFER** and press Enter. Type **1** (to turn this mode on) and press Enter.

▶

Parallel, collinear, concentric, and equal constraints always appear in pairs.

3. Type **REC** (for Rectangle) and press Enter. Click two more points to draw another arbitrarily sized rectangle adjacent and to the right of the first one (see Figure 12.1). AutoCAD automatically infers perpendicular and parallel constraints from the geometry of the second rectangle.

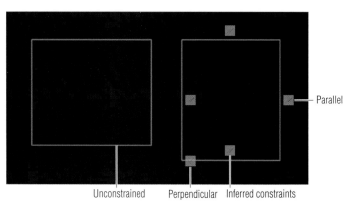

Parallel

Unconstrained   Perpendicular   Inferred constraints

F I G U R E   1 2 . 1   Drawing two rectangles, one unconstrained

4. Toggle off Infer Constraints mode by pressing Ctrl+Shift+I.

5. Select both rectangles with a crossing selection window. Hover the cursor over the upper-right grip of the left rectangle, select Stretch Vertex from the grip menu that appears, and stretch it up and to the right so that the rectangle deforms. Hover the cursor over the upper-right grip of the right rectangle, select Stretch Vertex from the grip menu, stretch it up and to the right, and click to set its new location. The rectangle remains a rectangle because of the constraints (see Figure 12.2). Press Esc to deselect.

Objects are never repositioned when inferring constraints or when using the Auto Constrain tool. Objects can be repositioned when applying constraints manually.

▶

6. Select the Parametric tab on the ribbon and select the Auto Constrain tool in the Geometric panel. Select the unconstrained rectangle on the left and press Enter. Two constraints are applied: perpendicular and horizontal (see Figure 12.3).

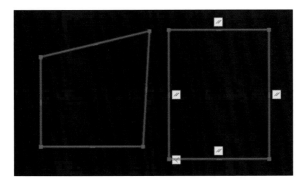

FIGURE 12.2 Stretching constrained geometry limits the types of transformation that can occur.

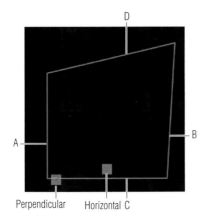

FIGURE 12.3 Applying constraints with the Auto Constrain tool

The order in which you select objects can be significant when you apply constraints. The second object will be repositioned in some cases, depending on the constraint that is applied and the shape and position of the objects.

7. Select the Parallel constraint tool in the Geometric panel. Click lines A and B shown in Figure 12.3. Line B is automatically repositioned to conform to the parallel constraint applied to line A.

8. Press the spacebar to repeat the GCPARALLEL (for Geometric Constraint Parallel) command. Click lines C and D shown in Figure 12.3.

9. Not only does the left rectangle have parallel and perpendicular constraints like the right rectangle, but it also has a horizontal constraint that was applied by the Auto Constrain tool. Select the right rectangle and press the Delete key.

10. Select the Equal constraint tool in the Geometric panel. Click lines A and C in Figure 12.3. The rectangle becomes a square (see Figure 12.4).

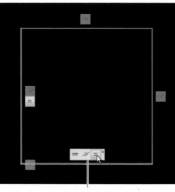

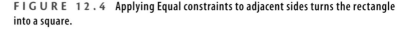

Constraint bar

FIGURE 12.4 Applying Equal constraints to adjacent sides turns the rectangle into a square.

11. Multiple constraints are grouped together in what is called a *constraint bar*. Position the cursor over the constraint bar, and you'll see a tiny Close box. Click it to hide the constraint bar.

12. Click the Show All button in the Geometric panel. The hidden constraint bar reappears.

13. Right-click the horizontal constraint and choose Delete from the context menu. The rectangle is no longer constrained horizontally (so you could rotate it if desired).

14. Click the Hide All button in the Geometric panel. The constraints are hidden but still active.

Your model should now resemble Ex12.1-end.dwg, which is available among this chapter's companion files.

Apply Dimensional Constraints

Dimensional constraints allow you to control object sizes with specific numerical values and to set up dynamic dimensional relationships with mathematical equations and formulas. User constraints are not tied to specific geometry but hold values calculated from dimensional constraints. In the following exercise, you will create dimensional constraints.

Exercise 12.2: Create Dimensional Constraints

To begin, open the file Ex12.2-start.dwg from this chapter's companion files.

1. Select the ribbon's Home tab, open the Layer drop-down menu in the Layers panel, and select Layer 2 to make it the current layer.

2. Select the Parametric tab on the ribbon. Select the Linear constraint tool in the Dimensional panel, and click *constraint points* A and B, shown in Figure 12.5. Constraint points highlight in red onscreen when you move the cursor near them. Click point C to locate the dimension line. Press Enter to accept the default dimension text. This dimensional constraint is automatically given the variable name d1.

Constraint points behave similarly to object snaps but are limited to endpoints, midpoints, center points, and insertion points.

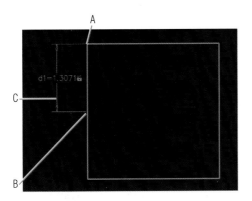

FIGURE 12.5 Creating a vertical linear dimensional constraint

3. Type C (for Circle) and press Enter. Draw an arbitrarily sized circle anywhere within the square.

4. Click the Linear constraint tool in the Dimensional panel, and click the first constraint point in the upper-left corner of the rectangle. Click the circle to accept its center as the second constraint point. Move the cursor upward and click to place the horizontal dimension line above the rectangle (see Figure 12.6). Move on to step 5 without pressing Enter.

5. Type d2=d1 and press Enter. The circle moves over so that it is horizontally centered within the rectangle and the constraint reads fx:d2=d1. The fx means the dimensional constraint is calculated by a function.

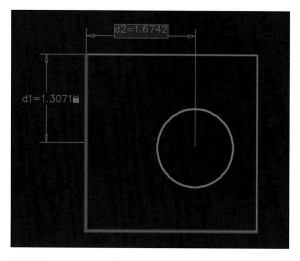

FIGURE 12.6 Creating a horizontal linear dimensional constraint

You can convert an existing dimension into a dimensional constraint with the DIMCONSTRAINT command.

6. Press the spacebar to repeat the DCLINEAR (for Dimensional Constraint Linear) command. Click the first constraint point in the upper-right corner of the rectangle. Click the circle to accept its center as the second constraint point. Move the cursor to the right and click to place the vertical dimension line to the right of the rectangle. Type **d3=d1** and press Enter. The circle is now centered within the square (see Figure 12.7).

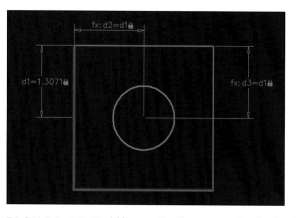

FIGURE 12.7 Adding another linear constraint that is calculated by a function

fx

Parameters Manager

7. Click the Parameters Manager button in the Manage panel to open the Parameters Manager. All the dimensional constraints that you have created are listed here (d1, d2, and d3). Click the fx button to create a new user parameter.

8. Type **P** (for Perimeter) as the user parameter name and press Enter. Double-click the Expression value, type **d1*8** (d1 times 8), and press Enter (see Figure 12.8). The perimeter of the square is equal to eight times the length of half of one of its sides. Close the Parameters Manager.

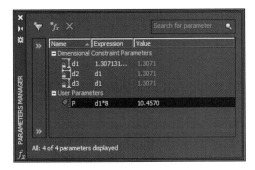

FIGURE 12.8 Adding a user parameter in the Parameters Manager

9. Select the Hide All button in the Dimensional panel.

Hide All

10. Select the Diameter constraint tool in the Dimensional panel, select the circle, click a point inside the circle to locate the dimension line, type **dia=P/PI**, and press Enter. The variable PI is hard-coded as 3.14159265; there is no need to define it as a user variable. The circumference of the circle is now equal to the perimeter of the square, traditionally called *squaring the circle* (see Figure 12.9).

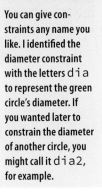

You can give constraints any name you like. I identified the diameter constraint with the letters dia to represent the green circle's diameter. If you wanted later to constrain the diameter of another circle, you might call it dia2, for example.

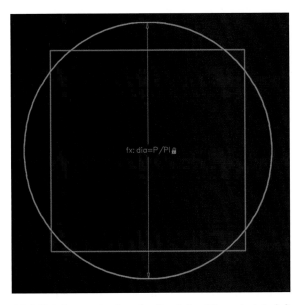

FIGURE 12.9 Squaring the circle with constraints defined by formulas

Your model should now resemble Ex12.2-end.dwg, which is available among this chapter's companion files.

Constrain Objects Simultaneously with Geometry and Dimensions

You can use geometric and dimensional constraints together to force objects to conform to your design intent. In the following exercise, you will draw two more circles and constrain their positions and sizes using a combination of geometric and dimensional constraints.

Exercise 12.3: Use Simultaneous Constraints

To begin, open the file Ex12.3-start.dwg.

1. Select the ribbon's Home tab, open the Layer drop-down menu in the Layers panel, and select Layer 3 to make it the current layer.

2. Type C (for Circle) and press Enter. Draw an arbitrarily sized circle anywhere within the square.

3. Select the ribbon's Parametric tab and then click the Concentric constraint tool in the Geometric panel. Select the green circle and then the yellow circle. The yellow circle immediately moves to conform to the geometric constraint so that it is concentric within the larger circle.

4. Select the Radius constraint tool in the Dimensional panel, select the yellow circle, and click a point inside the circle to locate the dimension line. Type **rad=d1** and press Enter. The yellow circle changes size so that it fits perfectly within the square (see Figure 12.10).

5. Select the Hide All button in the Dimensional panel.

6. Select the ribbon's Home tab, open the Layer drop-down menu in the Layers panel, and select Layer 4 to make it the current layer.

7. Type C (for Circle) and press Enter. Draw an arbitrarily sized circle anywhere above the square.

8. Select the ribbon's Parametric tab and click the Tangent constraint tool in the Geometric panel. Select the top line of the square as the first object and the magenta circle as the second object. The circle moves down to conform to the tangent constraint (see Figure 12.11).

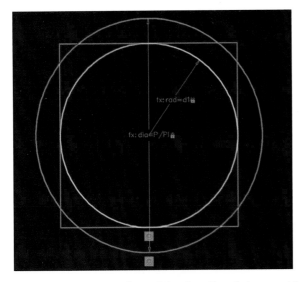

FIGURE 12.10 Constraining the yellow circle geometrically and dimensionally

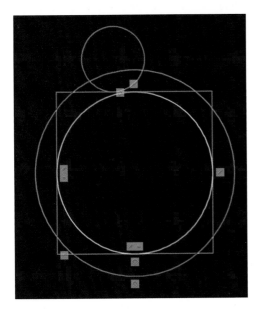

FIGURE 12.11 Applying a tangent geometric constraint

9. Press the spacebar to repeat the GCTANGENT (for Geometric Constraint Tangent) command. Select the yellow circle first and then select the magenta circle. The magenta circle moves on top of the yellow circle to conform to the new tangent constraint.

10. Click the Linear constraint tool in the Dimensional panel. Click the magenta circle, the yellow circle, and then a point off to the right to place the dimension line. Type **d4=dia/2** and press Enter (see Figure 12.12). The center of the magenta circle is anchored effectively at the top quadrant (or top cardinal point) of the green circle.

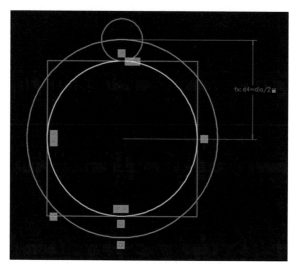

FIGURE 12.12 Adding the last dimensional constraint

All constraints are hidden but still active.

11. Click the Hide All button in the Dimensional panel, and click the Hide All button in the Geometric panel.

Your model should now resemble Ex12.3-end.dwg, which is available among this chapter's companion files.

Make Parametric Changes to Constrained Objects

Once you have intelligently applied geometric and/or dimensional constraints, it is easy to make parametric changes that affect the shape and/or size of multiple interconnected objects. In the following exercise, you will change a single parameter (d1) and see how it affects the objects you have constrained. In addition, you will add dimensions to two circles and uncover an amazing coincidence.

Exercise 12.4: Alter Constraint Parameters

To begin, open the file Ex12.4-start.dwg.

1. Select the ribbon's Parametric tab and click the Parameters Manager button in the Manage panel.

2. Double-click the d1 parameter's expression. Type 3 and press Enter. All parameter values are recalculated because they are all based on the first parameter you created earlier in this chapter (see Figure 12.13).

FIGURE 12.13 Changing a single parameter has a cascading effect.

3. Click the Zoom Extents tool in the Navigation bar. The form of the diagram remains unchanged; only the scale has changed.

4. The Earth's polar radius is 3949.9 miles (or 6356.8 km). Double-click the d1 parameter's expression. Type **3949.9** (or **6356.8** in metric) and press Enter. Close the Parameters Manager.

5. Click the Zoom Extents tool in the Navigation bar.

6. Select the ribbon's Home tab, open the Layer drop-down menu in the Layers panel, and select 0 to make it the current layer.

7. Select the ribbon's Annotate tab, open the Dimension menu in the Dimensions panel, and click the Radius tool. Select the yellow circle and then click a point inside the circle to locate the dimension object.

8. Press the spacebar to repeat the DIMRADIUS (Dimension Radius) command. Select the magenta circle and click a point outside the circle to locate the dimension object. Figure 12.14 shows the result.

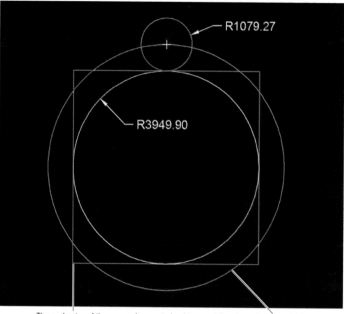

The perimeter of the square is constrained to equal the circumference of this circle.

FIGURE 12.14 **Dimensioning two radii in the squaring the circle diagram**

Your model should now resemble Ex12.4-end.dwg, which is available among this chapter's companion files.

The moon's polar radius is 1078.7 miles (or 1735.97 km). The diagram encodes the actual sizes of the earth and moon with 99.9 percent accuracy.

John Michell was the first to discover this geometric relationship, discussed in his book *City of Revelation* (Ballantine Books, 1973).

Now You Know

In this chapter, you learned how to apply geometric and dimensional constraints and how to alter constraint parameters to affect geometry. You now can include specific requirements in your drawing that alter the shape of your designs.

CHAPTER 13

Working with Layouts and Annotative Objects

There are two distinct spaces in which you can create drawings: *model space* and *paper space*. Typically, 2D drawings and 3D models are created in model space. *Layouts* in paper space bring together annotations and drawings ultimately to be plotted on paper or published electronically. *Viewports* display drawings at specific scales on layouts, which is where you'll draw title blocks that frame the drawings.

In this chapter, you'll learn to do the following:

▶ **Create annotative styles and objects**

▶ **Create layouts**

▶ **Adjust floating viewports**

▶ **Override layer properties in layout viewports**

▶ **Draw on layouts**

Create Annotative Styles and Objects

All the geometry you draw in the AutoCAD® program is created at its actual size. However, the heights of text, dimensions, and attributes present a potential problem. As drawings are scaled down from their real-world size to be represented on paper using viewport scale (which you'll learn more about in the "Adjust Floating Viewports" section later in this chapter), text, dimensions, and attributes are likewise scaled down to fit on paper.

Annotative objects allow you to automatically display text, dimensions, and attributes at different heights on the same drawing according to the viewport scale in which they are displayed. The purpose of annotative styles is to control the appearance of annotative objects such as text, dimensions, and attributes. I will discuss both text and dimensions in upcoming sections but will hold off on attributes until Chapter 15, "Working with Data." As you'll see, annotative objects change their sizes automatically to fit the drawing scale.

Exercise 13.1: Work with Annotative Text

In the following steps, you will configure an annotative text style to display text at 1/8" (or 0.4 cm) high on paper. All the text objects assigned to this style will automatically adjust their heights to 1/8" (or 0.4 cm) no matter in what scale the drawing is shown. In this way, annotative objects automatically change their sizes relative to other geometry in the drawing.

Begin by opening the file Ex13.1-start.dwg, which is among the companion files available for download from this book's web page, www.sybex.com/go/autocad2018essentials.

1. Type **ST** (for Style) and press Enter. Click the New button in the Text Style dialog box that appears. Type **Annotative** as the style name in the New Text Style dialog box and click OK.

2. Select Arial as the font name, select Annotative in the Size area, type **1/8"** (or **0.4 cm**) for Paper Text Height, and type **0.9** for Width Factor (see Figure 13.1). Click Apply and then click Close.

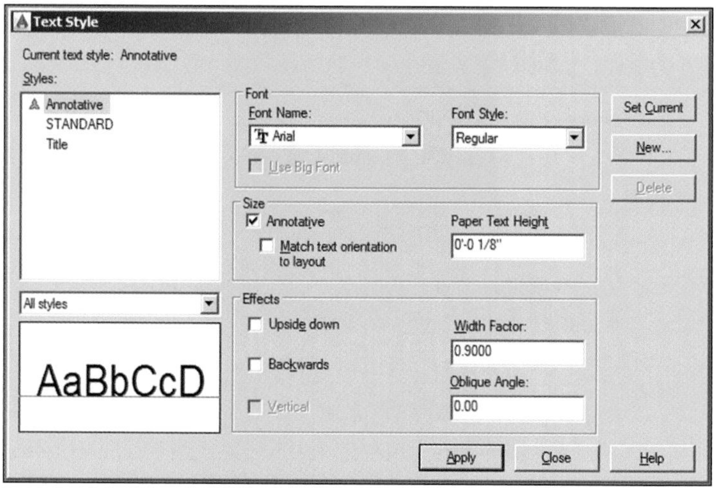

FIGURE 13.1   Creating an annotative text style

3. Select Zoom Realtime from the Navigation bar and zoom into the room with the round table at the top of the floor plan by dragging upward. Pan as necessary in Windows by dragging with the mouse wheel depressed. On the Mac, hold the spacebar and drag to pan.

4. Click the Multiline Text tool in the Annotation panel on the ribbon's Home tab. Select 1/16" = 1'-0" (or 1:200 for metric) from the drop-down menu in the Select Annotation Scale dialog box that appears (see Figure 13.2). Click OK.

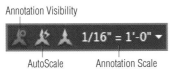

FIGURE 13.2 Selecting an annotation scale in model space

If you don't see the Select Annotation Scale dialog box (it can be suppressed), you can still set the annotation scale on the status bar.

5. Click the Customization button on the status bar and select Annotation Visibility, AutoScale, and Annotation Scale from the menu. New controls appear on the status bar (see Figure 13.3).

Annotation Visibility

AutoScale   Annotation Scale

FIGURE 13.3 Annotation controls on the status bar

Pressing Enter moves you to the next line in multiline text.

6. Click the first corner at some arbitrary point inside the round table. Type **J** (for Justify) and press Enter. The command prompt reads as follows:

    MTEXT Enter justification [TL TC TR ML MC MR BL BC BR] <TL>:

   Type **MC** (for Middle Center) and press Enter. Click the second point a short distance down and to the right. Type **Conference** and press Enter; then type **Room** and press Ctrl+Enter to end the MTEXT command.

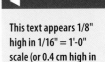

This text appears 1/8" high in 1/16" = 1'-0" scale (or 0.4 cm high in 1:200 scale).

7. Click the Move tool on the Modify panel, type **L** (for Last), and press Enter twice. Type **INS** (for Insert), press Enter, and click the text object. Type **CEN** (for Center), press Enter, hover the cursor over the circle, and press Enter to end the command. Click the circular table to center the text on it (see Figure 13.4).

FIGURE 13.4 Centering multiline text on the circular table

8. Toggle on Annotation Visibility and AutoScale on the status bar.

9. Change the Annotation Scale to 1/2" = 1'-0" (or 1:20 for metric) in the status bar. The text you created appears much smaller. This text will appear 1/8" high in 1/2" = 1'-0" scale (or 0.4 cm in 1:20 scale). Select the text object and observe both scales simultaneously (see Figure 13.5). Press Esc to deselect.

FIGURE 13.5 Annotative text shown in two scales

Your model should now resemble Ex13.1-end.dwg, which is available among this chapter's companion files.

ANNOTATION SCALES

Annotative objects do not automatically hold representations at all conceivable scales. You can add or delete scales for individual annotative objects in the right-click context menu.

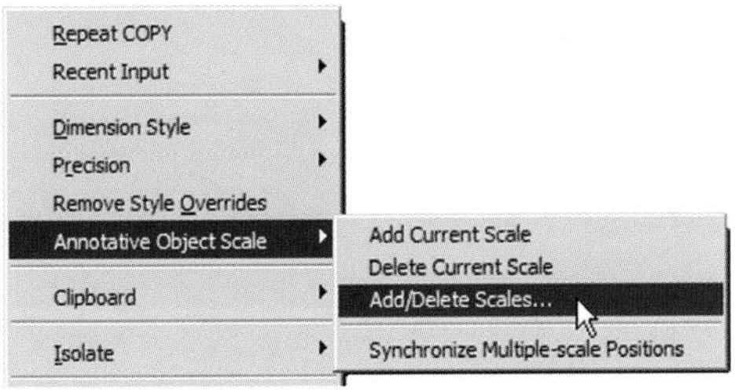

Exercise 13.2: Work with Annotative Dimensions

In much the same way as text, dimensions can be made annotative so that they change sizes when the annotative scale is changed. In the following steps, you will explore how to do this by creating an annotative dimension style and then adding an annotative linear dimension.

To begin, open the file Ex13.2-start.dwg from this chapter's companion files.

1. Type **D** (for Dimension Style) and press Enter. Click the New button in the Dimension Style Manager to bring up the Create New Dimension Style dialog box. Type **Annotative** in New Style Name and click the Annotative check box (see Figure 13.6). Then do the following:

   ▶ If you are using Imperial units, click Continue and then Close.

   ▶ If you are using metric units, click Continue. On the Primary Units tab of the Modify Dimension Style dialog box, select Decimal Units and a Precision of 0 (whole centimeters), click OK, and click Close.

Annotative styles can have any name. What makes a style annotative is the Annotative check box in the Create New Dimension Style dialog box.

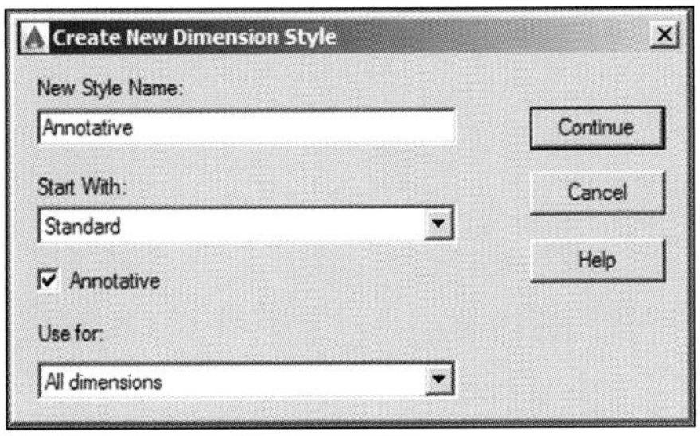

FIGURE 13.6 Creating an annotative dimension style

2. Toggle on Object Snap. Verify that endpoint running object snap mode is on by right-clicking the icon in the status bar.

3. Click the Linear dimension tool in the Annotation panel. Click points A, B, and C shown in Figure 13.7.

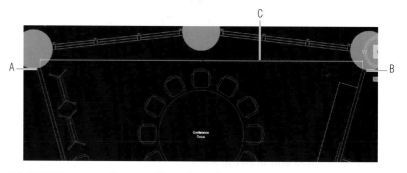

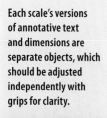

FIGURE 13.7 Drawing a linear dimension

4. Toggle on AutoScale if it is not already on. Select the 1/16" = 1'-0" (or 1:200 in metric) scale button in the Annotation Scale menu on the status bar. Select the larger dimension object and, using one of the dimension line grips at either end of the dimension line, move it upward so that the dimension has longer extension lines. Press Esc to deselect. Figure 13.8 shows the result.

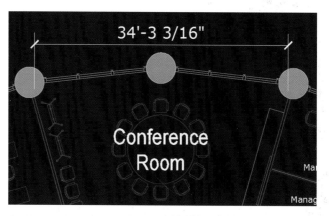

FIGURE 13.8 Moving the 1/16" = 1'-0" (or 1:200 in metric) scale dimension line upward for clarity

Your model should now resemble Ex13.2-end.dwg, which is available among this chapter's companion files.

Create Layouts

Think of layouts as sheets of virtual paper because that's what they represent. You will create layouts whether you ultimately plan to publish the drawing on paper or in electronic form. Each drawing can have multiple layouts to publish in a variety of formats.

Exercise 13.3: Configure Layouts

In the following steps, you will create two layouts, one for an 8.5" × 11" sheet of paper (or ISO A4) and another for a 30" × 42" drawing (or ISO A0), which are standard business and drawing sizes.

To begin, open the file Ex13.3-start.dwg from this chapter's companion files.

Layer Properties

1. Click the Layer Properties tool in the Layers panel on the ribbon's Home tab.

2. Click the New Layer button in the Layer Properties Manager that appears. Type **Z-Viewport** and press Enter. Double click Z-Viewport's status icon to set this layer as current (it changes to a green check mark). Click the printer icon in the Z-Viewport layer's Plot column to make this layer nonplotting (see Figure 13.9). Close the Layer Properties Manager.

Status	Name	On	Freeze	Lock	Color	Linetype	Lineweight	Transparency	Plot Style	Plot	New VP Freeze
	0	♀	☀	🔓	■ white	CONTINU...	—— Default	0	Color_7	⊟	🖶
	Z-Viewport	♀	☀	🔓	■ white	CONTINU...	—— Default	0	Color_7	⊟	🖶
	A-door	♀	☀	🔓	■ green	CONTINU...	—— Default	0	Color_3	⊟	🖶
	A-door-elev	♀	☀	🔓	□ 44	CONTINU...	—— Default	0	Color_44	⊟	🖶
	A-eqpt	♀	☀	🔓	□ 181	CONTINU...	—— Default	0	Color_181	⊟	🖶
	A-flor-fill	♀	☀	🔓	■ 232,234,253	CONTINU...	—— Default	0	Color_7	⊟	🖶
	A-flor-patn	♀	☀	🔓	□ blue	CONTINU...	—— Default	0	Color_5	⊟	🖶
	A-flor-shft	♀	☀	🔓	□ blue	CONTINU...	—— Default	0	Color_5	⊟	🖶

Current layer: Z-Viewport

Search for layer

All: 24 layers displayed of 24 total layers

FIGURE 13.9 Creating a nonplotting viewport layer and setting it as current

You can toggle between model space and any layout using the large icons that appear under the file tabs or by clicking the small tabs in the lower-left corner of the user interface.

Certification Objective

3. Hover the cursor over the current drawing's file tab and click Layout1 (see Figure 13.10).

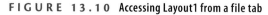

FIGURE 13.10 Accessing Layout1 from a file tab

▶

The viewport frame will not appear in the output because it is on a nonplotting layer. The contents of the viewport will be output, however.

4. The image in the drawing canvas changes as you enter paper space. A white representation of paper is displayed with an automatically created viewport through which you can see the drawing in model space. The viewport object is on the Z-Viewport layer. The dashed lines indicate the limits of the plotting device's printable area. Make a crossing selection across the entire layout—only the viewport is selected because there is only one object currently in paper space (see Figure 13.11). Press Esc.

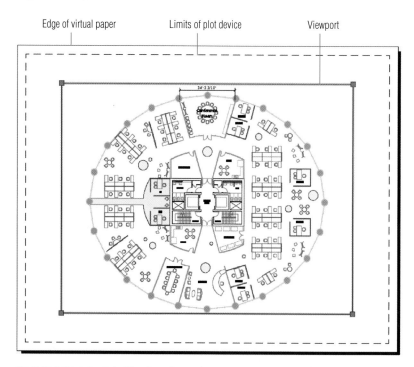

FIGURE 13.11 Viewing a layout in paper space

5. Select the ribbon's Output tab. Click the Page Setup Manager tool in the Plot panel, and click the Modify button in the Page Setup Manager dialog box that appears. When the Page Setup: Layout1 dialog box opens, select the DWG To PDF.pc3 plotter from the Name drop-down, choose monochrome.ctb from the Plot Style Table drop-down, check Display Plot Styles, and do the following:

Certification
Objective

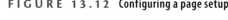 Page Setup Manager

▶ If you are using Imperial units, select ANSI Expand A (8.50 × 11.00 Inches) as the paper size (see Figure 13.12). Leave the plot scale at 1 inch = 1 unit. Click OK and then click Close.

◀

Available paper sizes depend on the plotter selection.

▶ If you are using metric units, select ISO Full Bleed A4 (297.00 × 210.00 MM) as the paper size. Set the plot scale to 10 mm = 1 unit. Click OK and then click Close.

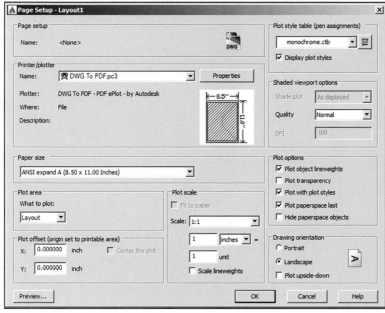

F I G U R E   1 3 . 1 2   Configuring a page setup

6. Click the plus icon adjacent to the Layout1 tab in the lower-left corner of the user interface to create a new layout. Layout2 appears as a tab; click it.

7. Click the Page Setup Manager in the Plot panel. Click the Modify button in the Page Setup Manager dialog box that appears to modify Layout2. Select the DWG To PDF.pc3 plotter, select monochrome.ctb

from the Plot Style Table drop-down, and check Display Plot Styles. Then do the following:

▶ If you are using Imperial units, select ARCH E1 (30.00 × 42.00 Inches) as the paper size. Leave the plot scale at 1 inch = 1 unit. Click OK and then click Close.

▶ If you are using metric units, select ISO A0 (841.00 × 1189.00 MM) as the paper size. Set the plot scale to 10 mm = 1 unit. Click OK and then click Close.

A single tiny viewport was automatically created on the current layer in the corner of the layout (see Figure 13.13). (You will configure this viewport in the next section and create an additional viewport.) Your model should now resemble Ex13.3-end.dwg, which is available among this chapter's companion files.

FIGURE 13.13   Selecting a larger paper size on Layout2

Adjust Floating Viewports

Think of floating viewports as windows that exist in paper space through which you see into model space. Viewports are termed *floating* because you can position and size their frames however you like in relation to the paper represented in a layout. You will configure a single floating viewport on Layout1 and two separate viewports on Layout2 to gain experience with viewports.

Exercise 13.4: Work on Layout1

In the following steps, you will set the scale of the building floor plan on Layout1 and then adjust its viewport to fit the floor plan.

To begin, open the file Ex13.4-start.dwg from this chapter's companion files.

1. Hover the cursor over the current drawing's file tab and select the large Layout1 icon that appears.

2. Double-click anywhere inside the viewport on Layout1 to switch into model space. The viewport's frame highlights with a thicker representation when displaying model space (see Figure 13.14). Move the cursor inside the viewport and observe that the crosshair cursor is available only within the viewport.

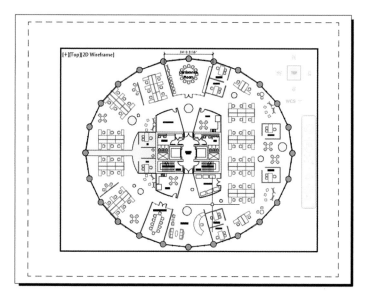

FIGURE 13.14 Model space active inside a floating viewport

3. Choose 1/16" = 1'-0" (or 1:200 in metric) from the Viewport Scale menu button on the status bar, as shown in Figure 13.15. The viewport zooms into the building core, which is in the center of the plan. At this exact zoom magnification, the plan appears in 1/16" scale (or 1:200) in the layout.

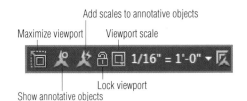

FIGURE 13.15 The status bar's appearance when a floating viewport is active

4. Double-click anywhere outside the viewport on Layout1 to switch back into paper space. Move the crosshair cursor across the drawing canvas and observe that it appears across the entire paper.

5. Viewport frames exist in paper space only. Click the single viewport frame to select it. Select the upper-right grip and move it upward and to the right until it is close to the upper-right corner of the paper but inside the plot device limits. Click the lower-left grip and move it to the lower-left corner inside the device limits (see Figure 13.16). Press Esc to deselect the viewport.

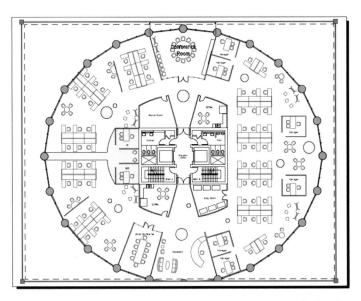

FIGURE 13.16 Adjusting the viewport in an attempt to display the entire floor plan at 1/16" scale (or 1:200 in metric)

6. Unfortunately, the plan doesn't quite fit on the page in 1/16" scale. Double-click anywhere inside the viewport to switch back into model space. Toggle on the Add Scales To Annotative Objects button in the status bar. Select 1/32" = 1'-0" (or 1:300 in metric) from the Viewport Scale menu button on the status bar. The drawing fits on the page, and new annotative objects are created in this scale.

7. Zoom in, select the single dimension object, and move its dimension line upward for clarity. Note, however, that by zooming, you have changed the viewport scale. Again, select 1/32" = 1'-0" (or 1:300 in metric) from the Viewport Scale menu button on the status bar and pan the drawing to the center of the page (see Figure 13.17).

You can add a custom scale such as 1:300 by selecting Custom from the Viewport Scale menu.

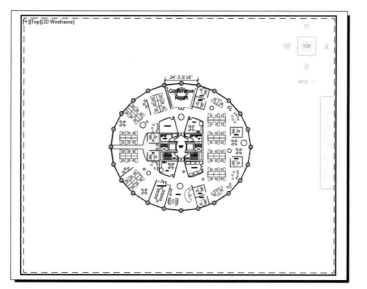

FIGURE 13.17 Finding the largest scale that will fit on the page

8. Double-click outside the viewport on Layout1 to switch back into paper space.

Your model should now resemble Ex13.4-end.dwg, which is available among this chapter's companion files.

Exercise 13.5: Work on Layout2

In the following steps, you will adjust the viewport on Layout2 and, in the process, discover that certain combinations of building geometry, viewport scales, and paper sizes do not always mesh. You will fix the problem by selecting a different viewport scale and then adjust the viewport to fit the floor plan. In addition, you'll create a viewport from scratch and adjust it.

To begin, open the file Ex13.5-start.dwg from this chapter's companion files.

You can reorder the sequence of layouts by dragging and dropping their tabs in the lower-left corner of the user interface.

Layout2
1. Select the Layout2 tab in the lower-left corner of the user interface.

2. Double-click inside the viewport to activate model space.

3. Choose 1/4" = 1'-0" (or 1:40 in metric) from the Viewport Scale menu on the status bar.

Changing the viewport scale automatically triggers a corresponding change in the annotation scale.

4. Double-click the layout outside of the viewport to switch back into paper space.

5. Viewport frames exist in paper space only. Click the viewport frame to select it. Select the upper-right grip and move it upward until it is close to the upper-right corner of the paper but inside the plot device limits. Click the lower-left grip and move it to the lower-left corner inside the device limits (see Figure 13.18). Press Esc to deselect.

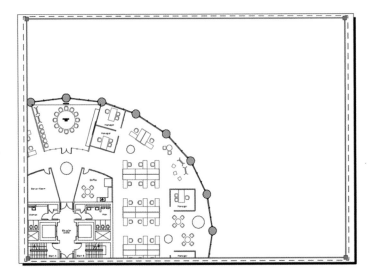

FIGURE 13.18 Scaling the viewport with grips

6. Double-click inside the viewport to switch back into model space. Drag the mouse wheel (but do not turn the wheel) to pan the drawing over within the viewport to center it on the paper. The 1/4" (or 1:50 in metric) scale drawing almost fits, but it's too tight to fit comfortably on ARCH E1 or ISO A0 paper.

You couldn't have known this without first creating the layout and trying to fit the drawing to the paper at this specific scale.

7. Verify that the option Add Scales To Annotative Objects is toggled on in the status bar and then select 3/16" = 1'-0" scale (or 1:60 in metric) in the Viewport Scale menu. The floor plan now fits the layout.

8. Double-click the paper outside the viewport to switch back into paper space. Select the viewport and grip-edit it so that it closely surrounds the plan geometry. Move the plan to the left on the paper to make room for another drawing on this layout. Figure 13.19 shows the result.

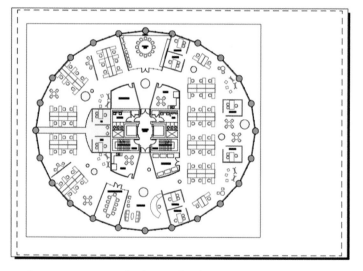

FIGURE 13.19 The drawing fits the paper at 3/16" scale (or 1:50 in metric).

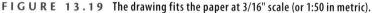

9. Type **MV** (for Make Viewport) and press Enter. Click two arbitrary corner points to the right of the existing viewport to create a new viewport. The MVIEW command ends.

Certification
Objective

10. Double-click within the new viewport to enter its model space. Select 1/2" = 1'-0" (or 1:20 in metric) in the Viewport Scale menu on the status bar; the viewports zoom into the Elevator Lobby again. Pan downward until you center the view on the conference room. Double-click outside the viewport to return to paper space. Figure 13.20 shows the result.

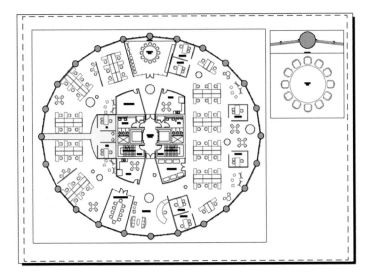

FIGURE 13.20 Creating and configuring a new viewport detailing the conference room

11. Select both viewport objects and then click the Lock Viewport icon on the status bar. Press Esc to deselect. Double-click inside the new viewport and roll the mouse wheel forward to zoom in. Whereas before when you locked the viewport only the space within the viewport zoomed in, now the entire layout zooms in.

Your model should now resemble Ex13.5-end.dwg, which is available among this chapter's companion files.

Override Layer Properties in Layout Viewports

Each viewport maintains its own set of layer properties that can override the drawing's basic layer properties. In the following steps, you will use this feature to turn off a selection of layers in a particular viewport while continuing to display these same layers in another viewport.

Exercise 13.6: Override Layer Properties

To begin, open the file Ex13.6-start.dwg from this chapter's companion files.

1. Double-click within the larger viewport on Layout2 that shows the entire floor plan to activate it and switch into floating model space.

2. Click the Layer Properties tool on the Layers panel on the ribbon's Home tab.

3. Expand the palette to the right by dragging its edge. Observe a set of properties in columns preceded with the letters *VP* (viewport). Click the icons in the VP Freeze column for layers A-furn, A-flor-fill, and A-flor-patn to freeze them in the current viewport (see Figure 13.21).

> You can override the color, linetype, line-weight, transparency, and plot style layer properties independently in each viewport if so desired.

F I G U R E   1 3 . 2 1   Freezing selected layers in the current viewport only

4. Double-click the layout outside the viewport to switch back into paper space. The furniture and furniture systems disappear from the current viewport, but the conference room's round table is still visible in the viewport on the right of Layout2 (see Figure 13.22). Close the Layer Properties Manager.

Your model should now resemble Ex13.6-end.dwg, which is available among this chapter's companion files.

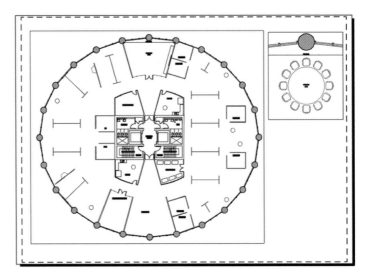

FIGURE 13.22 Furniture is visible in the viewport on the right but not in the left viewport, whose layer properties have been overridden.

Draw on Layouts

You can draw on layouts just as you can draw in model space. However, the types of content drawn on layouts will necessarily be of a different character, such as a title block, viewports, and (optionally) dimensions. Layouts have the measurements of physical sheets of paper and are not meant to hold real-world geometry directly (that's what model space is used for).

One way to draw directly on layouts is to use *title blocks*, which are borders surrounding the drawing that also have rectangles in which text identifying the sheet is placed. You can also draw dimensions directly on layouts. Dimensions added in paper space are associated with geometry in model space. If the real-world geometry changes, the dimensions will automatically update.

Exercise 13.7: Lay Out Geometry

In the following steps, you will draw a title block and add a dimension to the paper space of the layout. To begin, open the file Ex13.7-start.dwg from this chapter's companion files.

1. Type **LA** (for Layer Properties Manager) and press Enter. Click the New Layer icon, type **Z-Title**, and press Enter. Double-click the new layer to make it current. Select a Lineweight value of 0.039" (or 1.00 mm in metric) for a thick border. Close the Layer Properties Manager.

2. Click the Rectangle tool in the Draw panel. Click the corner points just inside the dashed limits of the plot device, as shown in Layout2. You cannot use object snap in this instance because the limits of the plot device rectangle is not an object that you can snap to.

3. Set the Text layer as current by selecting it in the Layer drop-down in the Layers panel.

4. Zoom into the smaller viewport on the right of Layout2.

5. Right-click the Object Snap icon in the status bar and toggle on quadrant snap. Click the Linear tool in the Annotation panel and click points A, B, and C shown in Figure 13.23. Points A and B are on the quadrants of the circle. A dimension measuring 9'-0" (274 in metric) appears on the layout in paper space that looks similar to the dimension you drew earlier in this chapter in model space.

Dimensions added in paper space are necessarily specific to each drawing and cannot be shown simultaneously in multiple viewports like annotative, model space dimensions can.

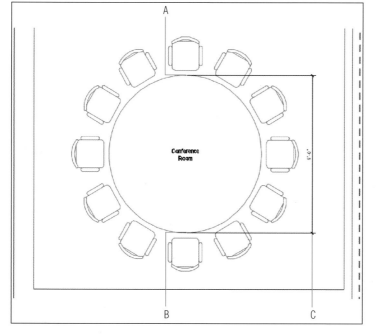

FIGURE 13.23 Drawing a dimension in paper space

TITLE BLOCKS

Drawings are legal documents and, as such, typically indicate the drawing scale, sheet name, and sheet number. This information is traditionally shown with text or attributes in a title block, which is drawn directly on the layout.

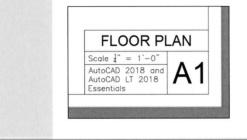

6. Double-click inside the smaller viewport that is displaying the conference table to switch into floating model space.

7. Click Maximize Viewport on the status bar. A blue border indicates that you are working in the model space of a viewport in maximized mode.

8. Select the circle representing the table and select its top quadrant grip. Type 4' 8 (**140** cm in metric) and press Enter to input the new radius. The circle grows slightly larger. Press Esc.

9. Click Minimize Viewport in the status bar. The drawing canvas returns to Layout2. The dimension in paper space is automatically updated with the value of 9'-4" (280 cm in metric).

10. Select the Output tab on the ribbon and click the Preview tool in the Plot panel. What you now see is what you would get if you published this drawing (see Figure 13.24). Press Esc to exit the preview.

The viewport frames do not appear in the plot preview because they are on a nonplotting layer.

Your model should now resemble Ex13.7-end.dwg, which is available among this chapter's companion files.

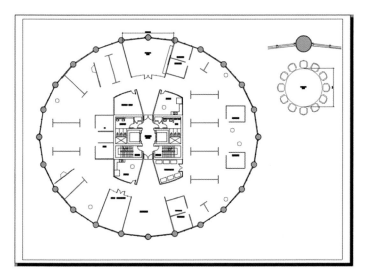

FIGURE 13.24   Plot preview of Layout2

Now You Know

In this chapter, you learned how to create annotative styles and objects, layouts, floating viewports, and title blocks. You also learned how to override layer properties within a floating viewport and magnify the contents to scale. In short, you know how to create complete blueprints of measured drawings.

CHAPTER 14

Printing and Plotting

Plotting is the term for producing output using a large-format printer (which is networked or directly connected to an AutoCAD® workstation) or exporting to an electronic drawing format. There is much more to plotting a drawing or publishing an entire sheet set than clicking the Print icon, however. Before you can successfully print, you must learn to configure a plotter and a plot style table; you'll then learn how to create professional output from model space and paper space. As you'll see in this chapter, you'll also have the option to keep everything in digital format and export DWF or PDF files that can be shared on the Internet with your partners and clients.

In this chapter, you'll learn to do the following:

▶ **Configure output devices**

▶ **Create plot style tables**

▶ **Use plot style tables**

▶ **Plot in model space**

▶ **Plot layouts in paper space**

▶ **Export to an electronic format**

Configure Output Devices

In the most general sense, everything you do on a computer is a form of *input*. Creating physical or even electronic drawings are forms of *output*. Output devices are more commonly known as printers.

Large-format (24" wide or larger) printers are marketed as "plotters" because of the history of technology. When I started my career more than 20 years ago, plotters had technical pens in them that you had to refill individually with ink. The paper (actually Mylar film) was rolled back and forth, and the pens literally plotted one line at a time. Thankfully, modern inkjet technology is much faster, so you no longer wind up with clogged pens and ink on your hands.

In the following sections, you will configure an output device by setting up a system printer and an AutoCAD plotter. Once these steps are completed, you won't have to perform them again on the same computer.

Exercise 14.1: Set Up a System Printer

The first thing you'll need to do is set up a system printer, which contains *drivers* that your operating system uses to control the output device. System printers are not specific to AutoCAD; device manufacturers supply drivers, which you then install to become printers on your system.

If you are reading this book at work, you undoubtedly already have a system printer or your CAD manager has installed one for you. For the purposes of this book, however, you will install a driver for the HP DesignJet T920 plotter (an industry workhorse), whether or not you own this device. You will be using the HP DesignJet T920 system printer in this chapter. The following steps guide you in installing this typical system printer:

1. Open your browser and type **HP DesignJet T920 eprinter driver** into your favorite search engine. Select the first search result or go to www.hp.com and search for Download Drivers and Software.

2. Download the appropriate driver for your system.

3. Install the HP DesignJet T920 HPGL2 driver following the manufacturer's instructions. Select File:Port in the installation options because you don't have access to the actual device. If you did have the physical device, you would select the relevant connection port, such as Ethernet, USB, or Wireless.

Exercise 14.2: Set Up an AutoCAD Plotter

> **AutoCAD for Mac doesn't use AutoCAD plotters but instead outputs directly to the system printers listed under System Preferences.**

Most programs send output directly to system printers, but AutoCAD is an exception. AutoCAD has another layer of software between the program and the operating system known as an AutoCAD plotter. In this section, you will set up an *AutoCAD plotter* that sends its output to the system printer, which in turn hands off the print job to the output device itself.

1. In a blank AutoCAD drawing, type **PLOTTERMANAGER** and press Enter. The Windows Explorer dialog box appears displaying the Add-A-Plotter Wizard and various AutoCAD plotters that have the .pc3 file extension (see Figure 14.1).

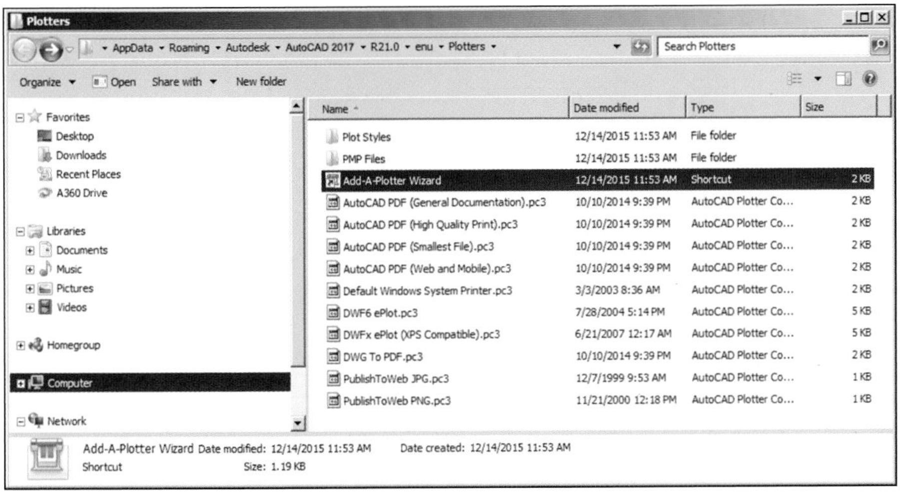

FIGURE 14.1 Explorer window showing two folders, the Add-A-Plotter Wizard, and various AutoCAD plotters

2. Double-click the Add-A-Plotter Wizard. Read the Introduction page and click Next.

3. Select the System Printer radio button and click Next.

PLOTTING RASTER IMAGES TO SCALE

Raster images of drawing layers can be output to scale from AutoCAD and enhanced in Adobe Photoshop for presentation. For more information on setting up and plotting to a raster plotter driver in AutoCAD, see my book *Enhancing Architectural Drawings and Models with Photoshop* (Sybex, 2010).

4. Select the HP DesignJet T920 HPGL2 system printer from the list in the Add Plotter – System Printer dialog box. The listed printers will differ on your computer depending on which drivers you (or your CAD manager) have already installed on your system. Click Next.

5. The next page allows you to import a legacy PCP or PC2 file from older versions of AutoCAD. Since you are creating a PC3 file from scratch, click Next to open the Add Plotter – Plotter Name page.

6. AutoCAD now suggests a name for the plotter that is identical to the name of the system printer. Type the name **HP DesignJet T920 Plotter** to differentiate the new printer name from the system printer. Click Next.

7. The final page of the Add-A-Plotter Wizard allows you to edit the newly created plotter driver itself. Click the Edit Plotter Configuration button to do this.

▶

Edit the Custom Properties in the Plotter Configuration Editor to access settings specific to the system printer driver.

▶

You should filter the list of paper sizes to display only the sizes you use.

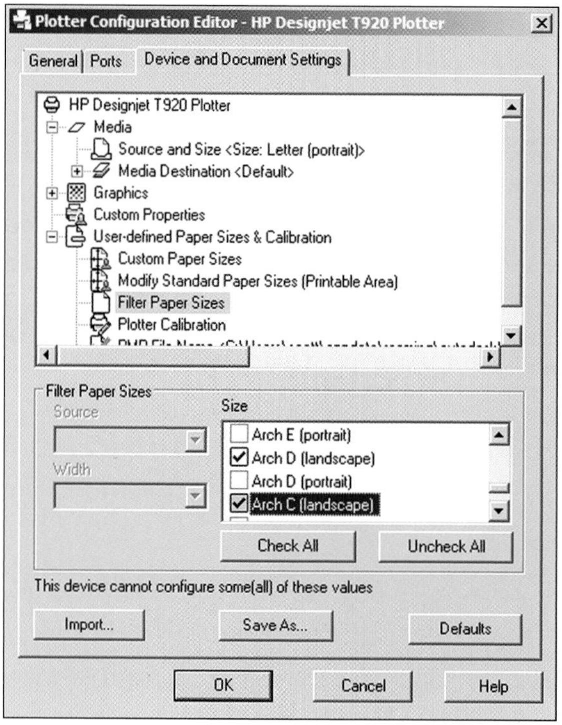

8. Select the Device And Document Settings tab and then select the Filter Paper Sizes node in the Plotter Configuration Editor dialog box. Click the Uncheck All button. Scroll down the list and select the following paper sizes: Arch C (landscape) and Arch D (landscape). Figure 14.2 shows the result.

FIGURE 14.2 Filtering out all unused paper sizes

9. Click OK to close the Plotter Configuration Editor. Click Finish to close the Add-A-Plotter Wizard.

10. The new AutoCAD plotter driver you just created, HP DesignJet T920 Plotter.pc3, appears in the Windows Explorer window that was opened in step 1. Close Windows Explorer.

Create Plot Style Tables

Plot style tables determine the final appearance of objects in terms of their color, linetype, lineweight, end cap, line fill, and screening percentage. Plot style tables take precedence over layer properties when the drawing is printed.

In addition to creating a system printer and AutoCAD plotter, you will need to create a plot style table or use an existing one. AutoCAD has two types of plot style tables:

Color-Dependent Plot Style Tables (CTB Files) These have been used since the days of pen plotters when you assigned a number of colors in AutoCAD to a specific physical pen. For example, red objects might plot using the 0.5 mm pen, and green and yellow objects might use the 0.7 mm pen. Many firms still use color-dependent plot style tables today.

Named Plot Styles (STB Files) These were a new feature in AutoCAD 2000. Named plot style tables offer greater flexibility as compared with color-dependent plot styles because plot criteria can be assigned by layer or by object rather than by color only. In the following exercise, you will create a named plot style. Named plot styles use the .stb file extension.

> ◄
> You cannot create or modify plot styles on the Mac version of AutoCAD—you can use only the default plot styles.

Exercise 14.3: Create a Named Plot Style Table

In this exercise, you will create a named plot style table. Plot style tables control the appearance of objects when they are plotted.

1. Type **STYLESMANAGER** and press Enter. Windows Explorer appears and displays a number of preset plot style table files.

2. Double-click the Add-A-Plot Style Table Wizard. Read the introductory page and then click Next.

3. Select Start From Scratch on the next page. Click Next.

4. Select the Named Plot Style radio button on the next page. This will create a named plot style having one default style called Normal. Click Next.

5. For lack of a more descriptive name, type **My plot style** on the File Name page. Click Next.

6. The final page of the wizard allows you to edit the newly created STB file itself. Click the Plot Style Table Editor button.

7. Select the Form View tab in the Plot Style Table Editor that appears. Click the Add Style button. Type **Black** and press Enter.

8. Open the Color drop-down and select Black (see Figure 14.3).

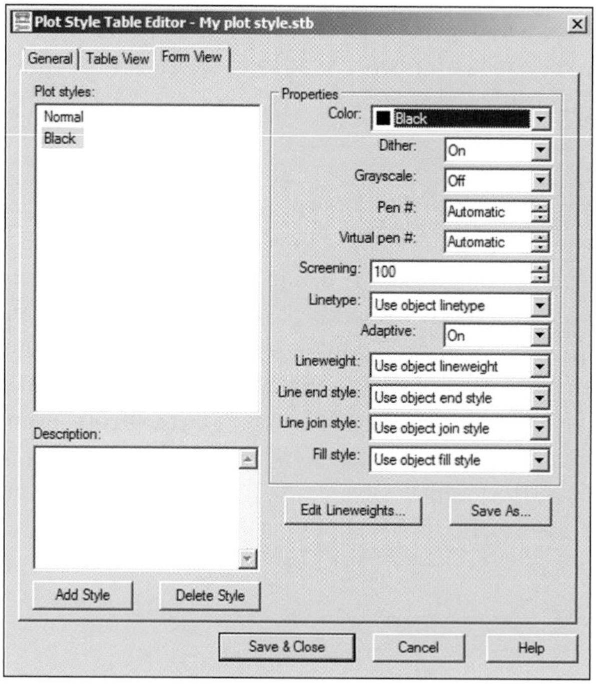

FIGURE 14.3 Creating a Black plot style

Screening refers to the intensity of ink sprayed on the paper while plotting. Selecting 100 directs the inkjet print head to spray at full intensity, whereas setting this value to 0 will not spray any ink. Intermediate values produce varying levels of grayscale.

9. Click the Add Style button again, type **20% Screen**, and press Enter. Highlight the value next to the word *Screening*, type **20**, and press Tab. Click Save & Close to close the Plot Style Table Editor.

10. Click Finish to close the Add-A-Plot Style Table Wizard. The named plot style table you just created, My plot style.stb, appears in the Windows Explorer window that was opened in step 1. Click the close box in Windows Explorer.

Use Plot Style Tables

New drawings are created using either color-dependent or named plot style tables. A setting in the Options dialog box controls this behavior. Existing drawings must go through a conversion process to switch from using one plot style table type to the other.

Exercise 14.4: Configure New Drawings for Named Plot Style Tables

In the following steps, you will configure new drawings to use named plot styles, and you will save a template that has a named plot style table assigned:

1. Type **OP** (for Options) and press Enter. Select the Plot And Publish tab in the Options dialog box that appears.

2. Click the Plot Style Table Settings button in the lower right of the Options dialog box. Select the Use Named Plot Styles radio button in the Plot Style Table Settings dialog box that appears. Select `My plot style.stb` from the Default Plot Style Table drop-down menu. Select Black from the Default Plot Style For Layer 0 drop-down menu. Select ByLayer from the Default Plot Style For Objects drop-down menu if it is not already selected (see Figure 14.4). Click OK and then click OK again to close both of the open dialog boxes.

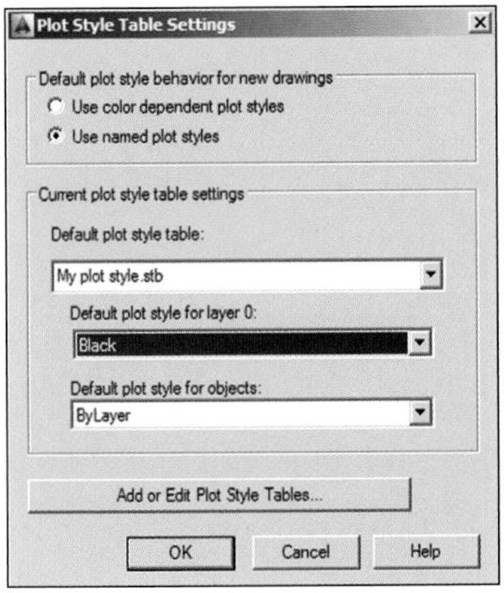

FIGURE 14.4 Configuring the default plot style behavior and settings for new drawings

After you decide (or your CAD manager decides for you) which type of plot style table to use consistently, you will want to save a template that records this preference so that you don't have to revisit this issue every time you create a new drawing.

3. Click the New button on the Quick Access toolbar. Click the arrow button adjacent to the Open button in the Select Template dialog box that appears. Choose Open With No Template – Imperial from the drop-down menu (see Figure 14.5).

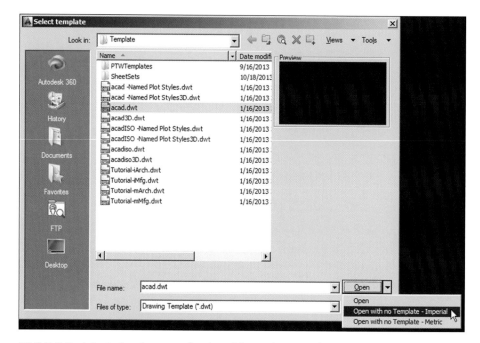

FIGURE 14.5 Creating a new drawing without using a template

4. Type **UN** (for Units) and press Enter. Choose Architectural units (or Decimal units in metric) with a precision of 1/4" (metric users choose a precision of 0.0). Set Units To Scale Inserted Content under the Insertion Scale area to Inches (or Centimeters in metric) (see Figure 14.6). Click OK.

5. Click the Save As button in the Quick Access toolbar. Change the Files Of Type drop-down in the Save Drawing As dialog box that appears to AutoCAD Drawing Template (*.dwt). Type **My template** in the File Name text box (see Figure 14.7). Click Save.

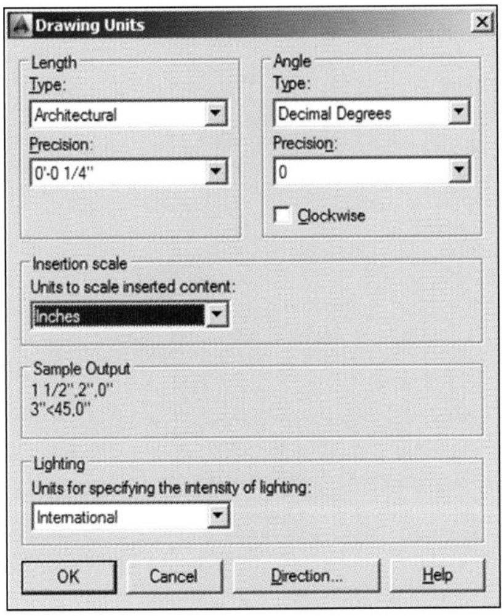

FIGURE 14.6 Setting architectural drawing units

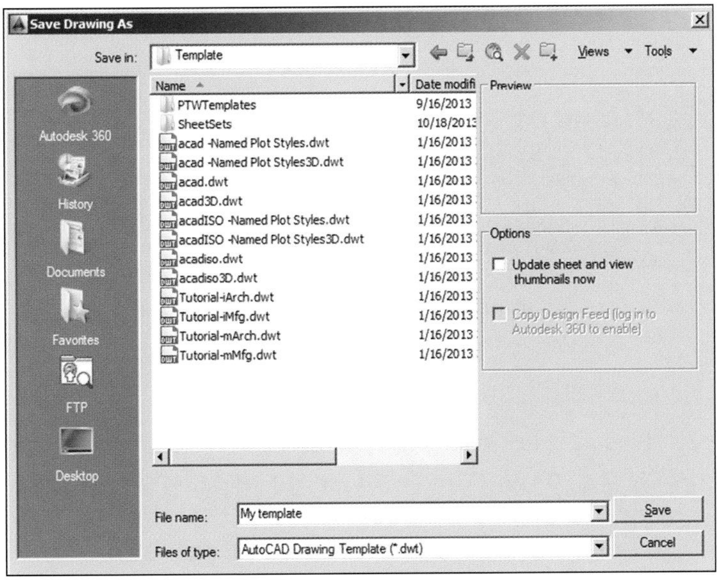

FIGURE 14.7 Saving a new drawing template

6. Type **Named plot styles and architectural units** in the Template Options dialog box that appears (see Figure 14.8). Click OK.

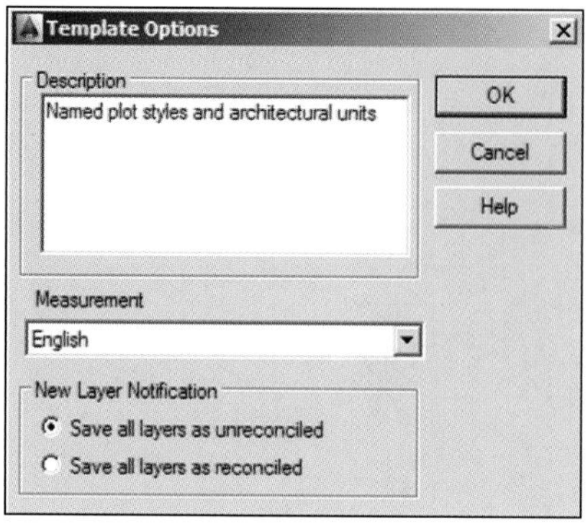

FIGURE 14.8   Describing the template

7. Type **CLOSE** on the command line and press Enter.

You can now create new drawings that have named plot styles (and architectural or decimal units) simply by selecting My Template—no other configuration is required.

SWITCHING PLOT STYLE TABLE TYPES IN EXISTING DRAWINGS

If you are switching from named plot styles to color-dependent plot styles in an existing drawing, use the CONVERTPSTYLES command to make the conversion. If you are going in the other direction and converting an existing drawing from color-dependent plot styles to named plot styles, you must first use the CONVERTCTB command and then use CONVERTPSTYLES.

Exercise 14.5: Assign Plot Styles by Layer or by Object

If you are working in a drawing that uses a color-dependent plot style table, then the plot styles are automatically configured by color. When working on a drawing that uses a named plot style table, you will need to assign named plot styles by layer or by object, as shown in the following exercise.

Start by opening the file Ex14.5-start.dwg, which is among the companion files available for download from this book's web page, www.sybex.com/go/autocad2018essentials.

1. Type **LA** (for Layer) and press Enter. Right-click any one of the layer names in the Layer Properties Manager that appears and choose Select All from the context menu. Click the word *Normal* in the Plot Style column. The plot style table you created earlier (My plot style.stb) is selected. Choose Black in the Select Plot Style dialog box (see Figure 14.9). Click OK. Now all the layers will plot in black.

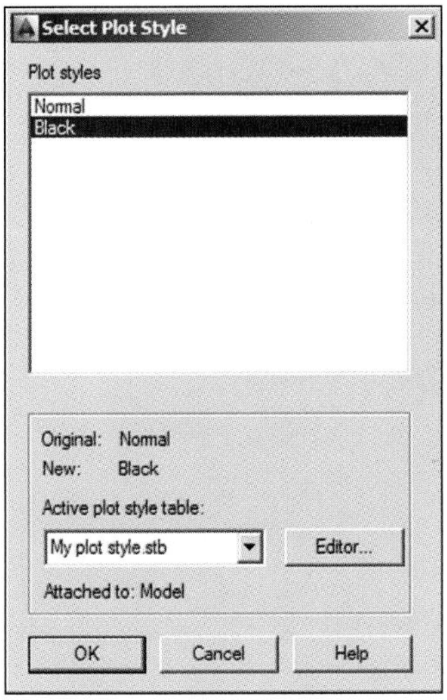

FIGURE 14.9 Selecting a plot style to assign to a layer

2. Click the Title layer in the Layer Properties Manager to select it; all the other layers automatically deselect. Click the Plot Style on the Title layer and change it to Normal in the Select Plot Style dialog box that appears (see Figure 14.10). The title text will now plot in red.

The Normal plot style in My plot style.stb outputs objects in color.

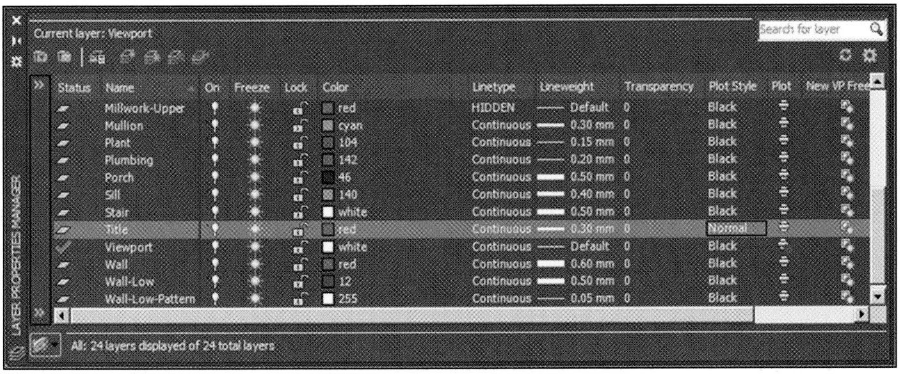

FIGURE 14.10 Configuring named plot styles by layer

Properties

3. Close the Layer Properties Manager.

4. Select the ribbon's View tab. Click the Properties button in the Palettes panel.

5. Click the solid hatch of the flooring in Marketing to select it (see Figure 14.11).

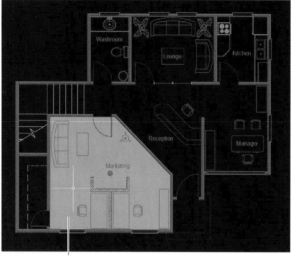

Select this hatch object.

FIGURE 14.11 Selecting a hatch object

6. Open the Plot Style drop-down in the Properties palette and select Other from the menu. Select 20% Screen in the Select Plot Style dialog box that appears. Click OK and 20% Screen is listed as the plot style for the Hatch object in the Properties palette (see Figure 14.12). This object will plot with reduced intensity, so the hatch appears lighter.

FIGURE 14.12 Changing the plot style assigned to a specific object

7. Press Esc to deselect. Close the Properties palette.

Your model should now resemble Ex14.5-end.dwg, which is available among this chapter's companion files.

Plot in Model Space

You can plot whatever you are working on in model space at any time. This is usually done to create a test plot so that you (or your colleagues) can check and possibly mark up the evolving design on paper. In the following steps, you will create a test plot in model space.

Exercise 14.6: Plot from Model Space

In this exercise, you will learn how to plot directly from model space. You will choose a drawing scale allowing the whole drawing to appear on the printed page.

Begin by opening the Ex14.6-start.dwg file from this chapter's companion files.

1. Click the Plot tool in the Quick Access toolbar. Open the Name drop-down menu under Printer/Plotter in the Plot – Model dialog box (see Figure 14.13). Observe that both a system printer and an AutoCAD plotter appear for the HP DesignJet T920 device. Click Cancel.

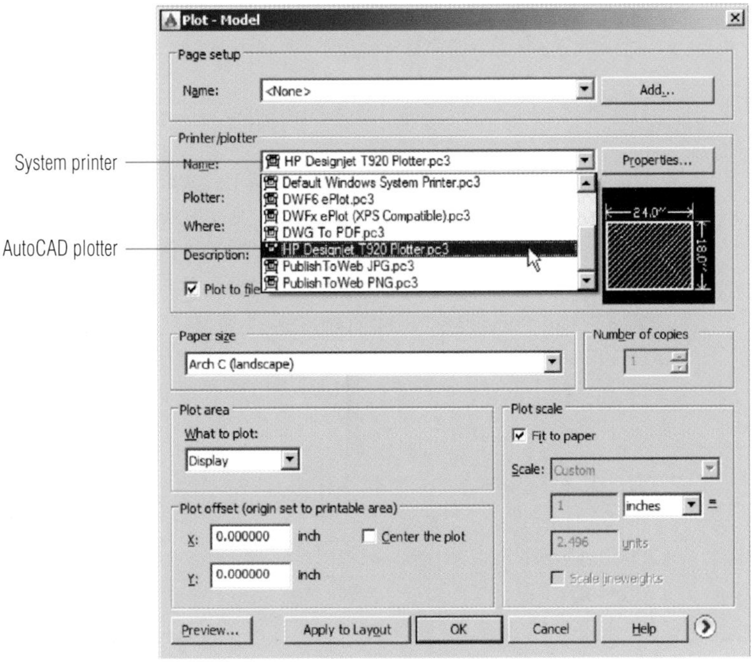

FIGURE 14.13 Selecting a plotter driver in the Plot dialog box

2. Type OP (for Options) and press Enter.

3. Select the Plot And Publish tab. Select Hide System Printers in the General Plot Options area (see Figure 14.14). Click OK.

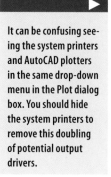

FIGURE 14.14   Hiding the system printer drivers in the Options dialog box

Certification Objective

4. Type **PLOT** and press Enter. Select HP DesignJet T920 Plotter .pc3 from the Name drop-down menu (no system printers appear). Select Arch C (landscape) in the Paper Size area and Extents in the What To Plot drop-down menu. Select Center The Plot in the Plot Offset area, deselect Fit To Paper in the Plot Scale area, and select 3/8" = 1'-0" from the Scale drop-down menu. Click the More Options button to expand the dialog box. Select My plot style.stb in the Plot Style Table area. Select Plot Stamp On in the Plot Options area (see Figure 14.15).

5. Check Plot Stamp On and then click the Plot Stamp Settings button, as shown in Figure 14.15. Select Drawing Name, Device Name, and Plot Scale in the Plot Stamp dialog box that appears (see Figure 14.16). Click OK.

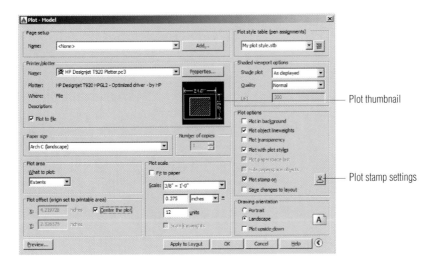

Plot thumbnail

Plot stamp settings

FIGURE 14.15 Configuring the Plot dialog box for output

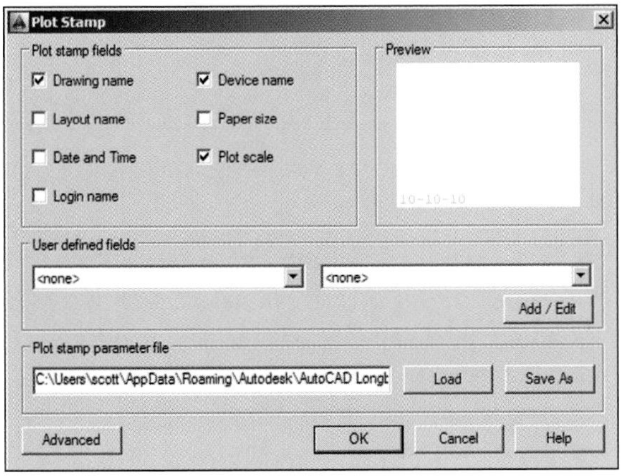

FIGURE 14.16 Configuring the Plot Stamp feature

6. Click the Preview button in the lower-left corner of the Plot – Model dialog box. Click Continue in the Plot – Plot Scale Confirm dialog box that appears. A preview window temporarily replaces the user interface (see Figure 14.17).

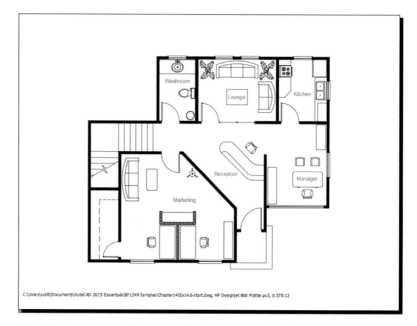

C:\Users\scott\Documents\AutoCAD 2015 Essentials\871249 Samples\Chapter14\Ex14.6-start.dwg, HP Designjet 800 Plotter.pc3, 0.375:12

FIGURE 14.17   What you see is what you get in the plot preview window.

7. Click the Plot icon in the upper-left corner of the plot preview. The plot is immediately sent to the hypothetical HP DesignJet T920 output device. If this device were really attached to your computer, it would start plotting within seconds. Once the plot has been sent, a notification window appears in the lower-right corner of the user interface (see Figure 14.18). The plot is complete; click the close box in the notification window.

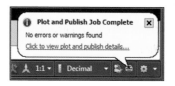

FIGURE 14.18   Plot notification window

Your model should now resemble Ex14.6-end.dwg, which is available among this chapter's companion files.

Plot Layouts in Paper Space

Layouts are the preferred plotting environment where you can display multiple scaled drawings within viewports, surrounded by title blocks containing text, or having dimensions in paper space. In the following exercise, you will create and plot two layouts from paper space.

Exercise 14.7: Plot from Paper Space

In this exercise, you will learn how to plot from a layout in paper space in 1:1 scale.

Begin by opening the Ex14.7-start.dwg file from this chapter's companion files.

1. Click the Layout1 tab in the lower-left corner of the user interface. A single viewport is automatically generated on the layout.

2. Click the ribbon's Output tab and click the Page Setup Manager icon in the Plot panel. Click the New button in the Page Setup Manager dialog box that appears. Click OK in the New Page Setup dialog box to accept the default name of Setup1.

3. In the Page Setup – Layout1 dialog box that appears, open the Name drop-down menu, and select HP DesignJet T920 Plotter.pc3. Then select Arch C (landscape) in the Paper Size drop-down menu. Select My plot style.stb in the Plot Style Table drop-down menu. Click OK.

4. The Page Setup Manager dialog box now lists Setup1 as a saved page setup. Select Display When Creating A New Layout (see Figure 14.19). Click the Set Current button and then click Close.

5. Double-click within the viewport to activate floating model space. Select 3/8" = 1'-0" from the Viewport Scale menu on the status bar. Double-click outside the viewport on the drawing canvas to return to paper space.

6. Select the viewport and stretch its grips to reveal and center the entire building, as shown in Figure 14.20. You might need to move the viewport to center the building on the page, depending on how you stretch the grips.

Layouts are always plotted at 1:1 scale in Imperial units. Metric layouts are also plotted at 1:1 scale, if 1 millimeter equals 1 drawing unit, or at 10:1 scale if you decide 1 centimeter equals 1 drawing unit.

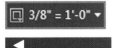

You will have to scroll down the list of viewport scales to find the 3/8" = 1'-0" scale.

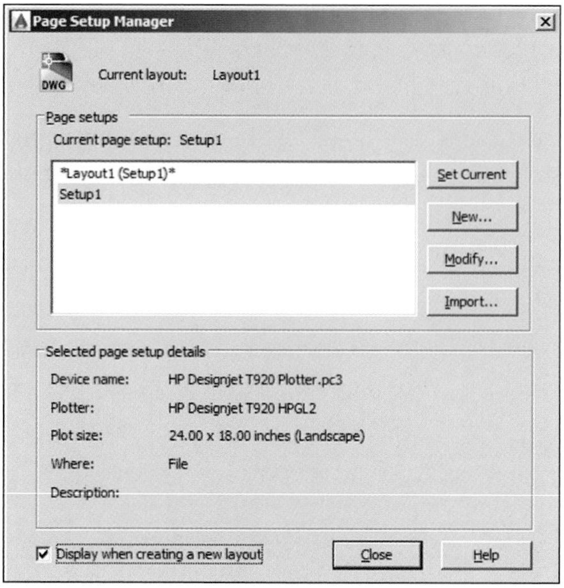

FIGURE 14.19 Saving a page setup for use in the next layout

FIGURE 14.20 Configuring Layout1 to display the drawing in 3/8" scale

7. Press Ctrl+P to execute the PLOT command. Deselect Plot Stamp On in the Plot dialog box that appears. Click OK, and the plot is processed. Close the plot notification window when it appears.

Certification Objective

8. Click the plus icon next to Layout1 in the lower-left corner of the user interface to create a new layout. Select the Layout2 tab.

9. Select Setup1 in the Page Setup Manager that appears and click the Set Current and Close buttons. Layout2 is configured the same way as Layout1.

10. Double-click inside the viewport to activate floating model space. Select 3/8" = 1'-0" from the Viewport Scale menu on the status bar.

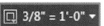

11. Type **LAYERSTATE** and press Enter. Select the Reflected Ceiling Plan layer state and then click the Restore button (see Figure 14.21).

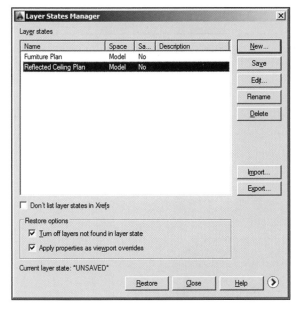

FIGURE 14.21 Restoring a layer state in floating model space

12. Double-click outside the viewport on the drawing canvas to return to paper space. Open the Application menu, choose the Print category, and then click Plot. Click the Preview button to open a preview window (see Figure 14.22).

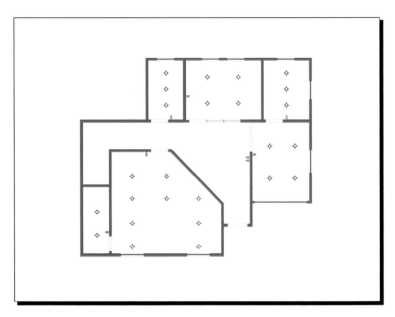

FIGURE 14.22 Previewing Layout2

You may remove the HP DesignJet T920 plotter from your system or use it to practice plotting.

13. Click the Plot icon in the upper-left corner of the preview window, and the plot is processed. Close the plot notification window.

Your model should now resemble Ex14.7-end.dwg, which is available among this chapter's companion files.

Export to an Electronic Format

To reduce the amount of paper you use and eliminate reprographics and drawing shipment costs, Windows users can consider exporting their drawings to electronic formats such as Design Web Format (DWF), Portable Document Format (PDF), or the Share Design View feature. Mac for AutoCAD users can't export to DWF (they can, however, save as PDF in the Plot dialog box). You can email, use File Transfer Protocol (FTP), or use an online service to transfer electronic files to your subcontractors and clients for collaboration or approval purposes.

Exercise 14.8: Export to DWF

In this exercise, you will export a drawing to the DWF format so it can be reviewed by others.

Begin by opening the Ex14.8-start.dwg file from this chapter's companion files.

1. Click the ribbon's Output tab and, in the Export To DWF/PDF panel, click the drop-down arrow under the Export icon. Select DWFx from the menu that appears.

2. Select All Layouts from the Export drop-down menu in the Save As DWFx dialog box (see Figure 14.23). Click Save.

DWFx files are written in Extensible Markup Language (XML) as opposed to Autodesk's proprietary DWF format.

Use Autodesk® Design Review if you want to view and mark up DWF or DWFx files.

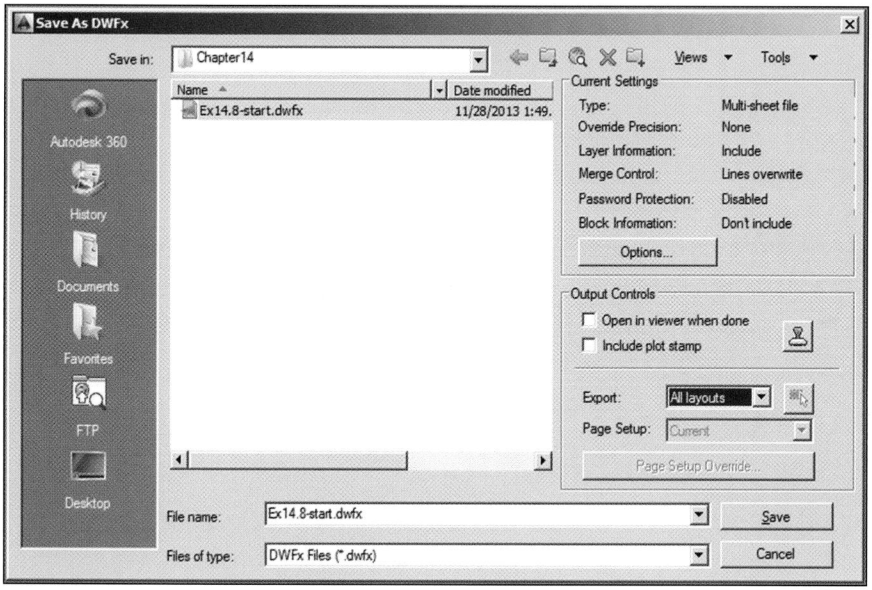

FIGURE 14.23 Save As DWFx

3. Double-click the Ex14.8-start.dwfx file on your hard drive. After a few moments, the vector drawing appears in the XPS Viewer, a program that is part of the Windows operating system. Drag the slider to the left at the bottom of the interface to zoom out (see Figure 14.24).

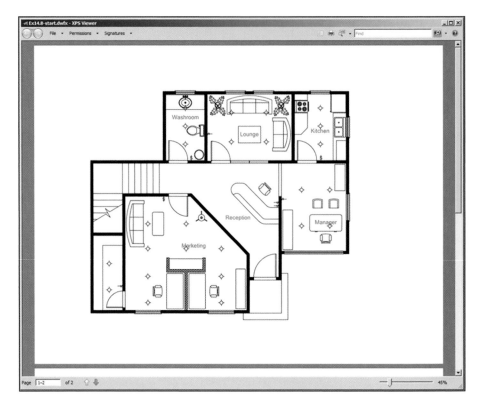

FIGURE 14.24 DWFx drawing displayed in Internet Explorer

Exercise 14.9: Export to PDF

In this exercise, you will export a drawing to the PDF format so it can be viewed and printed by others. AutoCAD has PDF export options that make creating a variety of types of PDF output easy.

Begin by opening the Ex14.9-start.dwg file from this chapter's companion files.

1. Click the ribbon's Output tab and, in the Export To DWF/PDF panel, click the Export To PDF Options button.

2. Change Vector Quality to 2400 dpi and reduce Raster Image Quality to 150 dpi (see Figure 14.25). Click OK.

F I G U R E 1 4 . 2 5 Export To PDF options

3. Click the drop-down arrow under the Export icon. Select PDF from the menu that appears. Before saving the file, select AutoCAD PDF (High Quality Print) from the PDF Preset drop-down menu (see Figure 14.26). Verify that Open In Viewer When Done is selected in the Output Controls area.

Named views and layer states are exported as bookmarks in PDFs. Hyperlinks will also be exported automatically.

F I G U R E 1 4 . 2 6 Choosing a PDF preset prior to saving

4. Click Save. The program your computer has associated with PDFs opens (in most cases, this will be Adobe Reader). Note that both of the drawing's layer states, Furniture Plan and Reflected Ceiling Plan, automatically appear as bookmarks in Adobe Reader (see Figure 14.27), but these are labeled with the filename and the words *Layout1* and *Layout2* are appended.

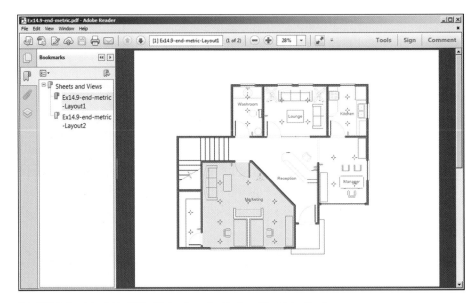

F I G U R E   1 4 . 2 7   PDF with bookmarks displayed in Adobe Reader

Exercise 14.10: Share Design Views

In this exercise, you will upload a drawing to a secure anonymous location with the Autodesk® A360 online service. Anyone using Chrome, Firefox, and other browsers supporting WebGL 3D graphics can view your design views without having AutoCAD, an Autodesk A360 account, or any other software.

Begin by opening the Ex14.10-start.dwg file from this chapter's companion files.

1. Click the ribbon's A360 tab and click the Share Design View button.

2. You are prompted to select whether you want to launch your browser now and wait for the file to upload or be notified with a bubble in the lower-right corner of AutoCAD's user interface when the upload is complete. Choose Publish And Display In My Browser Now (see Figure 14.28) and wait a few moments for the small file upload to complete.

You can use the command ONLINEDESIGNSHARE instead of the button on the A360 tab.

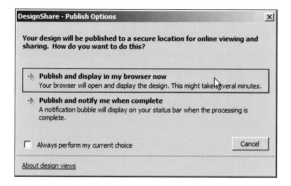

FIGURE 14.28   DesignShare – Publish Options

3. After a few minutes, your default browser will launch automatically and open an anonymous, encrypted link displaying the A360
Viewer. A list of all the drawing's model and sheet views appears in
the left pane (see Figure 14.29). Try navigating the drawing using the
pan and zoom controls. Open the Layer Manager and toggle off the
Electrical and Lighting layers if they are not already off.

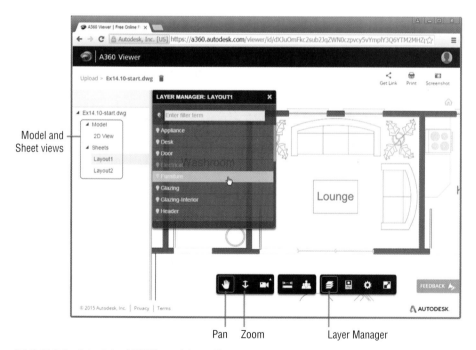

FIGURE 14.29   A360 Viewer's Layer Manager

▶

In AutoCAD 2018, you can now comment on Shared Design Views on the Autodesk A360 site, enabling more effective collaboration.

4. Check your email. The email account you used to register with A360 will receive a message from Autodesk A360 when your uploaded drawing is ready to share. You can click the View Design button in the email (see Figure 14.30) to open it in your browser or simply copy and paste the link to share with anyone who has a browser supporting WebGL (a standard widely supported in modern browsers; see `https://en.wikipedia.org/wiki/WebGL`).

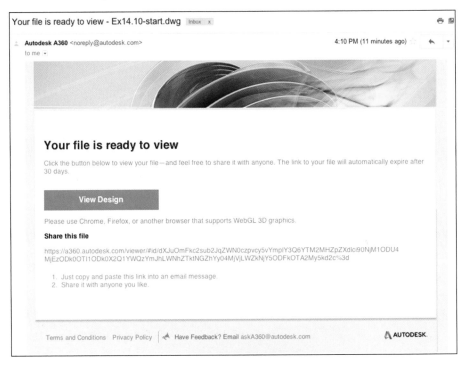

FIGURE 14.30 Autodesk 360 email with embedded View Design button

5. Save your work as `Ex14.10-end.dwg`.

Now You Know

In this chapter, you learned how to configure output devices, create plot style tables, use plot style tables, plot in model space, plot layouts in paper space, and export to electronic formats. You now know how to create professional output in AutoCAD.

CHAPTER 15

Working with Data

The AutoCAD® program has several features that allow you to manipulate data within your drawings. (Please note that the AutoCAD® LT program doesn't support these features.) In this chapter, you'll begin by geolocating project geometry. Then you will define *attributes* within a block definition in order to store nongraphical data. You'll proceed to enter values in several block references, and then you'll create a table to organize and display this data on a drawing layout. The data shown in the table will be a mixture of static text and dynamically linked fields that display textual information in model space. After creating this complex data management system, you'll change one of the attribute's values and watch as the fields displaying data in the table automatically update.

In this chapter, you'll learn to do the following:

▶ **Geolocate projects**

▶ **Import SketchUp models**

▶ **Define attributes and blocks**

▶ **Insert attributed blocks**

▶ **Edit table styles and create tables**

▶ **Use fields in table cells**

▶ **Edit table data**

Geolocate Projects

In AutoCAD, you can store your project's geographic location and site orientation with respect to true north within the drawing file. This information can be specified using road maps or aerial imagery all within AutoCAD, without your having to use another program to access this information (such as Google Earth).

When geolocated blocks or images are inserted or attached to your drawing files, they are aligned using the geographic data as the common point of reference. When each team member uses geolocated drawings, drawing coordination will be automatically streamlined. In the following steps, you will geolocate a drawing using the AutoCAD built-in mapping service.

Exercise 15.1: Geolocate a Drawing

The drawing is an elaboration on the diagram you dimensioned in Chapter 11, "Dimensioning."

In this exercise you will locate a project on the earth. Begin by opening the file Ex15.1-start.dwg (see Figure 15.1), which is among the companion files available for download from the book's web page, www.sybex.com/go/autocad2018essentials.

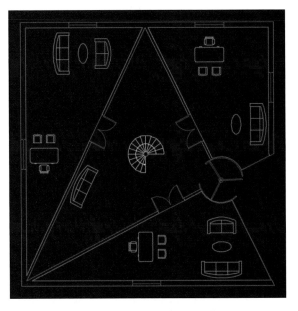

FIGURE 15.1 The diagram shown in Figure 11.1, converted into a floor plan for use in this chapter

1. Select the ribbon's Insert tab, open the Set Location flyout in the Location panel, and choose From Map. Use the navigation controls located in the upper right of the map in the Geographic Location dialog box to locate a hypothetical site for this structure. When you have zoomed in sufficiently to settle on a site location, right-click and choose Drop Pin Here from the context menu. A red pin icon appears on the map at the location where you right-clicked (see Figure 15.2).

FIGURE 15.2 Selecting a geographic location with aerial maps

2. Click the Next button at the bottom of the Geographic Location dialog box. Select the first item in the list of coordinate systems, NM-W in this example. This system has its origin point closest to the chosen site (see Figure 15.3).

3. Click Next. You are prompted on the command line to select a point within the drawing for the location corresponding to the pin on the map. Click the center of the spiral staircase at the center of the floor plan.

4. The command line reads as follows:

```
GEOGRAPHICLOCATION Specify the north direction angle or
[First point]<90>:
```

Press Enter to accept the default option of North at a 90-degree angle (up) and press Enter to end the GEOGRAPHICLOCATION command. An aerial map acts as an underlay to the drawing (see Figure 15.4).

Geographic Location - Set Coordinate System (Page 2 of 2)   ×

GIS Coordinate System: NM-W

Specify a coordinate system to
assign to the drawing.   Search for coordinate system 🔍

It is recommended you select a
coordinate system with an origin
close to your location.
The list is ordered by closest origin
to the set locaton.

Name	Reference	Unit	EPSG code
NM-W	NAD27	Foot	32014
HARN/NM.NM-W	HARN/NM	Meter	2827
HARN/NM.NM-WF	HARN/NM	Foot	2904
NM83-WF	NAD83	Foot	2259
NM83-W	NAD83	Meter	32114
NM83-C	NAD83	Meter	32113
NM-C	NAD27	Foot	32013
HARN/NM.NM-C	HARN/NM	Meter	2826
HARN/NM.NM-CF	HARN/NM	Foot	2903
NM83-CF	NAD83	Foot	2258
HARN/13.UTM-13	HARN/13	Meter	3743
TX-DOT27	NAD27	Ifoot	3080
TX-DOT83	NAD83	Ifoot	-
WGS72be/a.UTM-13N	WGS72-TBE/a	Meter	32413
WGS72.UTM-13N	WGS72	Meter	32213
WGS72be/b.UTM-13N	WGS72-TBE/b	Meter	32413
UTM84-13N	WGS84	Meter	32613
TXHP-NCF	HPGN	Foot	2917
TXHP-NC	HPGN	Meter	2845
NAD83/98.UTM-13N	CSRS	Meter	2151
UTMHP-13F	HPGN	Foot	-

Time Zone: (GMT-07:00) Mountain Time (US & Canada)   ▼

Drawing Unit: Inches   ▼

                           Back   Next   Cancel   Help

FIGURE 15.3   Choosing a coordinate system

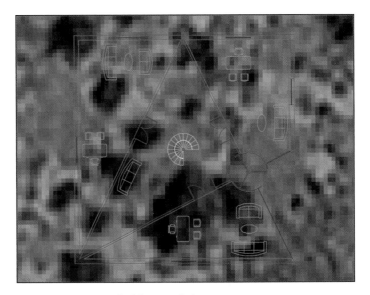

FIGURE 15.4   Aerial map underlay

5. After you have geolocated the drawing, a specialized Geolocation tab appears on the ribbon. To hide the map from the drawing window, go to the Online Map panel on the Geolocation tab, open the Map Aerial flyout, and select Map Off.

Your model should now resemble `Ex15.1-end.dwg`, which is available among this chapter's companion files.

USING DESIGN FEED

Design Feed is accessible from the Autodesk® 360 Ribbon tab. Use Design Feed to share text messages and images with your colleagues. Posts are created and read using AutoCAD or the free AutoCAD® WS app for mobile devices. Whenever you tag a colleague in a post, your post automatically appears in their Design Feed palette or AutoCAD WS app, and they also are notified by email. All posts are stored in Autodesk 360 no matter where they are created, so you can stay electronically connected to your colleagues in the office and in the field. You can also optionally geolocate your posts in drawings so that they refer to specific areas in the real world.

Import SketchUp Models

You can import SketchUp models into AutoCAD from SKP files and import models from the Trimble 3D Warehouse using one of the free Autodesk Exchange apps.

Exercise 15.2: Import a SketchUp Model

The ribbon's Add-ins tab has the Import SKP tool, which you will use to import a model from the 3D Warehouse in the following steps:

If you don't see the Import SKP tool, you can download it for free from the Autodesk App Store.

1. Open your web browser and go to https://3dwarehouse.sketchup .com to access the 3D Warehouse. Type **Cathedral Notre Dame de Paris** in the search bar and click the Search button. Select the Cathedral Notre Dame de Paris model by Alejandro Diaz, which is the top result as of the date of this book's publication (see Figure 15.5). Click the Download Model button, select SketchUp 2017 (.skp) from the menu that appears, and save it to your downloads folder.

FIGURE 15.5 Downloading a model from the 3D Warehouse

2. In AutoCAD, create a new blank document and select the 3D modeling workspace. Then select the Featured Apps tab and click the Import SKP tool. In the Select SKP File dialog box that appears, select the file you downloaded in the previous step and click the Open button.

3. Click any point in the drawing window to select an insertion point for the model.

4. Type **Z** (for Zoom) and press Enter. Type **E** (for Extents) and press Enter.

5. Hold down Shift and drag the mouse wheel or middle button to orbit the model so you can view the model in 3D. Zoom or pan the model to create a pleasing bird's-eye view of the cathedral.

◄

Refer to Chapters 16–18 for more on 3D modeling.

6. From the two separate in-canvas menus located in the upper-left corner of the drawing window, select Perspective and Shaded With Edges to better visualize the geometry (see Figure 15.6).

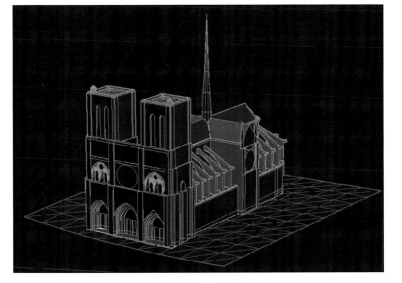

F I G U R E   1 5 . 6   Viewing the imported Notre Dame cathedral 3D model in AutoCAD

7. Close the drawing without saving.

Define Attributes and Blocks

Blocks can be defined with *attributes* that contain any manner of textual information relevant to the object in question. Let's explore this topic in an exercise. First you'll alter the Annotative text style that will be used by the attributes you create. Then you'll create attribute definitions to store employees' names and ID numbers. Finally, you'll define a simple block composed of two rectangles containing the attribute definitions.

Exercise 15.3: Define Attributes and a Block

In this exercise you will create attribute definitions and include them in a block definition. To begin, open Ex15.3-start.dwg from this chapter's companion download.

1. Type **ST** (for Style) and press Enter. Select the Annotative style in the Styles list on the left side of the Text Style dialog box. Select romans.shx in the Font Name drop-down menu. Type 1/8" (or 0.30 cm) in the Paper Text Height box (see Figure 15.7). Click Apply, select Set Current, and then click Close.

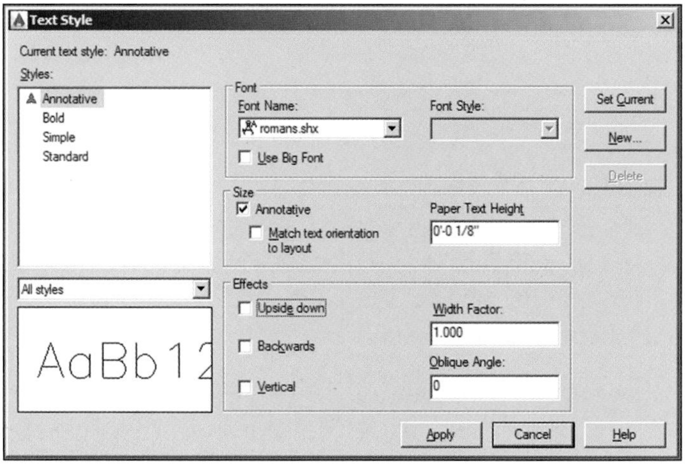

FIGURE 15.7 Setting the height of the Annotative text style

2. Click the Rectangle tool in the Draw panel of the ribbon's Home tab. Click a point at some arbitrary distance from the building as the start point, type @3',1' (or @90,25 for metric), and press Enter.

3. Click the Copy tool in the Modify panel, select the rectangle you just drew, and press Enter. Press F3 to toggle on Endpoint object snap if it is not already on, click the upper-left corner of the rectangle, and then click its lower-left corner to create two vertically stacked rectangles. Press Enter to end the COPY command.

4. Click the Line tool in the Draw panel, and click points A, B, and C in Figure 15.8. Press Enter to end the LINE command.

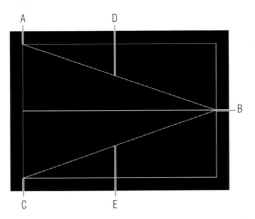

FIGURE 15.8 Drawing simple geometry to form the basis of an attributed block

5. Select 1/4" = 1'-0" scale (or 1:40 scale for metric) from the Annotation Scale menu on the status bar.

6. Right-click the Object Snap toggle on the status bar and turn on Midpoint running object snap mode if it is not already on.

7. Expand the Block panel and click the Define Attributes tool to open the Attribute Definition dialog box. Type **NAME** as the tag, **Employee Name?** as the prompt, and **Smith** as the default. Set Justification to Middle Center and Text Style to Annotative (see Figure 15.9).

8. Click OK to close the Attribute Definition dialog box. Click the midpoint at point D in Figure 15.8. Figure 15.10 shows the result.

UNDERSTANDING THE PARTS OF AN ATTRIBUTE

Tag, Prompt, and Value, along with a number of additional settings and optional modes, define every attribute. Tag is the programming name (typically capitalized without any spaces in the tag). Prompt is the question you'll be asking the person who inserts the attributed block, prompting them to enter the attribute value. The value is entered only when the attributed block is inserted and not when the attribute is defined (see the next section, "Insert Attributed Blocks"). The optional Default setting displays a default value when the attributed block is eventually inserted into a drawing.

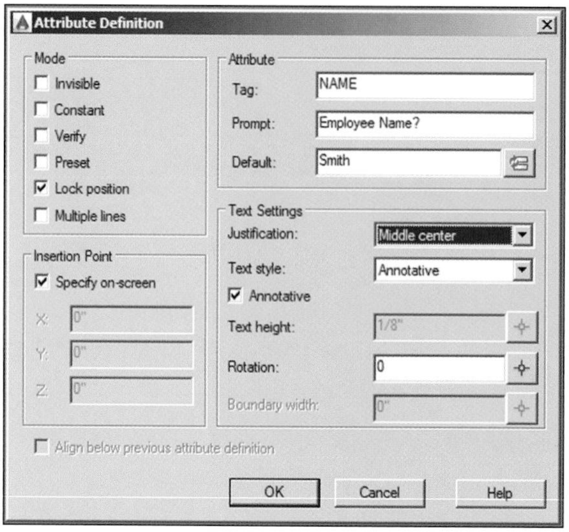

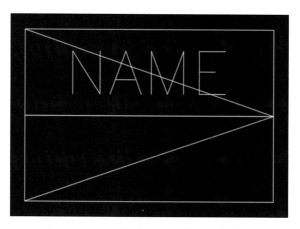

FIGURE 15.9 Specifying the properties of an attribute definition

FIGURE 15.10 Placing an attribute definition in relation to the block definition geometry

9. Press the spacebar to repeat the ATTDEF command. Type **IDNO** as the tag, **Identification number?** as the prompt, and **1234** as the default (see Figure 15.11). Set Justification to Middle Center and click OK. Click the midpoint of the lower diagonal line at point E in Figure 15.8.

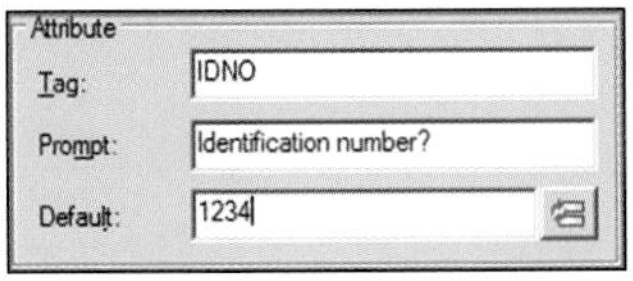

FIGURE 15.11 Creating another attribute definition

10. Click the Erase tool in the Modify panel, select the two diagonal lines, and press Enter.

11. Click the Create Block tool in the Block Definition panel and type **Employee Data** in the Name text box.

12. Click the Pick Point icon in the Base Point area and then click point C in Figure 15.8.

13. Click the Select Objects icon, click the NAME attribute definition, and then click IDNO. Select both rectangles and press Enter. Click the Delete radio button in the Objects area of the Block Definition dialog box and select Inches (or Centimeters) in the Block Unit dropdown menu (see Figure 15.12). Click OK, and the attribute definitions and geometry disappear as expected.

The order in which you select attribute definitions when defining them as a block determines the order in which their prompts will appear in block references.

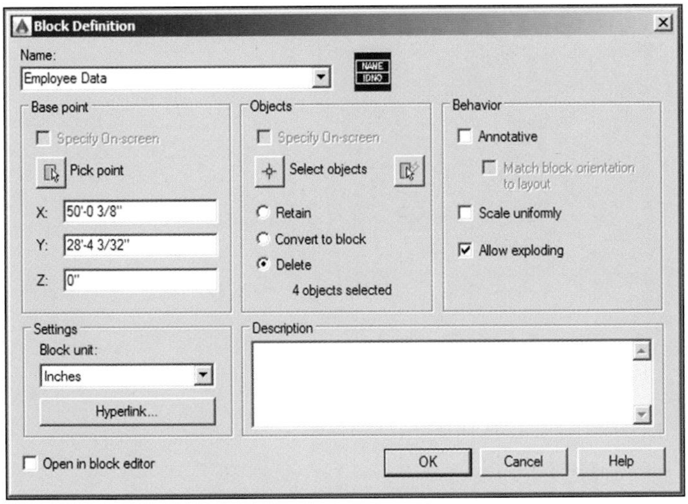

FIGURE 15.12 Defining a block with attribute definitions

Your model should now resemble `Ex15.3-end.dwg`, which is available among this chapter's companion files.

Insert Attributed Blocks

After you have (or your CAD manager has) gone to the trouble of defining blocks with attributes, inserting them and entering values is easy. In the following steps, you'll insert three Employee Name blocks and enter appropriate values in each block reference.

Exercise 15.4: Insert Block References with Attributes

In this exercise you will insert a block and enter attribute values. To begin, open `Ex15.4-start.dwg` from this chapter's companion download.

1. On the ribbon's Home tab, set the Symbol layer as current in the Layer drop-down menu in the Layers panel.

2. Switch to the ribbon's Insert tab. Click the Insert tool in the Block panel. Scroll down the list of icons in the block gallery and select Employee Data (see Figure 15.13).

FIGURE 15.13 Inserting the Employee Data block you defined in the previous section

3. Click a point in the center of the room on the upper right. Press Enter to accept the default of 0 degrees if prompted to specify a rotation angle. In the Edit Attributes dialog box that appears, type **Bruno** in the Employee Name text box and type **108** in the Identification Number text area. The block reference appears in the room with the values you typed in (see Figure 15.14).

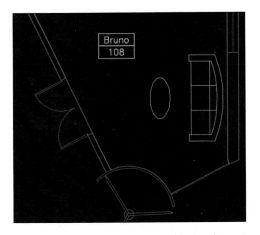

F I G U R E 1 5 . 1 4   Inserting a block and entering its attribute values

4. Type **I** (for Insert) and press Enter twice. Click a point in the center of the room on the left. Type **Andreae** as the employee name, press Tab, and type **864** as the identification number in the Edit Attributes dialog box. Click OK.

5. Press the spacebar to repeat the INSERT command and press Enter. Click a point in the center of the room on the bottom. Type **Dee** as the employee name, press Tab, and type **273** as the identification number in the Edit Attributes dialog box. Click OK. Figure 15.15 shows the result.

Your model should now resemble Ex15.4-end.dwg, which is available among this chapter's companion files.

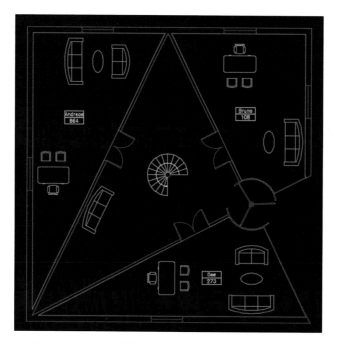

FIGURE 15.15 Three Employee Data blocks inserted and their attribute values entered

Edit Table Styles and Create Tables

Tables are like having Microsoft Excel or another spreadsheet program within AutoCAD. The overall appearance of tables is controlled by table styles. Cell spacing, borders, and background coloring are controlled by individual table cells. In the following steps, you'll adjust a table style, create a new table, and begin adding content to its cells.

Exercise 15.5: Alter a Table Style and Make a Table

In this exercise you will alter a table style and then use it to make a table. To begin, open Ex15.5-start.dwg from this chapter's companion download.

1. Expand the Annotate panel on the Home ribbon tab and open the drop-down menu in the Tables panel. Select Manage Table Styles and then click the Modify button in the Table Style dialog box that appears.

2. In the Modify Table Style: Standard dialog box that appears, open the Cell Styles drop-down menu and select Title.

3. Select the Text tab within the Modify Table Style: Standard dialog box. Open the Text Style drop-down menu and select Bold. Double-click the Text Height text box, type 3/8 (or 0.80 cm), and press the Tab key (see Figure 15.16).

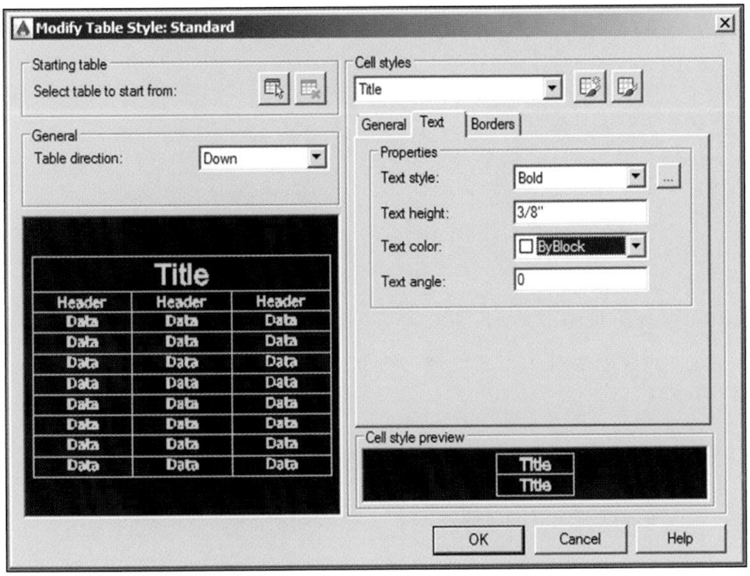

Table cell styles have three types: Title, Header, and Data.

FIGURE 15.16 Editing the Title cell style text properties

4. Open the Cell Styles drop-down menu and select Header. Open the Text Style drop-down menu and select Bold. Double-click the Text Height text box, type 1/4 (or 0.50 cm), press Tab, and observe the preview image update.

5. Open the Cell Styles drop-down menu again and select Data. Open the Text Style drop-down menu and select Simple. Double-click the Text Height text box and type 1/4 (or 0.50 cm). Press Tab to update. The updates to the table style are complete. Click OK and then click Close to end the TABLESTYLE command.

6. Hover the cursor over the current drawing's file tab and select Layout1.

7. On the ribbon's Home tab, open the Layer drop-down menu in the Layers panel, and set the Table layer as current.

8. Click the Table tool in the Annotation panel. Set the number of columns to 4 and data rows to 3 in the Insert Table dialog box. Set Column Width to 1" (or 2.50 cm) (see Figure 15.17). The Title, Header, and Data cell styles you customized within the Standard table style will be used by default. Click OK.

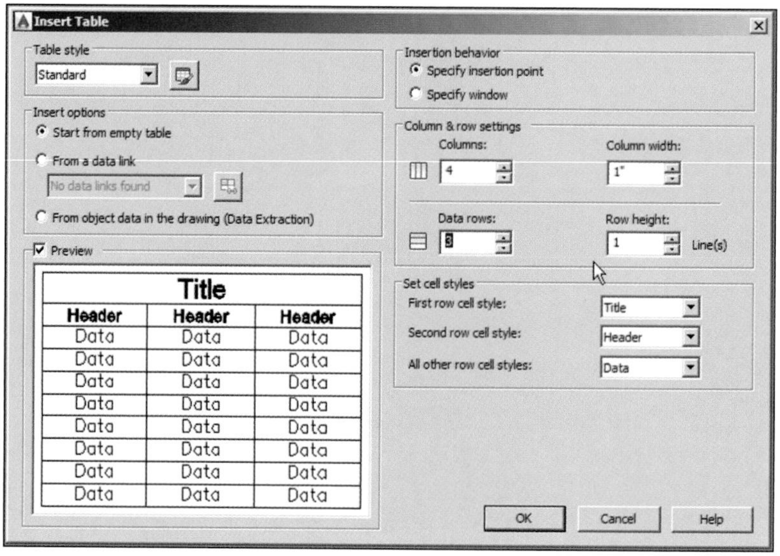

FIGURE 15.17 Specifying the number of columns and rows and their width and height

LINKING TO TABLES IN EXTERNAL SPREADSHEETS

Select the From A Data Link radio button in the Insert Table dialog box and click the Launch The Data Link Manager icon to the right of the drop-down to link dynamically to a spreadsheet in Microsoft Excel.

9. Click approximately at point A in Figure 15.18 to place the empty table on the layout.

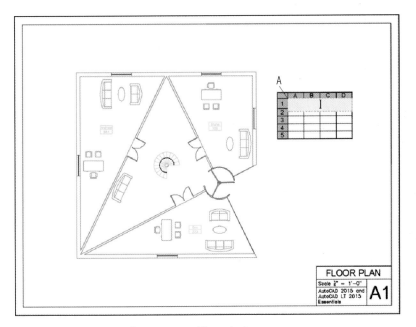

FIGURE 15.18 Placing a new table on the layout

10. The cursor is highlighted within the table's top cell. Zoom into the table by turning the mouse wheel. Type **Room Schedule** and press the Tab key. Type **Employee**, press Tab, and type **ID No**. Press Tab again. The Tab key advances to the next cell from left to right and then from top to bottom at the end of each row.

11. Type **Area (ft** (for Imperial) or **Area (m** (for metric).

12. Right-click to open the context menu. Select Symbol ➤ Squared as shown in Figure 15.19. Type) and press Tab. Now the column header indicates an area in square feet (or square meters). Click outside the table on the layout to deactivate it.

> You can insert or delete any number of rows and columns using tools on the Table Cell tab's Rows and Columns panels.
> ◄

Delete Column(s)

13. Click in the table to highlight it and then select cell D2 to highlight it for editing. Click the Delete Column(s) tool in the Columns panel within the ribbon's contextual Table Cell tab.

14. Use the arrow keys to move between cells in the table. Press the left arrow key twice to move to cell A2. Each cell has four grips. Click cell

A2's right grip and move it to the right to stretch column A wider. Click a point a short distance to the right to set the column width approximately as shown in Figure 15.20.

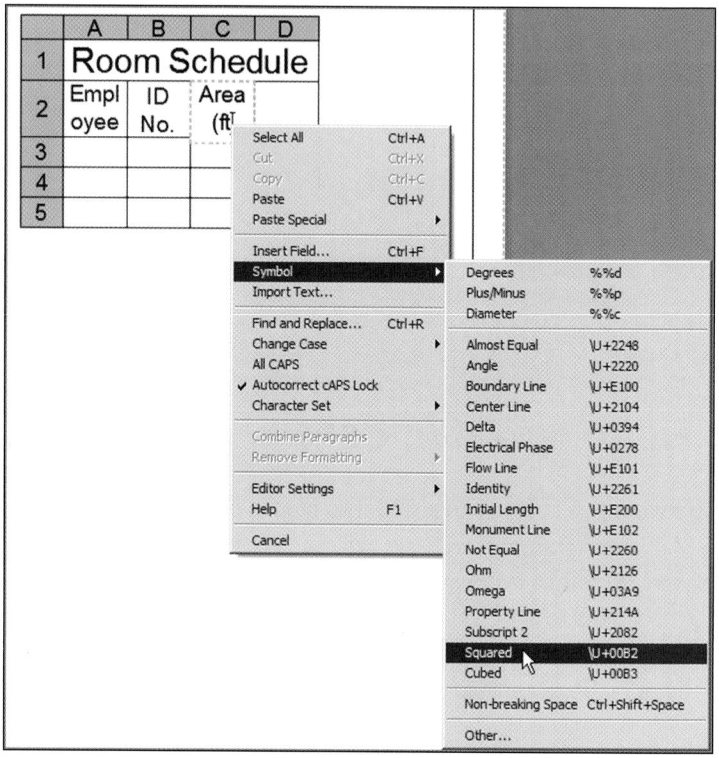

FIGURE 15.19 Accessing the symbol for squared

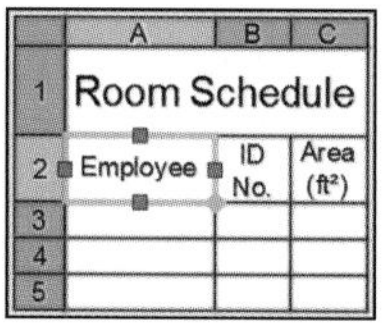

FIGURE 15.20 Resizing a column with cell grips

15. Press the right arrow key to move to cell B2. Click B2's right grip and stretch it to the right so that its entire header fits on one line. Repeat for cell C2. Press Esc to deselect. Figure 15.21 shows the result.

Room Schedule		
Employee	ID No.	Area (ft²)

FIGURE 15.21 Formatted table

Your model should now resemble Ex15.5-end.dwg, which is available among this chapter's companion files.

Use Fields in Table Cells

Fields are variables that are inserted into blocks of text that can change what they display over time. For example, you can insert a date field onto a title block that will update to show the current date every time the drawing is plotted. You can also link fields to objects in the drawing so that the field will display any one of the object properties. In the following steps, you'll insert fields into cells within the table you designed in the previous section.

Exercise 15.6: Create Fields

In this exercise you will create fields that display area values. To begin, open Ex15.6-start.dwg from this chapter's companion download.

1. Select cell A3, which is the first data cell in the Employee column. Double-click within this cell to activate the Text Editor contextual tab on the ribbon. Click the Field tool on the Insert panel.

2. In the Field dialog box that appears, open the Field Category drop-down menu and select Objects. Select Object in the Field Names list. Click the Select Objects button and select the attribute Bruno in the room on the upper right.

When selecting objects in the Field dialog box, you can select objects in floating viewports even when you are in paper space.

Fields are displayed against a gray background to identify them as fields onscreen. The gray field background does not appear in plotted output.

3. In the Property list that appears, select Value (see Figure 15.22). Click OK. The word *Bruno* appears in table cell A3.

FIGURE 15.22 Accessing the attribute value in the Field dialog box

4. Press the down arrow and move to cell A4. Right-click and choose Insert Field from the context menu. Click the Select Objects button and select the attribute Andreae in the room on the left. Choose Value from the Property list and click OK.

5. Repeat the previous step, selecting the attribute Dee in the room at the bottom for cell A5.

6. Continue adding fields in column B, selecting each attribute value as shown in Figure 15.23.

7. Double-click in cell C3 to activate the Text Editor. Press Ctrl+F to open the Field dialog box. Click the Select Objects button and select the magenta line in the doorway of Bruno's office. Choose Area from the Property list. Choose Architectural (or Decimal for metric) from the Format list. The preview shows the area value as 347.014 SQ. FT. or 322388.23 (in square centimeters).

FIGURE 15.23 Inserting fields that link to attribute values in model space

8. Click the Additional Format button. Then do the following:

   ▶ For Imperial units, remove the SQ. FT. text from the Suffix text box and type **1/144** in the Conversion Factor text box to convert from square inches to square feet. Click OK, and the fraction is converted to decimal form (see Figure 15.24). Click OK again.

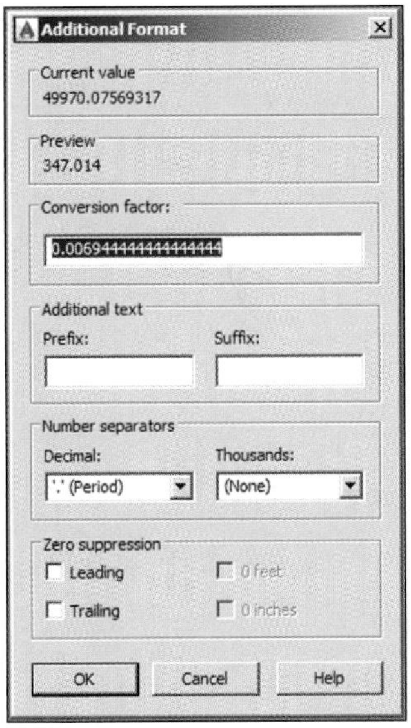

FIGURE 15.24 Converting units in the Additional Format dialog box

   ▶ For metric, type **1/10000** in the Conversion Factor text box in order to convert square centimeters to square meters. Click OK twice.

AutoCAD automatically inserts a factor that converts from square inches to square feet in the Additional Format dialog box.

9. Press the down arrow to move to cell C4. Repeat the previous two steps, selecting the magenta line in Andreae's office and displaying its area value in square feet (or square meters).

10. Press the down arrow to move to cell C5. Repeat steps 7 and 8, selecting the magenta line in Dee's office and displaying its area value in square feet (or square meters). Click outside the table on the layout to deselect the table. Figure 15.25 shows the result.

Room Schedule		
Employee	ID No.	Area (ft²)
Bruno	108	347.014
Andreae	864	439.451
Dee	273	346.052

FIGURE 15.25 Adding all the relevant fields to the table

Your model should now resemble Ex15.6-end.dwg, which is available among this chapter's companion download files.

Edit Table Data

Beyond filling in a table with all the relevant information, you can also format it to display the data in an aesthetically pleasing fashion. You can change justification, alter border color and/or lineweight, and even change the background color of chosen cells to highlight them. In the following steps, you'll format cells, add a row and a formula, and finally change an attribute and regenerate the drawing to see the table update.

Exercise 15.7: Alter Table Data

In this exercise you will edit the data in table cells. To begin, open Ex15.7-start.dwg from this chapter's companion download.

1. Click the word *Dee* (cell A5 in the table) to activate the ribbon's Table Cell contextual tab. Click the Insert Below button in the Row panel.

2. Press the down arrow and move to cell A6. Hold down Shift and click cell B6. Open the Merge Cells menu in the Merge panel and select Merge By Row. Cells A6 and B6 are merged. Type **Total** and click outside the table on the layout to deactivate Text Editing mode (see Figure 15.26).

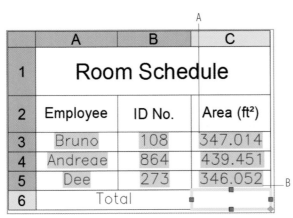

FIGURE 15.26 Merging two cells and typing the word *Total*

3. Click the cell to the right of the word Total to activate cell C6. Click the Formula button in the Insert panel and select Sum. Click points A and B shown in Figure 15.27. Press Enter to accept the formula =Sum(C3:C5).

FIGURE 15.27 Selecting a range of cells for a formula

4. Select the number 163082.582 (or 1052147.80 for metric) that appears in cell C6 (total area in square inches or square centimeters). Hold down Shift and click cell C3. Open the Data Format menu on the Cell Format panel and select Custom Table Cell Format from the context menu.

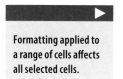

Formatting applied to a range of cells affects all selected cells.

5. Click the Additional Format button in the Table Cell Format dialog box that appears. Type **1/144** (or **1/10000** for metric) in the Conversion Factor text box and click OK to close the Additional Format dialog box.

6. Select Decimal in the Format list in the Table Cell Format dialog box. Open the Precision drop-down menu and select 0.0 (see Figure 15.28). Click OK.

FIGURE 15.28 Formatting a range of cells

7. Open the text justification menu (currently set at Top Center) in the Cell Styles panel and select Top Right. Cells C3 through C6 are right-justified.

8. Select cell B3, hold down Shift, and click cell B5. Change the justification to Top Right in the Cell Styles panel. Select cell A3, hold down Shift, and click cell A5. Change its justification to Top Left. Select merged cell AB6. Change its justification to Top Right. Click outside the table to deselect. Figure 15.29 shows the result.

9. Type **TABLESTYLE**, press Enter, and click the Modify button in the Table Style dialog box. In the Modify Table Style: Standard dialog box that appears, select Data from the Cell Styles drop-down menu

if it is not already selected. Select the General tab if it is not already selected, highlight the Horizontal text box in the Margins area, type 1/8 (or 0.15 for metric), and press Tab. Type 1/8 (or 0.15 for metric) and click OK and then Close. There is a bit more space around the data cells.

Room Schedule		
Employee	ID No.	Area (ft²)
Bruno	108	347.0
Andreae	864	439.5
Dee	273	346.1
Total		1132.5

FIGURE 15.29 **Table after adding a total row and justifying its data cells**

10. Click the words *Room Schedule* to select merged cell ABC1. Open the Table Cell Background Color drop-down in the Cell Styles panel and choose More Colors. Select the True Color tab in the Select Color dialog box that appears. Type **36,36,36** in the Color text box and press Tab (see Figure 15.30). Click OK.

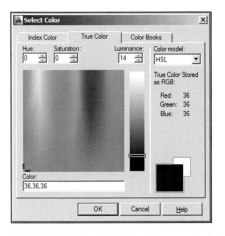

FIGURE 15.30 **Selecting a very dark table cell background color**

11. Double-click in cell ABC1 to activate the Text Editor contextual tab on the ribbon. Drag a selection encompassing the entire phrase Room Schedule. Open the Color drop-down in the Formatting panel and choose More Colors. Select the True Color tab in the Select Color dialog box that appears. Type 255,255,255 in the Color text box, press Tab, and click OK. White text now appears on a black background.

Edit Borders

12. Select cell ABC1, hold Shift, and click cell C6 to activate all the table's cells. Click the Edit Borders icon in the Cell Styles panel. Open the Lineweight drop-down menu and select 0.70 mm. Click the Outside Borders button to apply the properties and click OK (see Figure 15.31). A thicker line will appear around the outside borders of the table when the layout is plotted. Click outside the table to deselect it.

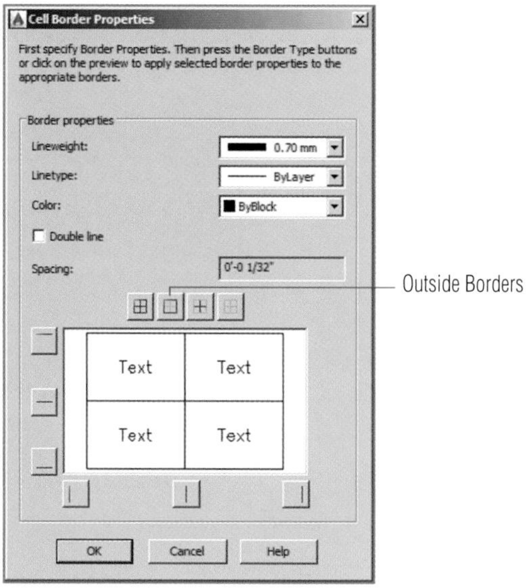

FIGURE 15.31 Changing cell border properties

13. Click the border of the table to select the entire table itself. Click the Uniformly Stretch Table Height grip in the lower-left corner and move it upward until the table reaches its maximum compactness (see Figure 15.32). Press Esc to deselect the table.

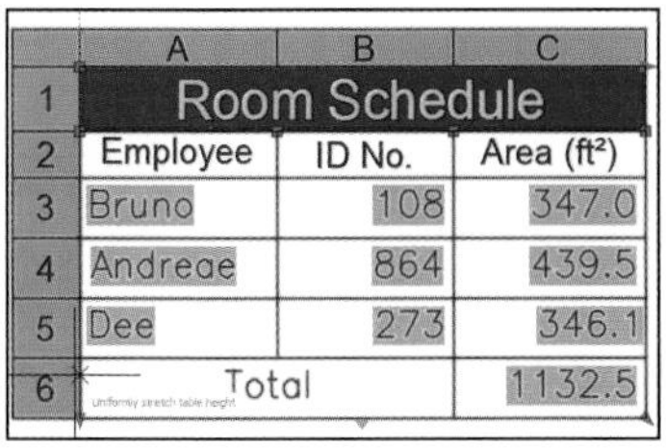

	A	B	C
1	Room Schedule		
2	Employee	ID No.	Area (ft²)
3	Bruno	108	347.0
4	Andreae	864	439.5
5	Dee	273	346.1
6	Total		1132.5

FIGURE 15.32 Stretching the table's height uniformly upward to compact its cells

14. Now you'll change an attribute value and observe that this change appears automatically in the table through the fields linked to the attribute values. Click the Maximize Viewport icon in the status bar. Double-click the Employee Data block in Dee's office to open the Enhanced Attribute Editor. Type **Newton**, press Enter, type 33, and press Enter again (see Figure 15.33). Click OK to end the EATTEDIT command.

The table in Layout1 has automatically been updated, and it lists Newton and his newly entered identification number.

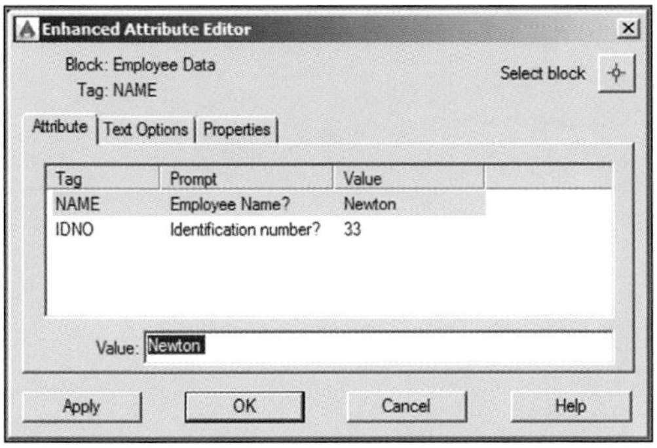

FIGURE 15.33 Editing attribute values in a maximized viewport

15. Click the Minimize Viewport icon in the status bar.

16. On the ribbon's Home tab, expand the Draw panel; then open the Revision Cloud flyout menu and select Rectangular. Click two opposite corner points around the Room Schedule to indicate the area of the drawing that has changed (see Figure 15.34).

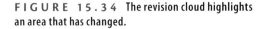

FIGURE 15.34 The revision cloud highlights an area that has changed.

17. Click the revision cloud object and use its grips to resize it so that the cloud surrounds Newton and his ID number 33 because this is more specifically the data that has changed.

18. Select the Output tab and click the Preview icon on the Plot panel. The gray background in the fields disappears, and you see the table exactly as it would plot (see Figure 15.35). Press Esc to exit preview mode.

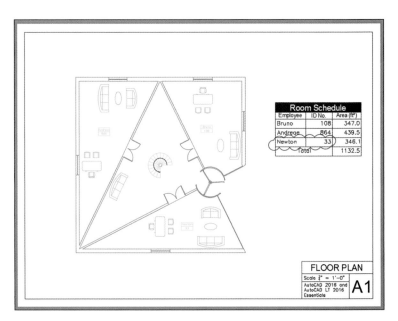

FIGURE 15.35 The final appearance of the drawing

Your model should now resemble Ex15.7-end.dwg, which is available among this chapter's companion download files.

Now You Know

In this chapter, you learned how to geolocate projects, import SketchUp models, define attributes and blocks, insert attributed blocks, edit table styles and create tables, use fields in table cells, and edit table data. Now you can work with a wide variety of data types and display information in tables on layouts.

CHAPTER 16

Navigating 3D Models

The only tools you need to navigate 2D drawings are Pan and Zoom, which are simple to use. However, getting around 3D models can be a bit more challenging. This chapter will delve into how to navigate 3D models in the AutoCAD® 2018 program. (Please note that the AutoCAD LT® software doesn't support these features.) You'll learn various methods for visualizing and navigating 3D models, from selecting visual styles to using preset isometric views. You'll also learn how to orbit into custom views and interactively navigate in perspective.

In this chapter, you'll learn to do the following:

▶ **Use visual styles**

▶ **Work with tiled viewports**

▶ **Navigate with the ViewCube®**

▶ **Orbit in 3D**

▶ **Use cameras**

▶ **Navigate with SteeringWheels®**

▶ **Save views**

Use Visual Styles

Visual styles control the way models appear in each viewport. The default visual style is 2D Wireframe, which is what you have been using in previous chapters. Consider for a moment how 3D models are displayed on a 2D screen—an illusion. Creating the illusion of where objects are situated in space requires some visual indication as to which objects are in front of other *occluded objects*. A wireframe representation does not give this indication. Rather, occluded objects need to be either hidden or covered by the shading of other objects according to the visual style that is selected.

Visual styles are never photorealistic like a rendering can be (see Chapter 18, "Presenting and Documenting 3D Design"), but many offer more realistic real-time views of your model compared to wireframe representations. In the following steps, you will sample the visual styles available in AutoCAD.

The model in this chapter is a conceptual model of the O2 Arena in London that you will build in Chapter 17, "Modeling in 3D." The O2 Arena (designed by architect Richard Rogers) was originally known as the Millennium Dome because it opened on January 1, 2000. This distinctive, mast-supported, dome-shaped cable network structure was one of the venues for the London 2012 Summer Olympics (see Figure 16.1).

FIGURE 16.1   You will navigate a 3D conceptual model of the O2 Arena in this chapter.

> Symbolizing the number of days, weeks, and months in a year, the O2 Arena is 365 meters in diameter and 52 meters high and is supported by 12 masts. It is also on the Prime Meridian that runs through Greenwich.

Exercise 16.1: Explore Visual Styles

In this exercise you will experiment with different visual styles. Begin by opening the file Ex16.1-start.dwg, which is available for download from this book's web page at www.sybex.com/go/autocad2018essentials.

1. Select the 3D Modeling workspace from the Quick Access toolbar.

2. Select the ribbon's Home tab if it is not already selected and open the Visual Styles drop-down menu at the top of the View panel (see Figure 16.2).

FIGURE 16.2 Selecting a visual style

The sample file is displayed in 2D Wireframe visual style by default.

3. Select the Wireframe icon. The UCS icon displays a colorful axis tripod in this 3D visual style (see Figure 16.3).

AutoCAD 2018 has a new geometric modeler (ASM), providing improved security and stability.

FIGURE 16.3 Wireframe visual style

Visual Styles

4. Select the ribbon's View tab and select the Visual Styles icon in the Palettes panel to alter visual style settings. Scroll down the list of Available Visual Styles In Drawing and select Shaded With Edges. Change Color to Tint in the Face Settings group (see Figure 16.4).

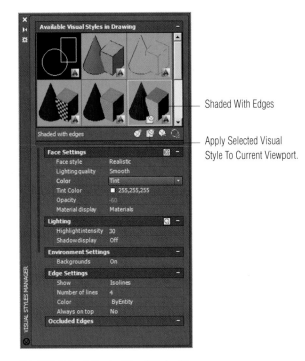

FIGURE 16.4   Visual Styles Manager

5. Select the Apply Selected Visual Style To Current Viewport button, as shown in Figure 16.4. Close the Visual Styles Manager. Figure 16.5 shows the result in the drawing canvas.

6. On the Home tab, open the Visual Styles drop-down menu in the View panel and select Save As A New Visual Style. The command prompt reads as follows:

```
VSSAVE Save current visual style as or [?]:
```

Type **Tinted with edges** and press Enter. These words appear on the Visual Styles drop-down menu, showing that this is now the current visual style.

> By saving a visual style, you can recall it later after switching to another visual style.

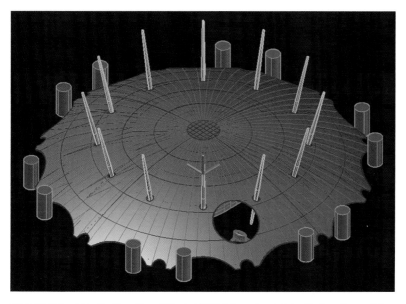

FIGURE 16.5 The altered Shaded With Edges visual style displays the model tinted with white.

7. You can also change visual styles using the in-canvas controls located in the upper-left corner of the viewport. Select the Visual Style Controls to open a menu (see Figure 16.6).

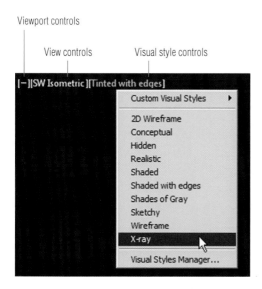

FIGURE 16.6 In-canvas controls

8. Choose X-ray from the in-canvas menu that appears. Figure 16.7 shows the result: a transparent, shaded view with edges.

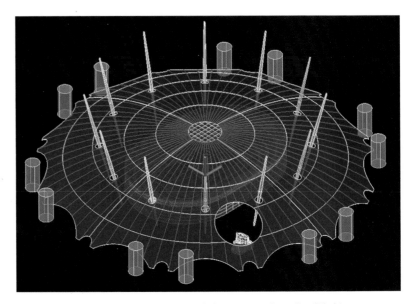

FIGURE 16.7 The X-ray visual style lets you see through solid objects.

Your model should now resemble Ex16.1-end.dwg, which is available among this chapter's companion files.

Work with Tiled Viewports

Tiled viewports can exist only in model space with the system variable TILEMODE equal to 1. Floating viewports exist only on layouts.

Tiled viewports allow you to visualize a 3D model from different simultaneous vantage points. By starting a command in one viewport and finishing it in another, you can more easily transform objects in 3D. To help you get a better grasp of how this works, the following exercise shows you how to divide the single default viewport into three tiled viewports.

Exercise 16.2: Tile Viewports

In this exercise you will subdivide the drawing window into multiple tiled viewports in model space, in contrast to the floating viewports that can be placed on layouts. To begin, open Ex16.2-start.dwg from this chapter's files available from this book's web page.

1. Type **VPORTS** and press Enter. In the Viewports dialog box that appears, select Three: Right in the Standard Viewports list. Open the Setup drop-down menu and select 3D (see Figure 16.8). Click OK.

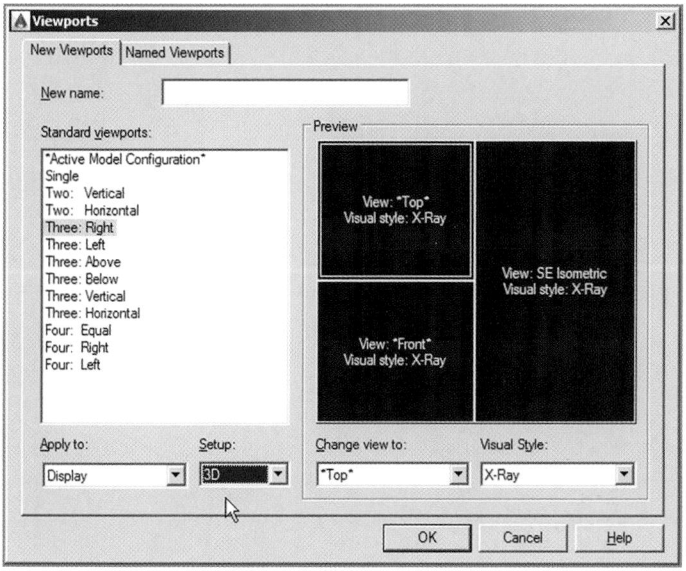

FIGURE 16.8 Configuring viewports

2. Click anywhere inside the lower-left viewport showing the front view to activate it. Open the in-canvas Visual Style Controls menu in this viewport and select Shaded. Click anywhere inside the viewport showing the top view to activate it. Open the in-canvas Visual Style Controls menu in this viewport and select Wireframe. Figure 16.9 shows the result.

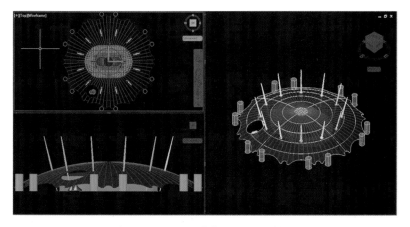

FIGURE 16.9 Three viewports, each displaying a different view and visual style

You can maximize or minimize viewports as needed at any time to get a better view of a 3D object.

Observe that what was formerly a plus (+) symbol in the in-canvas Viewport menu is now a minus (−) symbol.

Autodesk uses the same ViewCube and SteeringWheel navigation controls in many 3D applications, including the AutoCAD, Autodesk® Revit®, Autodesk® Inventor®, and Autodesk® 3ds Max® programs.

3. Select the plus (+) symbol in the lower-left viewport displaying the front view to open the in-canvas Viewport menu. Select Maximize Viewport. The front view fills the drawing canvas.

4. Double-click the minus symbol to minimize this viewport.

5. Click anywhere inside the right viewport showing the SE Isometric view to activate it. Double-click this viewport's plus symbol to maximize it. The SE Isometric view once again fills the drawing canvas.

Your model should now resemble Ex16.2-end.dwg, which is available among this chapter's companion files.

Navigate with the ViewCube

The ViewCube is a 3D navigation interface that lets you easily rotate through numerous preset orthogonal and isometric views. The ViewCube's instant visual feedback keeps you from getting lost in 3D space, even when you orbit into a custom view.

The ViewCube helps you visualize the relationship between the current user coordinate system (UCS) and the world coordinate system (WCS).

In the following steps, you will experiment with the ViewCube and learn how to view a 3D model from almost any angle.

Exercise 16.3: Use the ViewCube to Navigate

In this exercise you will learn how to use the ViewCube. To begin, open Ex16.3-start.dwg from the companion files for this chapter.

1. Open the ViewCube menu (see Figure 16.10) and select Set Current View As Home.

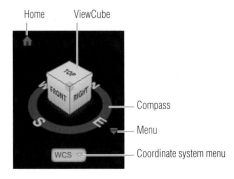

FIGURE 16.10 ViewCube navigation interface

2. Hover your cursor over the ViewCube and observe that different parts highlight in blue as you pass over them. Click the word *Right*. The view changes to an orthogonal view of the right side of the model (also known as an *architectural elevation*).

You can select from a short list of preset views using the in-canvas View Controls menu as an alternative to the ViewCube.

3. The ViewCube rotates with the view change. Hover the cursor over each of the elements on the right face and observe there are four corners, four edges, plus the right face itself that highlights in blue. In addition, there are four arrows facing the cube and two curved arrows in the upper right. Each of these interface elements rotates the view in a specific direction, as indicated in Figure 16.11.

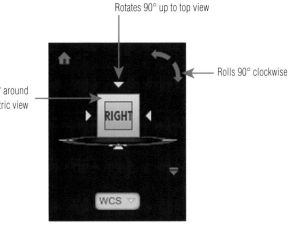

Rotates 90° up to top view

Rolls 90° clockwise

Rotates 45° up and 45° around the compass to SE isometric view

FIGURE 16.11 Additional ViewCube controls

4. Spend some time navigating with the ViewCube, rotating into multiple different views. Try Bottom, Left, Back, SE Isometric, and NW Isometric.

5. Click the Home icon in the ViewCube interface to return to the initial view.

6. Select the UCS icon at the center of the 3D model to activate it. Drag the tip of the blue z-axis. The command prompt reads as follows:

```
** Z AXIS DIRECTION **
Specify a point on Z axis:
```

Click an arbitrary point in the drawing canvas to rotate the UCS. Observe that the ViewCube rotates relative to the current UCS (see Figure 16.12). This feedback can help you visualize where the XY drawing plane is (parallel to the Top face of the ViewCube).

ViewCube is rotated with respect to compass.

FIGURE 16.12 ViewCube aligned to the current UCS

Your model should now resemble Ex16.3-end.dwg, which is available among this chapter's companion files.

Orbit in 3D

As you learned in the previous section, the ViewCube is limited to rotating the view in 45° increments. Although the ViewCube might get you close to the angle from which you want to view a 3D model, you will often need to orbit to the optimal viewing angle to see particular geometry best. Orbiting refers to rotating the view at any arbitrary angle.

Exercise 16.4: Orbit

In this exercise you will orbit your point of view around the model. Let's assume you want to get a close look at the ventilation towers that appear under a large elliptical hole in the dome membrane. To begin, open Ex16.4-start.dwg from this chapter's companion files.

1. Click the ViewCube's edge between the Top and Front faces and zoom into the ventilation towers, as shown in Figure 16.13.

Ventilation towers

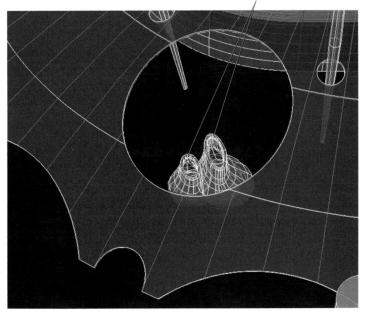

FIGURE 16.13 Using the ViewCube to view the ventilation towers

2. Position the cursor over the compass ring surrounding the ViewCube and drag it to the right to get a better view of the ventilation towers so that the hole in the dome membrane appears more circular.

3. Click the Orbit tool in the Navigation bar. Drag down in the drawing canvas to orbit your point of view upward until you can see the ventilation towers unobstructed by the dome membrane (see Figure 16.14). Press Esc to end the `3DORBIT` command.

4. Hold down Shift and drag the mouse wheel to orbit (without roll) about the ventilation towers once more. You will find that it is not possible to gain an eye-level view of the towers without other objects obstructing the view. You will learn how to set up this type of view using a camera in the next section.

5. Click the Undo icon in the Quick Access toolbar to return to the previous viewpoint.

> The Orbit tool is constrained so that it doesn't roll by default. Use `3DFORBIT`, the free orbit tool, to orbit with roll.

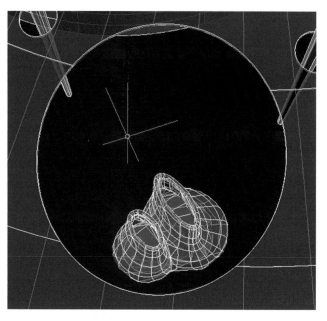

FIGURE 16.14   Orbiting for a better view of the subject

Your model should now resemble Ex16.4-end.dwg, which is available among this chapter's companion files.

Use Cameras

AutoCAD uses virtual cameras to set up views similar to those achieved in the real world with physical cameras. The CAMERA command creates a camera object that you can manipulate in an isometric view to position the viewpoint in relation to the camera target.

Exercise 16.5: Utilize Virtual Cameras

In this exercise you will use a virtual camera to help you compose a perspective view of the 3D model. To begin, open Ex16.5-start.dwg from this chapter's companion files.

1. Open the in-canvas View Controls menu and select SW Isometric.

2. Zoom out by rolling the mouse wheel backward.

3. Toggle off Object Snap in the status bar.

4. Type **CAMERA** and press Enter. Click points A and B, as shown in Figure 16.15, and press Enter.

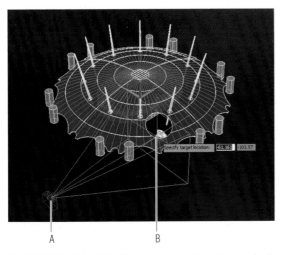

FIGURE 16.15 Placing a camera in an isometric view

5. Select the camera object. Select the Shaded visual style in the Camera Preview window that appears. Drag the Lens Length/FOV grip to the right and click approximately at point A to expand the field of view (see Figure 16.16).

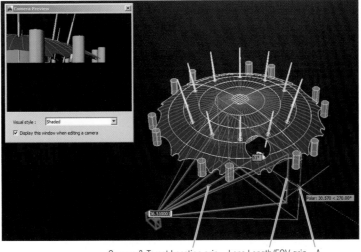

Camera & Target Location grip   Lens Length/FOV grip   A

FIGURE 16.16 Adjusting a camera in an isometric view

You will correct the fact that the camera is "on the ground" in the next step.

6. Drag the Camera & Target Location grip forward until the camera is under the outer edge of the dome. Figure 16.17 shows the Camera Preview window.

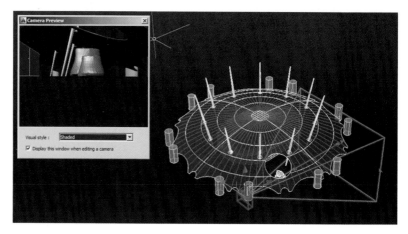

FIGURE 16.17 Camera Preview window showing the new position of the camera "on the ground"

Camera views are in perspective so that objects diminish in size according to their distances from the camera.

7. Right-click in the drawing window and choose Set Camera View from the context menu that appears. Drag the mouse wheel downward to move the camera and its target upward, as shown in Figure 16.18.

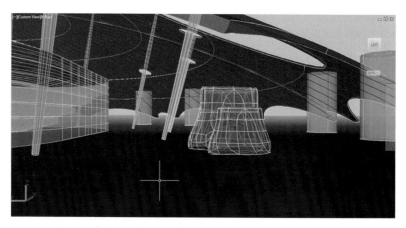

FIGURE 16.18 Looking through the camera

Your model should now resemble Ex16.5-end.dwg, which is available among this chapter's companion files.

Navigate with SteeringWheels

SteeringWheels are interactive navigation controls that Autodesk uses in many 3D applications, including AutoCAD. In the following steps, you will use the Full Navigation SteeringWheel feature (displaying all eight navigation tools) to compose a view under the dome.

Exercise 16.6: Use SteeringWheels to Navigate

In this exercise you will learn how to navigate with a SteeringWheel. To begin, open Ex16.6-start.dwg from this chapter's companion files.

1. Open the SteeringWheel menu in the Navigation bar and select Full Navigation Wheel. The SteeringWheel control appears in the drawing canvas in close proximity to the cursor (see Figure 16.19).

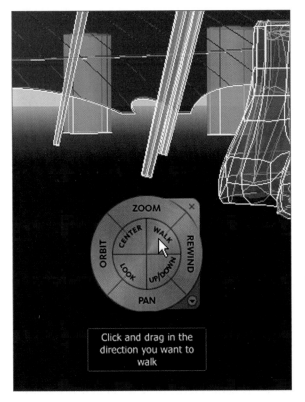

FIGURE 16.19 Full navigation SteeringWheel interface

2. Position the cursor over the Walk tool within the inner donut hole of the Full Navigation SteeringWheel. Click and hold the mouse button and observe a walk circle appear in the lower portion of the drawing canvas. Drag the cursor relative to the walk circle to move in that direction (see Figure 16.20). The further from the walk circle you drag, the faster you walk in that direction. Release the mouse button.

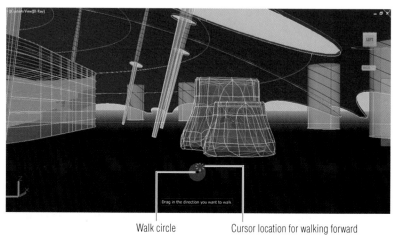

Walk circle   Cursor location for walking forward

FIGURE 16.20 Walking under the dome

3. Position the cursor over the Look tool in the SteeringWheel's inner ring. Click and hold the mouse button and drag upward to rotate the camera to look up at the hole in the dome above the ventilation towers. Release the mouse button.

ADDITIONAL STEERINGWHEELS

There are nine commands that appear on variations of SteeringWheels: Zoom, Pan, Orbit, Rewind, Center, Forward, Walk, Up/Down, and Look.

There are three basic SteeringWheels: Full Navigation, View Object, and Tour Building. The latter two wheels have four commands—each command is suitable to its purpose of navigating around an object or touring through a building.

Each one of the basic wheels has a corresponding mini-wheel with the same commands as the larger interface. I suggest starting with the basic wheels and then graduating to mini-wheels as you gain experience. Mini-wheels are more efficient because you don't have to move the mouse as far to select navigation commands.

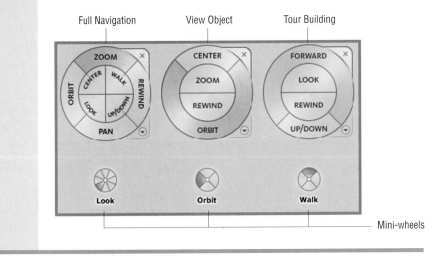

4. Position the cursor over the Rewind tool in the SteeringWheel's outer ring. Drag to the left to go backward in the history of movements made using the SteeringWheel (see Figure 16.21). Drag back to the point before you looked up. Press Esc to exit the SteeringWheel.

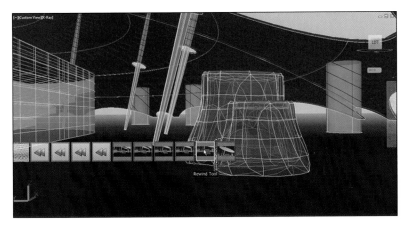

FIGURE 16.21   Interactively rewinding through navigation history

Your model should now resemble Ex16.6-end.dwg, which is available among this chapter's companion files.

Save Views

Named views allow you to save where you are in space so that you can recall these positions in the future. In the following exercise, you will save the current position in the viewport, change the view, switch out of perspective, and then return to the saved view.

Exercise 16.7: Save Views

In this exercise you will learn how to save a view. To begin, open Ex16.7-start.dwg from the Chapter 16 companion files.

> Many different properties can be saved with views, including Camera Position, Layer Snapshot, UCS, Live Section, Visual Style, and Background.

1. Type **V** (for view) and press Enter. Click the New button in the View Manager dialog box that appears.

2. In the New View / Shot Properties dialog box that appears, type **Camera2** as the view name (see Figure 16.22). Click OK twice to close both open dialog boxes.

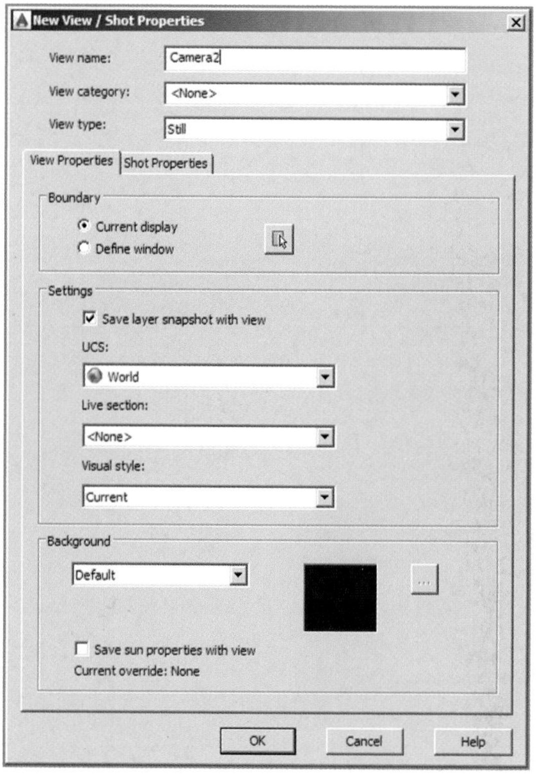

FIGURE 16.22 Saving a new view

3. Click the upper-left corner of the left face of the ViewCube to switch to the NW Isometric view. The model is still in perspective even after switching out of the Camera2 view (see Figure 16.23).

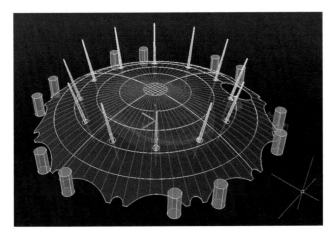

FIGURE 16.23 Perspective overview of the 3D model

4. You can toggle in and out of perspective view at any time. Open the in-canvas View Controls menu and select Parallel to switch out of perspective.

5. Type **V** (for view) and press Enter. Select Camera2 in the list of Model Views in the View Manager dialog box (see Figure 16.24). Click Set Current, Apply, and then OK.

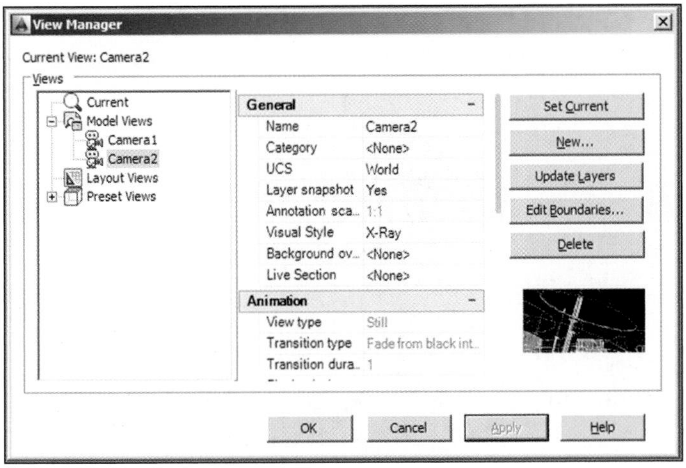

FIGURE 16.24 Restoring a view

Your model should now resemble ex16.7-end.dwg, which is available among this chapter's companion files.

Now You Know

In this chapter, you learned how to use visual styles, work with tiled viewports, navigate with the ViewCube and SteeringWheel controls, orbit in 3D, use cameras, and save views. Now you know how to get around and control the display of objects in three-dimensional space.

CHAPTER 17

Modeling in 3D

The AutoCAD® program has three different 3D modeling toolsets comprising surfaces, solids, and meshes, reflecting the historical evolution of computer graphics. Each toolset was initially developed to suit specific industries: surfaces for industrial design, solids for engineering, and meshes for games and movies. Each toolset has its particular strengths and limitations that become evident the more you use it. Yet AutoCAD allows you to pick the best tool for the job no matter what type of work you do so that you can find the best solutions for your models.

In this chapter, you'll learn to do the following:

▶ **Create surface models**

▶ **Edit surface models**

▶ **Create solid models**

▶ **Edit solid models**

▶ **Smooth mesh models**

▶ **Live-section models**

Create Surface Models

In this chapter, you will create a conceptual model of the O2 Arena in London, the same model used in Chapter 16, "Navigating 3D Models."

In AutoCAD, *surfaces* are defined as infinitely thin shells that do not contain any mass or volume. To create surfaces in this chapter, you'll use two-dimensional profile shapes (provided as part of this chapter's companion files, available for download from the book's web page at www.sybex.com/go/autocad2018essentials). You will begin the following exercise by creating a planar surface and then revolving, sweeping, and extruding 2D profiles into 3D surfaces.

Exercise 17.1: Make Planar Surfaces

The sample file is displayed in the Shaded With Edges visual style so that surfaces will be visible when you create them.

Planar surfaces differ from flat bounded areas like circles and closed polylines in that they display surfaces rather than edges only, in shaded visual styles. Open the file Ex17.1-start.dwg from this chapter's companion files available on this book's web page.

 1. Select the 3D Modeling workspace from the Quick Access toolbar.

2. Select the ribbon's Home tab if it is not already selected and click the Make Current tool in the Layers panel. Select the circle at the center of the drawing to set the Dome Membrane layer as current.

 3. Select the ribbon's Surface tab and click the Surface Associativity toggle in the Create panel if it is not already highlighted in blue.

Like dimensions, surfaces can optionally be associated with the profile shapes that define them. Altering the shape of a profile immediately changes the form of its associated surface.

 4. Select the Planar tool in the Create panel. The command prompt reads as follows:

        PLANESURF Specify first corner or [Object] <Object>:

   Press Enter to accept the default Object option. Select the blue circle at the center of the drawing and press Enter. A planar surface appears as the PLANESURF command ends.

5. Click the SW corner of the ViewCube® to move to a SW isometric viewpoint. The blue planar surface you just created is visible at the top of the dome (see Figure 17.1).

FIGURE 17.1 Creating a planar surface at the top of the dome

Your model should now resemble Ex17.1-end.dwg.

Exercise 17.2: Revolve a 2D Profile to Create a 3D Model

Much like you would turn wood on a lathe, you create 3D surfaces by revolving open profiles such as lines, arcs, or polylines around an axis. In the following steps, you will revolve a single arc to generate the exterior surface of the dome. To begin, open Ex17.2-start.dwg from this chapter's companion files.

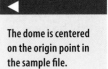

1. Select the ribbon's Surface tab and toggle off the Surface Associativity icon in the Create panel.

2. Select the Revolve tool on the Create panel of the ribbon's Surface tab. Select the blue arc running from the planar surface at the top of the dome down to the white circle at the periphery and press Enter.

3. The command prompt reads as follows:

   ```
   REVOLVE Specify axis start point or define axis by
   [Object X
   Y Z] <Object>:
   ```

   Type **0,0** and press Enter.

4. The command prompt now reads as follows:

   ```
   REVOLVE Specify axis endpoint:
   ```

   Type **0,0,1** and press Enter. Press Enter again to accept the default angle of revolution (360 degrees). The REVOLVE command ends, and the dome surface appears (see Figure 17.2).

> The dome is centered on the origin point in the sample file.

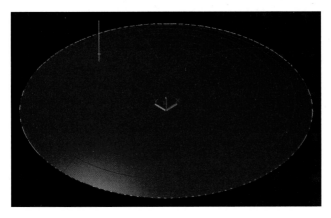

FIGURE 17.2   Revolving an arc to generate the dome surface

5. Type **E** (for Erase) and press Enter. Type **P** (for Previous) and press Enter. Press Enter again to erase the arc that generated the dome surface.

THREE-DIMENSIONAL CARTESIAN COORDINATES

The Z direction extending above and below the ground plane can be specified within Cartesian coordinates simply by adding a second comma followed by the Z value. For example, the coordinates of a point one unit above the origin point are 0,0,1.

6. Type **LA** (for Layer) and press Enter to open the Layer Properties Manager. Double-click the icon representing the Arena layer to set it as current.

7. Click the Dome Membrane layer's lightbulb icon to toggle it off.

8. Click the Auto-hide toggle so that the palette collapses when the cursor isn't over it (see Figure 17.3).

Auto-Hide toggle

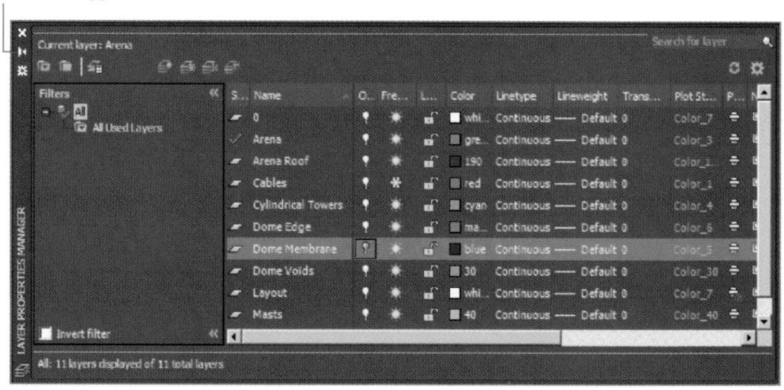

FIGURE 17.3 Changing layer properties

Your model should now resemble Ex17.2-end.dwg.

Exercise 17.3: Sweep Out 3D Geometry

The SWEEP command gives you the ability to create surfaces by pushing an open profile through space following a path. In these steps, you will model the area within the O2 Arena and its internal roof by sweeping open shapes along closed paths. To begin, open Ex17.3-start.dwg from this chapter's companion files.

1. Select the Sweep tool on the Create panel of the ribbon's Surface tab. Select the green arena profile shown in Figure 17.4 and press Enter.

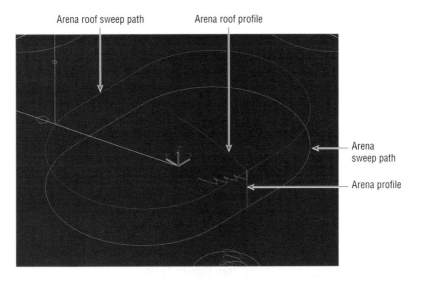

FIGURE 17.4 Profiles and sweep paths representing the 02 Arena

2. The command prompt reads as follows:

    ```
    Select sweep path or [Alignment Base point Scale Twist]:
    ```

    Select the arena sweep path as shown in Figure 17.4. Figure 17.5 shows the resulting 3D arena.

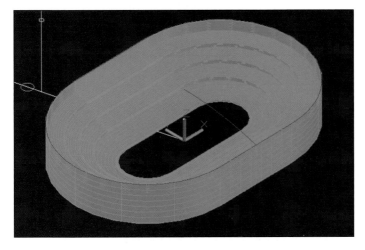

FIGURE 17.5 Arena created by sweeping a profile along a path

3. Hover the cursor over the Layer Properties Manager's title bar to reveal the palette. Double-click the Arena Roof layer's icon to set it as current.

4. Press the spacebar to repeat the SWEEP command. Select the arena roof profile and press Enter. Select the arena roof sweep path. Figure 17.6 shows the result.

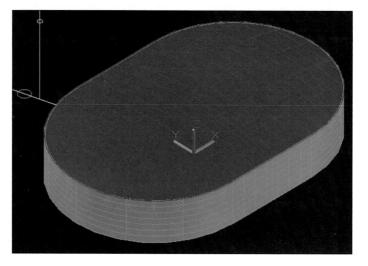

FIGURE 17.6 Sweeping the arena roof

5. Hover the cursor over the Layer Properties Manager's title bar to reveal the palette. Double-click the Dome Edge layer's icon to set it as current. Toggle off the Arena and Arena Roof layers.

Your model should now resemble Ex17.3-end.dwg.

Exercise 17.4: Extrude 2D Geometry into 3D

Extruding means pushing forcibly through a die, like hot steel beams being extruded at a foundry. In the following steps, you will extrude the boundary representing the edge of the dome membrane as a curtain-like wall. In the next section, you will use this curtain to trim off the outer portion of the membrane. To begin, open Ex17.4-start.dwg from this chapter's companion files.

1. Select the Extrude tool on the Create panel of the ribbon's Surface tab. Select the magenta dome edge (see Figure 17.7) and press Enter.

🔲 Extrude

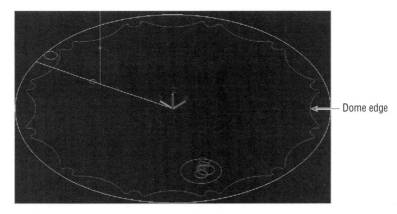

FIGURE 17.7   Selecting the dome edge

2. The command prompt reads as follows:

```
Specify height of extrusion or [Direction Path Taper
angle]
```

Type 50 and press Enter. A 3D curtain-like wall rises up out of the 2D edge.

3. Hover the cursor over the Layer Properties Manager's title bar to reveal the palette. Toggle on the Dome Membrane layer. Double-click the Dome Membrane layer's icon to set it as current. Figure 17.8 shows the result.

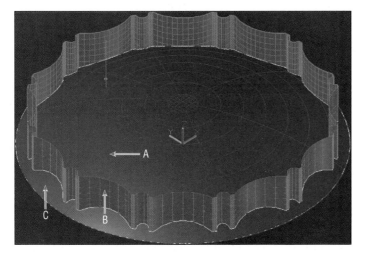

FIGURE 17.8   An extruded surface (in magenta) poking through the dome membrane (in blue)

Your model should now resemble Ex17.4-end.dwg.

Edit Surface Models

Surface models have editing tools that modify existing surface boundaries. In the following sections, you will modify surface boundaries by using other surfaces or by projecting edges onto existing surfaces and using these projections to modify boundaries or cut holes in surfaces. In addition, you will project 2D objects onto 3D surfaces without altering the surfaces at all.

Exercise 17.5: Trim Surfaces with Other Surfaces

In the following steps, you will trim off the portion of the dome membrane that extends beyond the curtain wall extrusion you generated in the previous section. To begin, open Ex17.5-start.dwg from this chapter's companion files.

1. Switch to the 3D Modeling workspace if it's not selected already in the Quick Access toolbar.

2. Select the Trim tool on the Edit panel of the ribbon's Surface tab. The command prompt reads as follows:

   SURFTRIM Select surfaces or regions to trim or [Extend PROjection direction]:

   Click point A in Figure 17.8 and press Enter.

3. The command prompt now reads as follows:

   SURFTRIM Select cutting curves, surfaces, or regions:

   Click point B in Figure 17.8 and press Enter.

4. The prompt reads as follows:

   SURFTRIM Select area to trim [Undo]:

   Click point C in Figure 17.8 and press Enter. The SURFTRIM command ends.

5. Hover the cursor over the Layer Properties Manager's title bar to reveal the palette. Click the Sun icon to freeze the Dome Edge layer. Figure 17.9 shows the resulting trimmed dome membrane.

Your model should now resemble Ex17.5-end.dwg.

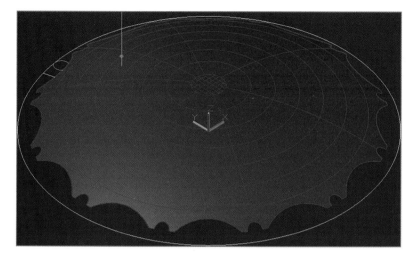

FIGURE 17.9 Trimmed dome membrane

Exercise 17.6: Project Edges on Surfaces

In the following steps, you will project a series of 2D objects onto a 3D surface. More specifically, you will project the large hole for the ventilation towers, 12 smaller holes accommodating the structural masts, and numerous cables onto the surface of the dome membrane. To begin, open Ex17.6-start.dwg from this chapter's companion download.

1. Using the in-canvas controls in the top-left corner of the viewport, click the Visual Style menu and select Wireframe. (You want to see through the dome but cannot in the Shaded With Edges visual style.)

2. Hover the cursor over the Layer Properties Manager's title bar to reveal the palette. Double-click the Dome Voids layer's icon to set it as current.

3. Zoom into the area where there is a large orange circle with a series of light blue circles and ellipses inside it.

4. Toggle on Auto Trim in the Project Geometry panel.

5. Select the Project To UCS tool in the Project Geometry panel on the ribbon's Surface tab. The command prompt reads as follows:

   PROJECTGEOMETRY Select curves, points to be projected or [PROjection direction]:

   Click the large orange circle and press Enter.

6. The command prompt now reads as follows:

   ```
   PROJECTGEOMETRY Select a solid, surface, or region
   for the target of the projection:
   ```

   Select the blue dome membrane. A new orange spline appears on the surface of the trimmed dome (see Figure 17.10), and the PROJECTGEOMETRY command ends.

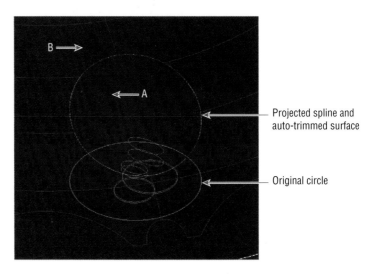

FIGURE 17.10 Projecting the ventilation tower cutout upward onto the dome membrane's surface

7. Type **E** (for Erase) and press Enter. Click points A and B in Figure 17.10 to create a crossing window that selects both the dome and the projected spline.

8. Type **R** (for Remove) and press Enter.

9. Type **L** (for Last) and press Enter twice to erase the projected spline but not the dome.

10. Pan over to the small orange circle with a white line running through it.

11. Toggle off Auto Trim in the Project Geometry panel.

12. Select the Project To UCS tool in the Project Geometry panel, select the small orange circle, and press Enter. Select the blue dome. A new projected spline appears on the dome surface (see Figure 17.11).

You will array this projected spline around the dome in the next section.

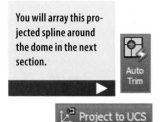

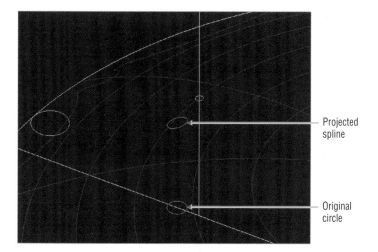

Projected spline

Original circle

FIGURE 17.11 Projecting one mast void upward onto the dome membrane's surface

13. Type E (for Erase) and press Enter. Select the original small orange circle on the ground and press Enter.

14. Select the ribbon's Home tab and click the Isolate tool in the Layers panel. Type S (for Settings) and press Enter. Type O (for Off) and press Enter twice. Select the blue dome membrane and press Enter.

15. Hover the cursor over the Layer Properties Manager's title bar to reveal the palette. Click the Cables layer's snowflake and darkened lightbulb icons both to thaw and to toggle the layer on. Double-click the Cables layer's icon to set it as current (see Figure 17.12).

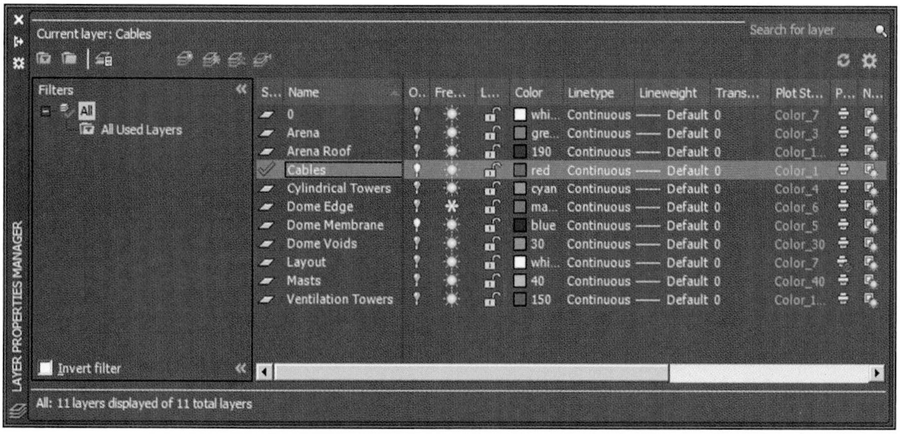

FIGURE 17.12 Changing layer states

16. Click the Top of the ViewCube. Click the Rotate Clockwise icon in the ViewCube interface if necessary so North is up.

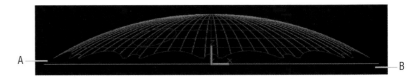 17. Select the ribbon's Surface tab and click the Project To View tool in the Project Geometry panel. Select all the objects in the drawing canvas with a crossing selection and press Enter. The command prompt reads as follows:

```
PROJECTGEOMETRY Select a solid, surface, or region
for the target of the projection:
```

Select the blue dome. Although the PROJECTGEOMETRY command ends, you can't see the projected objects in the top view.

18. Click the Front arrow below the ViewCube. Type **E** (for Erase) and click points A and B in Figure 17.13 to select all the lines on the ground. Press Enter to erase the selection.

FIGURE 17.13 Selecting lines on the ground in the Front view for deletion

19. Click the upper-left corner of the ViewCube to switch into an SW Isometric viewpoint. Type **LAYUN** (for Layer Unisolate) and press Enter.

Your model should now resemble Ex17.6-end.dwg.

Exercise 17.7: Trim Surfaces with Edges

You already trimmed one surface when you projected the large orange circle onto the dome using Auto Trim mode in the previous exercise. You won't use Auto Trim in the next exercise because you need to retain the projected object. In the following steps, you will first array this projected spline around the dome and then manually trim all 12 voids through which the structural masts will ultimately pass. To begin, open Ex17.7-start.dwg from the companion files.

1. Hover the cursor over the Layer Properties Manager's title bar to reveal the palette. Click the Dome Voids layer's darkened lightbulb icon to toggle on this layer.

2. Type **AR** (for Array), press Enter, select the small orange spline that you projected on the dome in the previous exercise, and press Enter. Type **PO** (for Polar) and press Enter. The command prompt reads as follows:

```
ARRAY Specify center point of array or
[Base point Axis of rotation]:
```

Type **0,0** and press Enter.

3. The command prompt now reads as follows:

```
ARRAY Select grip to edit array or [Associative Base
point Items Angle between Fill angle ROWs Levels
ROTate items eXit]:
```

Type **I** (for Items) and press Enter. Type **12** and press Enter. Type **AS** (for Associative), type **N** (for No), and press Enter. Press Enter to end the ARRAY command. Twelve splines appear arrayed around the dome (see Figure 17.14).

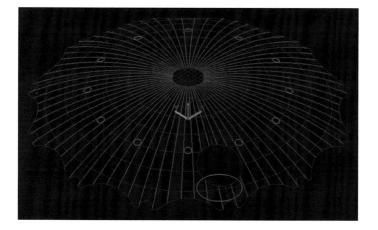

FIGURE 17.14 Arraying projected splines around the dome

You cannot trim a surface with an array object. By making a nonassociative array, you end up with individual objects that can be used.

4. Open the in-canvas Visual Style Controls menu and select Shaded With Edges.

5. Select the Trim tool on the Edit panel of the ribbon's Surface tab. Select the dome, press Enter, select one of the orange splines, and press Enter. Click inside the spline and press Enter. A hole in the shape of the spline is cut in the dome.

6. Repeat the previous step 11 times, one for each remaining orange spline.

7. Hover the cursor over the Layer Properties Manager's title bar to reveal the palette. Click the Cylindrical Towers layer's darkened lightbulb icon to toggle this layer on and then double-click the layer's icon to set it as current. Toggle off the Dome Voids layer. Figure 17.15 shows the result.

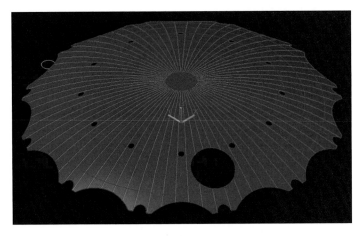

FIGURE 17.15 Trimming holes in the dome to accommodate the masts

Your model should now resemble `Ex17.7-end.dwg`.

Create Solid Models

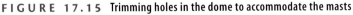

The EXTRUDE, REVOLVE, LOFT, and SWEEP commands have Mode options that allow you to select either Solid or Surface.

If surfaces cover 2D floor spaces, then solid models enclose 3D volumes. Only with solid objects can you use the MASSPROP command to calculate engineering properties such as volume, centroid, moments of inertia, and so on. Many of the solid modeling tools are the same as the surface modeling tools. If you start these commands with a closed path such as a circle, ellipse, or closed polyline, you will end up with a solid object, whereas open paths generate surfaces. In the following sections, you'll extrude and loft solid objects.

Exercise 17.8: Extrude Solid Objects

The difference between a surface extrusion and a solid extrusion is what's in the middle: nothing in the case of the surface model and "mass" in the case of the solid. In the next section, you'll see how to affect the solid "mass" with Boolean tools. In the following steps, you'll extrude a circle into a solid and array it around the dome. To begin, open `Ex17.8-start.dwg` from this chapter's companion files.

1. Switch to the 3D Modeling workspace if it's not selected already in the Quick Access toolbar.

2. Select the ribbon's Solid tab and click the Extrude tool in the Solid panel. Select the cyan circle at the edge of the dome and press Enter. The command prompt reads as follows:

   ```
   EXTRUDE Specify height of extrusion or [Direction
   Path Taper angle] <50.000>:
   ```

   Type 30 and press Enter. The 2D circle becomes a 3D solid cylinder.

3. The O2 Arena features cylindrical towers in pairs. Type **MI** (for Mirror) and press Enter. Type **L** (for Last) and press Enter twice. The command prompt reads as follows:

   ```
   MIRROR Specify first point of mirror line:
   ```

   Type 0,0 and press Enter.

4. The command prompt now reads as follows:

   ```
   MIRROR Specify second point of mirror line:
   ```

   Type 0,1 to specify a mirror line running along the y-axis and press Enter. Press Enter once more to accept the default (not to erase the source objects). Figure 17.16 shows the resulting pair of cylinders.

When you are specifying the mirror line, only its direction matters—the distance and units do not.

FIGURE 17.16 Extruding and mirroring one pair of solid cylindrical towers

5. You need to place six pairs of cylinders around the dome. Type **AR** (for Array) and press Enter. Select both cylindrical towers and press Enter. Type **PO** (for Polar) and press Enter. The command prompt reads as follows:

```
ARRAY Specify center point of array or
[Base point Axis of rotation]:
```

Type **0,0** and press Enter. Type **I** (for Items) and press Enter. Type **6** (for the number of items) and press Enter. Press Enter to accept the default and end the ARRAY command. Figure 17.17 shows the result.

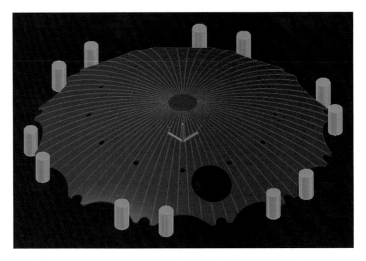

FIGURE 17.17 Arraying pairs of cylindrical towers around the dome

6. Switch to Wireframe using the in-canvas Visual Style Controls menu so that you can see through the dome.

7. Hover the cursor over the Layer Properties Manager's title bar to open the palette. Toggle on the Masts layer. Double-click the Masts layer to set it as current. Zoom into the yellow vertical line with a hexagon around its midpoint; this represents a structural mast.

8. Click the Extrude tool in the Solid panel. Select the hexagon at the midpoint of the vertical line and press Enter. The command prompt reads as follows:

```
EXTRUDE Specify height of extrusion or
[Direction Path Taper angle] <30.000>:
```

Type **T** (for Taper Angle) and press Enter.

Profiles of extruded items are automatically deleted.

9. The command prompt now reads as follows:

   ```
   EXTRUDE Specify angle of taper for extrusion <15.00>:
   ```

   Type 1 and press Enter. Toggle on Endpoint object snap if it is not already running and click the top endpoint of the vertical line to specify the height of the extrusion. Figure 17.18 shows the result.

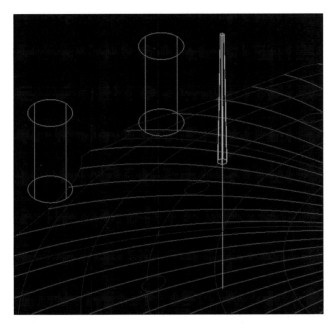

FIGURE 17.18 Extruding half of a tapering hexagonal solid mast

10. Select the Extract Edges tool on the Solid Editing panel, select the mast, and press Enter. The Extract Edges tool creates wireframe geometry for solid objects.

11. Zoom in on the hexagonal bottom of the mast. Type **J** (for Join) and press Enter. Click points A and B shown in Figure 17.19 to create a crossing window that selects the lines, making a hexagon, and press Enter.

12. Select the Extrude tool in the Solid panel, type **L** (for Last), and press Enter twice.

13. Type **T** (for Taper Angle), press Enter, and then press Enter again to select the default one-degree taper angle. Zoom and click the lower endpoint of the vertical yellow line to extrude the lower half of the mast down to the ground.

The extracted edges are coincident with the original edges of the solid object.

◄

 Extract Edges

 Extrude

◄

You will unify, rotate, and array the masts around the dome in the "Edit Solid Models" section.

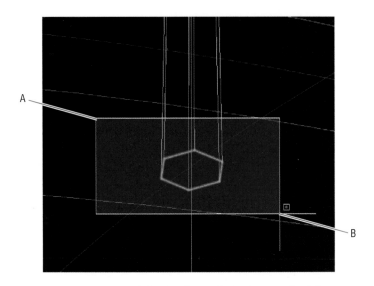

FIGURE 17.19 Joining six edges to form a hexagonal polyline

Your model should now resemble Ex17.8-end.dwg.

Exercise 17.9: Loft Solid Objects

Lofting is a modeling technique that lets you create a 3D model from a series of 2D cross sections. In the following steps, you will loft two ventilation towers from a series of circles and ellipses. To begin, open Ex17.9-start.dwg from this chapter's companion files.

The ventilation towers serve a pair of road tunnels passing under the Thames in London. These towers were *in situ* prior to the construction of the O2 Arena.

1. Hover the cursor over the Layer Properties Manager's title bar to open the palette. Toggle on Ventilation Towers and then double-click the layer to set it as current. Toggle off the Dome Membrane and Cables layers.

2. Switch to Shaded With Edges using the in-canvas Visual Style Controls menu.

Normal means perpendicular to the surface in question.

3. Zoom in on the collection of blue circles and ellipses. Select the Loft tool from the drop-down menu under Sweep on the Solid panel and press Enter. Select profiles A, B, C, and D shown in Figure 17.20 and press Enter twice. Select the loft object, open the grip menu that appears, choose Normal To Start And End Sections, and press Esc.

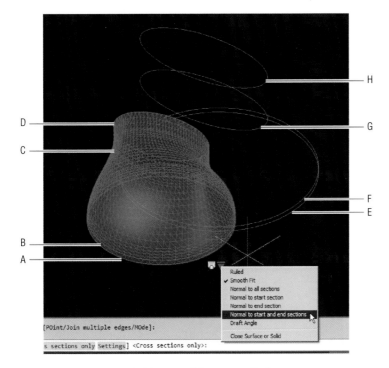

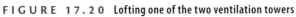

FIGURE 17.20 Lofting one of the two ventilation towers

4. Press the spacebar to repeat the LOFT command. Select profiles E, F, G, and H, shown in Figure 17.20, and press Enter twice. Select the new loft object, open the grip menu that appears, choose Normal To Start And End Sections, and press Esc. Figure 17.21 shows the result.

FIGURE 17.21 Lofted ventilation towers

Your model should now resemble Ex17.9-end.dwg.

Edit Solid Models

Solid-editing tools provide an alternative set of modeling possibilities as compared with surface tools. Boolean tools (named after mathematician George Boole) allow you to unify, subtract, and intersect solids (set theory terms) to create new forms. You will explore these tools in the following section and learn about a variety of specialized solid-editing tools.

Exercise 17.10: Perform Boolean Operations

In the following steps, you will unify the top and bottom parts of the mast with the UNION command. You will then rotate and array 12 masts around the dome. To begin, open Ex17.10-start.dwg from the companion files.

1. Switch to the 3D Modeling workspace if it's not selected already in the Quick Access toolbar.

2. Switch to Wireframe using the in-canvas Visual Style Controls menu.

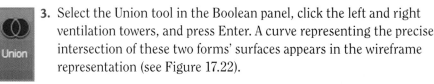

3. Select the Union tool in the Boolean panel, click the left and right ventilation towers, and press Enter. A curve representing the precise intersection of these two forms' surfaces appears in the wireframe representation (see Figure 17.22).

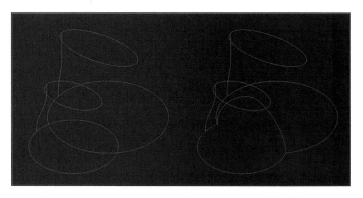

FIGURE 17.22 Wireframe representations of two separate lofted ventilation towers (left) and a single object (right) created with Boolean Union

4. Pan over to the mast objects you extruded in the previous section. Hover the cursor over the Layer Properties Manager's title bar to open the palette. Double-click the Masts layer to set it as current.

5. Select the Union tool in the Boolean panel. Drag a crossing window through both mast solids to select them and press Enter. Although nothing has changed visually, the two solids have been unified as a single object. Zoom into the base of the mast.

6. Select the ribbon's Home tab and click the 3D Rotate tool in the Modify panel. Select the mast and press Enter. Click the lower endpoint of the vertical line, which is at the center of the mast, to act as the base point. A 3D rotate gizmo appears (see Figure 17.23).

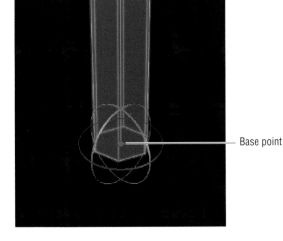

Base point

FIGURE 17.23 3D rotate gizmo displaying three colored rings representing the x-, y-, and z-axes

7. Click the red ring to select the x-axis. The command prompt reads as follows:

```
3DROTATE Specify angle start point or type an angle:
```

Type –14, and press Enter.

8. Click the 3D Rotate tool in the Modify panel again; then select the mast and press Enter. Click the same base point shown in Figure 17.23 and click the green axis ring to select the y-axis. Type 4 and press Enter.

9. Zoom out and select the Erase tool in the Modify panel. Select the edges you extracted from the mast in the previous section and the vertical mast line (see Figure 17.24) and press Enter.

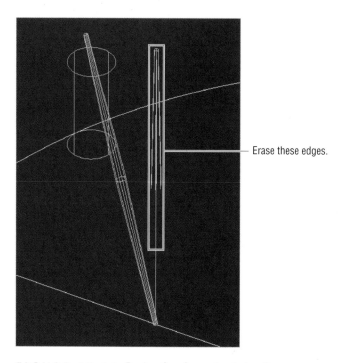

Erase these edges.

FIGURE 17.24 Erasing the edges extracted earlier

10. Type **AR** (for Array) and press Enter. Select the solid mast and press Enter. Type **PO** (for Polar) and press Enter. Type **0,0** (as the center point of the array) and press Enter.

11. Type **I** (for Items) and press Enter. The command prompt reads as follows:

```
ARRAY Enter number of items or [Angle between
Expression] <4>:
```

Type **12** and press Enter two more times to complete the command.

12. Hover the cursor over the Layer Properties Manager's title bar to reveal the palette. Toggle on the Dome Membrane layer. Switch to Shaded With Edges using the in-canvas Visual Style Controls

menu. Zoom out to view the entire model. Figure 17.25 shows the result.

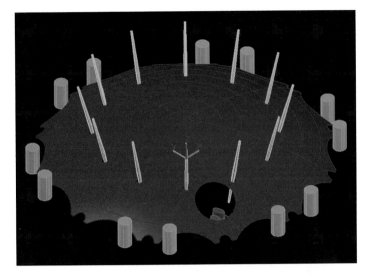

FIGURE 17.25 Arraying rotated masts around the dome

Your model should now resemble Ex17.10-end.dwg.

Exercise 17.11: Edit Solids

Rather than edit a whole solid object, it is possible to select parts of the object (called *subobjects*) for editing. In the following steps, you will offset a subobject, create an interior shell, and then use the AutoCAD Presspull tool on two faces to perform an automatic Boolean subtraction. To begin, open Ex17.11-start .dwg from this chapter's companion files.

1. Select the Isolate tool in the Layers panel, type S (for Settings), and press Enter. Type O (for Off) and press Enter twice. Select the ventilation towers and press Enter. Zoom into the ventilation towers.

2. Select the ribbon's Solid tab and then select the Offset Edge tool in the Solid Editing panel. Click the top face of the left tower. The command prompt reads as follows:

   OFFSETEDGE Specify through point or [Distance Corner]:

   Type D (for Distance) and press Enter. Type 1 and press Enter.

3. The command prompt now reads as follows:

```
Specify point on side to offset:
```

Click the center of the top-left face to offset the edge internally. Click the top face of the right tower. Type **D** (for Distance) and press Enter. Type 1 and press Enter. Click the center of the top-right face and press Enter to end the OFFSETEDGE command. Figure 17.26 shows the result.

FIGURE 17.26 Offsetting edges on the tops of the ventilation towers

4. Switch to Wireframe using the in-canvas Visual Style Controls menu.

5. Select the Shell tool on the right side of the Solid Editing panel. Select the side of the ventilation towers (not the offset top faces) and press Enter. Type 1 (the same distance you offset in the previous step) and press Enter twice to end the SOLIDEDIT command. A hollow interior shell is generated within each ventilation tower. However, the tops are still solid because the shell is inset 1 unit from all sides (including the top).

6. Select the Presspull tool on the Solid panel. Click point A in Figure 17.27, keep the cursor above the towers, type –1, and press Enter. Click point B, type –1, and press Enter twice.

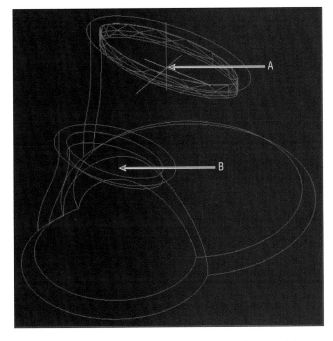

F I G U R E   1 7 . 2 7   Using Presspull to remove the tops of the ventilation towers

7. Switch to Shaded With Edges using the in-canvas Visual Style Controls menu. Now you can see the voids you cut in the tops of the ventilation towers in the previous step.

8. Type **LAYUN** (for Layer Unisolate) and press Enter.

9. Select the Thicken tool on the Solid Editing panel. Select the dome membrane and press Enter. The command prompt reads as follows:

```
THICKEN Specify thickness <1.000>
```

Type **–0.5** and press Enter. The dome surface thickens into a solid shell (see Figure 17.28).

Presspull

Thicken

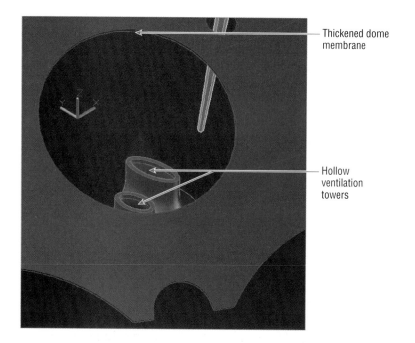

Thickened dome
membrane

Hollow
ventilation
towers

FIGURE 17.28 Thickening the dome membrane into a solid shell

Your model should now resemble Ex17.11-end.dwg. Figure 17.29 shows the completed 3D model.

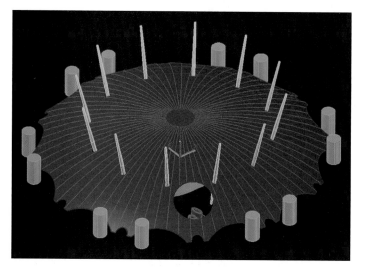

FIGURE 17.29 Completed O2 Arena 3D conceptual model

Smooth Mesh Models

Mesh objects are represented by discrete polygonal surfaces that can be *smoothed*, meaning their geometrical forms can be rounded out. Mesh objects are ideal for representing organic or sculptural forms.

Exercise 17.12: Create, Edit, and Smooth Mesh

In the following steps, you will create a mesh object, edit its faces, smooth, and refine it. To begin, open Ex17.12-start.dwg from this chapter's companion files.

1. Switch to the 3D Modeling workspace if it is not already selected in the Quick Access toolbar.

2. Zoom into the area to the left of the Ventilation towers.

3. Select the Mesh panel on the ribbon and click the Mesh Box tool. Click an arbitrary first corner point somewhere to the left of the ventilation towers. Type 20, press Tab, type 7, and press Enter. Move the cursor above the object, type 5, and press Enter to specify the height of the mesh box (see Figure 17.30).

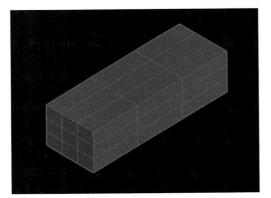

FIGURE 17.30 Creating a mesh box

4. Click the Extrude Face tool in the Mesh Edit panel, select the three faces on the top right of the mesh object, and press Enter. Type 5 and press Enter to extrude the selected faces (see Figure 17.31).

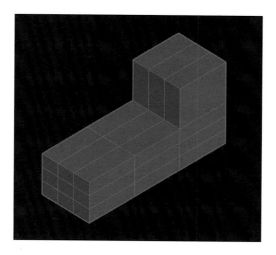

FIGURE 17.31 Extruding selected mesh faces

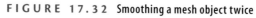Smooth More

5. Click the Smooth More tool in the Mesh panel, select the mesh object, and press Enter. Repeat this procedure to smooth the mesh even more (see Figure 17.32).

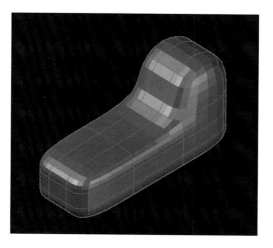

FIGURE 17.32 Smoothing a mesh object twice

Refine Mesh

6. Click the Refine Mesh tool in the Mesh panel, select the mesh object, and press Enter. A denser, smoother mesh is the result (see Figure 17.33).

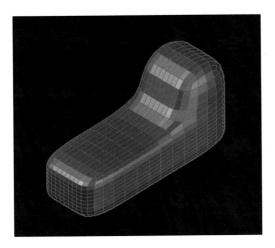

FIGURE 17.33 Refining a smoothed mesh

Your model should now resemble Ex17.12-end.dwg.

Live-Section Models

A section is a cut through a 3D model displaying 2D line work where the model and cutting plane intersect. A live section is a dynamic cutting plane that you can move in relation to the model, helping you visualize the model's interior with a combination of 2D and 3D geometry. In AutoCAD there are four types of live section cuts: plane, slice, boundary, and volume.

Exercise 17.13: Create and Edit a Section Plane

Let's create a section plane and then move it to see the dynamic feature. To begin, open Ex17.13-start.dwg from this chapter's companion files.

1. Switch to the 3D Modeling workspace if it is not already selected in the Quick Access toolbar.

2. On the ribbon's Home tab, click the Section Plane tool in the Section panel. With Ortho mode on, click points A and B shown in Figure 17.34 to create a vertical section plane.

Live sectioning uses your computer's graphics card processor. It might not work properly if your hardware is not recommended at www.autodesk.com/graphics-hardware.

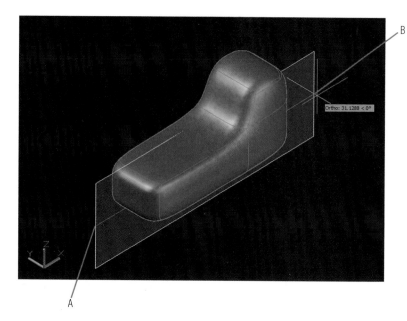

FIGURE 17.34 Drawing a section plane

3. Move the section plane over a short distance so that it still intersects the model and observe that the live section automatically updates.

4. Open the downward-facing triangular grip and select Slice from the context menu that appears. Type **0.5** in the Slice Thickness text box in the ribbon's Adjust panel that appears while you have the Section Object selected. A 3D slice is all that is visible of the object (see Figure 17.35).

5. Change the grip menu to Volume and then adjust the top and left grips to describe a volume less than the total volume of the object. The object is sliced along three planes.

6. Select the section object, type **SECTIONPLANESETTINGS**, and press Enter. Change the color under Intersection Boundary to Green. Under Intersection Fill, change Face Hatch to Predefined/ANSI31 and change Hatch Scale to 6. Scroll down; under Cut-Away Geometry, change Show to Yes, Color to Red, and Face Transparency to 80. The result shows the intersection boundary as a thin green line, the intersection fill with a cross-hatch pattern, and the cutaway geometry in transparent red (see Figure 17.36). Click OK.

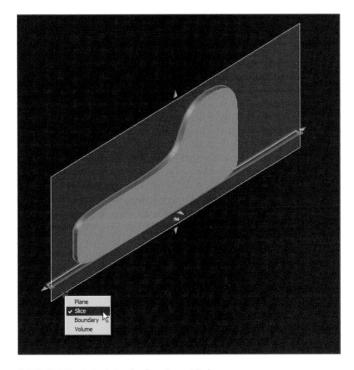

FIGURE 17.35 Configuring a 3D slice

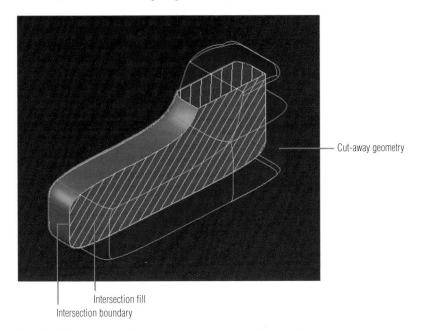

Cut-away geometry

Intersection fill

Intersection boundary

FIGURE 17.36 Changing the appearance of a live section

7. Select the section object. Open the Isolate Objects control on the status bar and select Hide Objects from the menu that appears.

Your model should now resemble Ex17.13-end.dwg.

Placing the section object on a layer that is off also hides the plane.

Now You Know

In this chapter, you learned how to create surface and solid modeling objects and how to edit and section them. You now have the skills to begin creating your own 3D models in AutoCAD.

CHAPTER 18

Presenting and Documenting 3D Design

Wireframe, hidden line, and shaded views are helpful means of visualizing models during the design process. However, visual styles leave something to be desired when you are communicating designs to your clients. The general public has come to expect designers to be able to produce the kind of realistic computer-generated imagery regularly seen in movies. This chapter will help you learn to do that by teaching you how to create realistic presentation images using the advanced rendering system in the AutoCAD® program. After you gain client approval, you still need to document your 3D design with relevant 2D plans, elevations, sections, and detail drawings so that your design can be communicated to the building or manufacturing trades. You will learn how to generate these drawings directly from models using the model documentation features.

In this chapter, you'll learn to do the following:

▶ **Assign materials**

▶ **Place and adjust lights**

▶ **Create renderings**

▶ **Document models with drawings**

Assign Materials

Materials describe the way objects interact with light. AutoCAD comes with an extensive library of real-world materials, including numerous types of concrete, metal, glass, brick, paint, leather, carpet, plastic, and so on. In the following steps, you will transfer materials from the Autodesk library to a sample model and then assign them to objects layer by layer.

Exercise 18.1: Apply Materials

Begin by opening the file Ex18.1-start.dwg, which is among the companion files available for download from this book's web page, www.sybex.com/go/autocad2018essentials. This is a model of this author's house (see Figure 18.1).

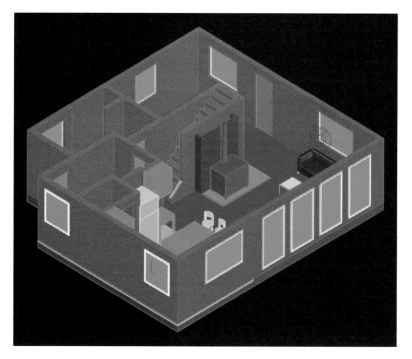

FIGURE 18.1 3D house model

1. Select the 3D Modeling workspace from the drop-down menu on the Quick Access toolbar.

2. Select the ribbon's View tab and click the Materials Browser toggle in the Palettes panel. In the Materials Browser palette that appears, expand the name column so you can read the material names. Click the Category column header to sort the list by category. Scroll down and locate the Fabric category in the Autodesk library. Click the upward-facing arrow icon in the Velvet – Black row to load this material into the document (see Figure 18.2).

There is no visual indication that a material has been loaded. Clicking the upward-facing arrow icon once is enough to load a material.

FIGURE 18.2 Loading a material from the Autodesk library into the document

3. Continue loading materials by single-clicking the materials listed by category in Table 18.1.

All drawings have a global material (flat gray) by default.

TABLE 18.1 Loading materials from the Autodesk library

Category	Subcategory	Material
Flooring	Stone	Flagstone
Flooring	Stone	Flagstone Light Pink
Flooring	Wood	Natural Maple – Antique
Glass	Glazing	Clear
Masonry	Brick	Uniform Running – Burgundy
Metal	(none)	Chrome Satin 1
Metal	Steel	Stainless – Brushed
Paint	(none)	Black
Plastic	(none)	Laminate Light Brown
Wall Paint	Matte	Cool White
Wall Paint	Matte	Flat – Antique White
Wood	(none)	Beech
Wood	(none)	Birch – Solid Stained Dark No Gloss

You can also assign materials by dragging them from the Materials Browser onto specific objects in the drawing canvas.

▶

🖾 Attach By Layer

4. Drag the horizontal separator that splits the Materials Browser into two panes down. Figure 18.3's top pane shows all the materials loaded into the current drawing. Close the Materials Browser.

5. Select the ribbon's Visualize tab. Expand the Materials panel and select the Attach By Layer tool. Click the Layer header to sort the list of layers in reverse alphabetical order. Click the Layer header again to sort in alphabetical order. Drag materials from the left side and drop them on the right side according to

Table 18.2. Figure 18.4 shows the dialog box with all the necessary materials assigned to specific layers. Click OK to close the Material Attachment Options dialog box.

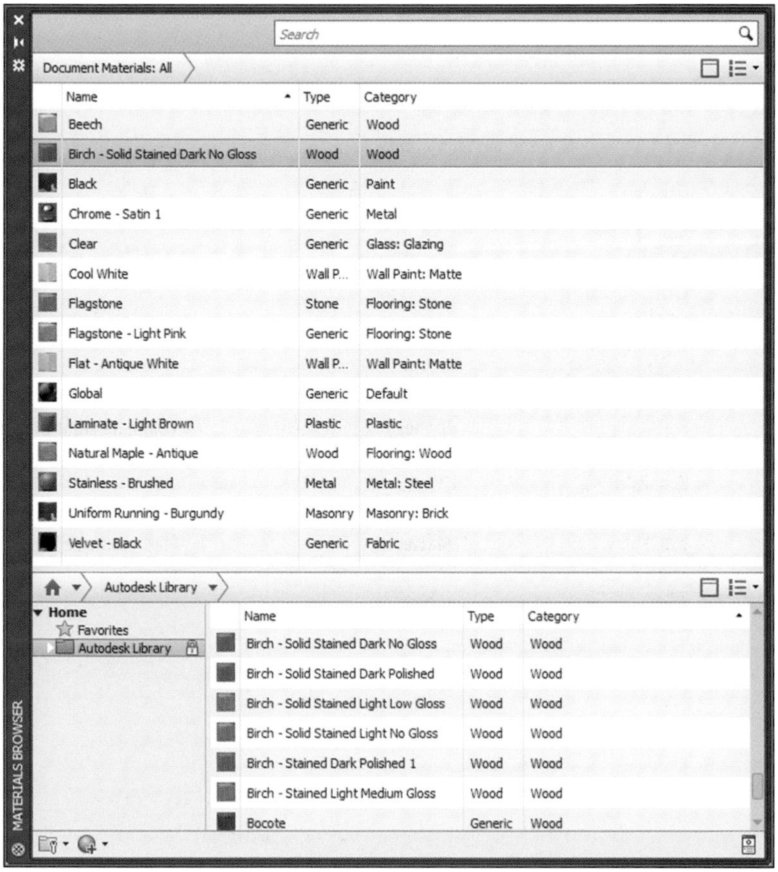

FIGURE 18.3 List of materials loaded into the current drawing

6. Texture maps do not normally appear in the viewport in the Shaded With Edges visual style. Select Realistic using the in-canvas Visual Style Controls menu. Figure 18.5 shows the texture maps in the viewport.

Your model should now resemble Ex18.1-end.dwg.

Texture maps are images used within materials to represent realistic surfaces.

T A B L E 1 8 . 2 Assigning materials to layers

Material	Layer
Global	0
Uniform Running – Burgundy	Brick
Beech	Cabinets
Cool White	Ceiling
Cool White	Ceiling2
Laminate Light Brown	Counter
Global	Defpoints
Birch – Solid Stained Dark No Gloss	Door
Cool White	Downlight
Stainless – Brushed	Equip
Natural Maple – Antique	Floor1
Flagstone	Floor2
Flagstone Light Pink	Floor3
Velvet – Black	Seat-Cushion
Chrome Satin 1	Seat-Frame
Stainless – Brushed	Sink
Birch – Solid Stained Dark No Gloss	Stairs
Beech	Stool
Black	Stove
Clear	Table-Glass
Chrome Satin 1	Table-Legs
Flat – Antique White	Wall
Flat – Antique White	Wall2

Material	Layer
Cool White	Window-Frame
Clear	Window-Glazing
Black	Woodstove

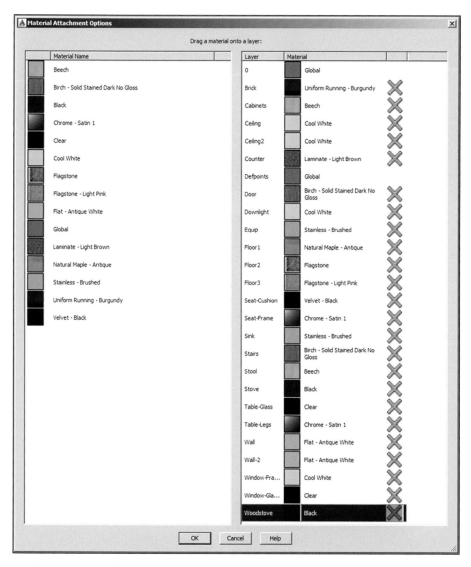

FIGURE 18.4 Assigning materials to layers by dragging from the left pane to the right pane in the Material Attachment Options dialog box

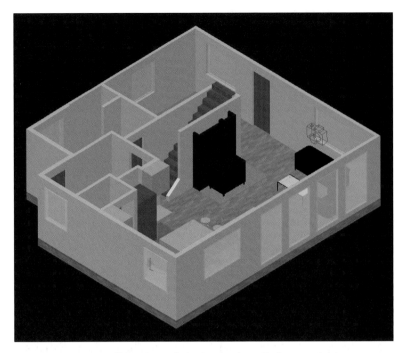

FIGURE 18.5 Using the realistic visual style to display materials' texture maps

Place and Adjust Lights

Without light, nothing would be visible. AutoCAD uses what is called default lighting to illuminate objects in the viewport while you are building 3D models. The default lights are positioned behind the viewer and emit even illumination so that you can always see what is in the viewport. However, *default lighting* is not realistic and must be turned off as soon as you create artificial or natural light. You will add artificial lights (a series of spotlights mounted in the ceiling) and natural lights simulating the sun and sky light diffused throughout the atmosphere.

The absolute size of the model matters when you are using photometric lights. Natural light can easily overpower artificial light in terms of intensity.

Exercise 18.2: Add Artificial Lights

In the real world, artificial lights are electrical lighting fixtures that are one of the hallmarks of the modern world. In AutoCAD, artificial lights include point, spot, and direct sources. Point sources illuminate in all directions, spot sources illuminate in a cone, and direct lights simulate light coming evenly from a particular direction, illuminating everything like the sun.

AutoCAD has two different lighting methods: standard and photometric. Standard lights were used before AutoCAD 2008, and they are still available so that lights in older DWG files will still be compatible in the current version.

However, I strongly urge you to use photometric lights, which are much more realistic. Photometric lights use real-world lighting intensity values (in American or International lighting units), and light coming from photometric light decays with the inverse square of distance, just like light does in the real world.

In the following steps, first you will change lighting units to turn on the photometric lighting system, and then you will add a series of artificial lights to illuminate an architectural interior. To begin, open Ex18.2-start.dwg from this chapter's companion files.

1. Switch to the 3D Modeling workspace if it's not selected already in the Quick Access toolbar.

2. Select the ribbon's Visualize tab and expand the Lights panel. Open the Generic Lighting Units menu (used only for the standard lighting method) and select American Lighting Units (or International Lighting Units in metric).

> AutoCAD for Mac users can change lighting units with the UNITS command.

3. Click the word Top in the ViewCube® to switch to a floor plan view. Rotate the view clockwise so that North is up. Choose Zoom Extents in the Navigation bar and switch to the Wireframe visual style using the in-canvas control.

4. Select the ribbon's Home tab and expand the Layers panel. Select the Turn All Layers On tool. Light fixtures (down lights) are visible in the viewport (see Figure 18.6).

5. Zoom in on the upper-left light by turning the mouse wheel forward. Do the following:

   ▶ If you're a Windows user, select the ribbon's Visualize tab and, on the Lights panel, open the Create Light menu and select Spot.

   ▶ If you're a Mac user, type **LIGHT**, press Enter, type **S** (for Spot), and press Enter.

6. Select Turn Off The Default Lighting when the Lighting – Viewport Lighting Mode dialog box appears (see Figure 18.7).

7. The command prompt reads as follows:

   > Point filters such as .xy, .xz, and .yz allow you to specify the listed coordinate values by clicking in the drawing. Typing the missing coordinate then specifies the 3D coordinates.

```
SPOTLIGHT Specify source location <0,0,0>:
```

   Type .xy and press Enter. Click a point visually centered on the light fixture (but do not use center object snap).

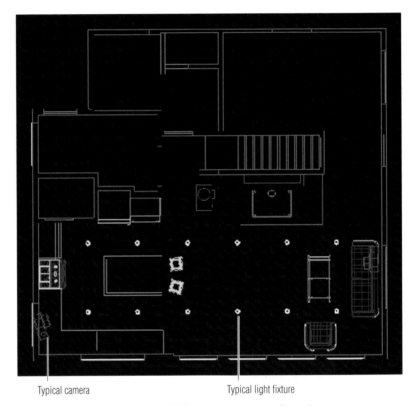

Typical camera   Typical light fixture

FIGURE 18.6 Viewing light fixture geometry on a floor plan

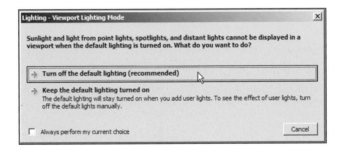

FIGURE 18.7 Turning off default lighting when adding the first artificial light source

8. The command prompt now says (need Z). Type **96** (the ceiling height) and press Enter. The command prompt now reads as follows:

```
SPOTLIGHT Specify target location <0,0,-10>:
```

Type .xy, press Enter, and click the same center point as you did in the previous step. The command prompt now says (need Z).

9. Type 0 (the floor height) and press Enter. Press Enter again to end the SPOTLIGHT command.

10. Press the F8 key if Ortho is not already on. Type CO (for Copy) and press Enter. Type L (for Last) and press Enter twice. Click a point near the light fixture, zoom out by turning the mouse wheel backward, move the cursor down to the light fixture in the bottom row, and click in the drawing canvas to create the second spotlight. Press Enter to end the COPY command.

11. Press the spacebar to repeat the last command, type P (for Previous), and press Enter. Type L (for Last) so that you have a selection of two lights, and press Enter twice to end Select Objects mode. Click the start point under the last spotlight and zoom out. The command prompt reads as follows:

```
COPY Specify second point or [Array]
<use first point as displacement>:
```

Type A (for Array) and press Enter. Type 6 (for the number of items) and press Enter.

12. Type F (for Fit) and press Enter. Move the cursor under the rightmost light fixture (see Figure 18.8), and click to specify the second point of the array. Press Enter to exit the ARRAY command.

Placing lights within block definitions can help keep the source and fixture together.

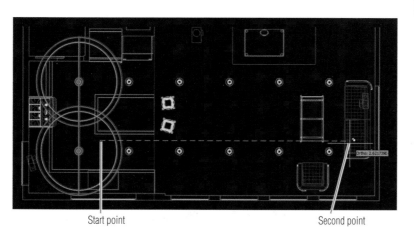

Start point   Second point

FIGURE 18.8 Copying spotlights in a rectangular array

13. Type V (for View) and press Enter. Double-click Camera1 in the View Manager (see Figure 18.9). Click Apply and OK.

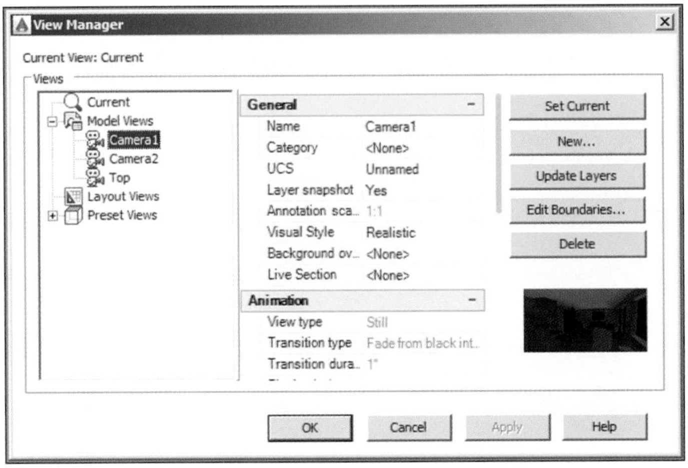

FIGURE 18.9 Selecting a predefined camera view

14. Click the Lights panel menu (a small icon in the lower-right corner of the Lights panel) to open the Lights In Model palette (see Figure 18.10). Select the first spotlight in the list, hold Shift, and select the last spotlight in the list to select them all.

FIGURE 18.10 Selecting lights in the Lights In Model palette

15. Right-click the selected lights in the Light Lister and choose Properties. Select the Lamp Color property and click the icon to the right of the drop-down menu to open the Lamp Color dialog box. Select the Kelvin Colors radio button, type **5000**, and press Tab. The resulting color changes (see Figure 18.11). Click OK.

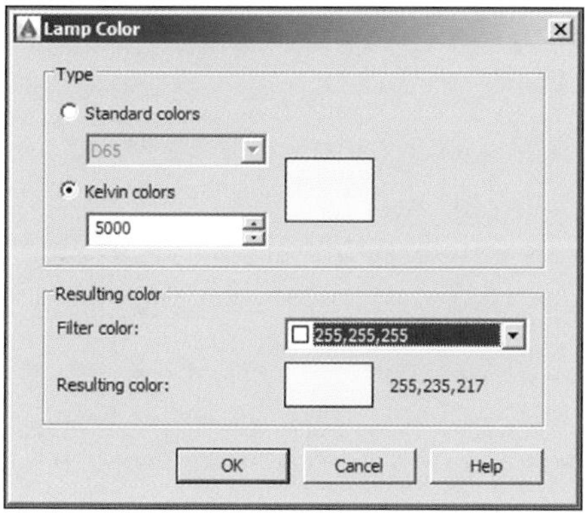

◄

Real-world lamps are typically rated by a color standard and/or color temperature (measured in degrees Kelvin). The Tool palettes have a set of real-world lamps ready for use.

FIGURE 18.11 Specifying lamp color by temperature

◄

The viewport shows direct illumination only. Reflected and transmitted light must be rendered.

16. In the Properties palette, change Lamp Intensity to **15000**, Hotspot Angle to **30**, and Falloff Angle to **60**. Figure 18.12 shows the resulting light glyphs in the drawing canvas. Close the Properties and Lights In Model palettes. Press Esc to deselect all.

FIGURE 18.12 Selected spotlights reveal light coverage as seen in the camera view.

Your model should now resemble Ex18.2-end.dwg.

Exercise 18.3: Simulate Natural Light

AutoCAD can simulate the light of the sun and/or the light scattered in the sky by the atmosphere for any location on Earth and for any time of year and time of day. In the following steps, you will configure the model to use a simulated sun and sky with specific time and space coordinates. To begin, open Ex18.3-start.dwg from the Chapter 18 companion files.

1. Switch to the 3D Modeling workspace if it's not selected already in the Quick Access toolbar.

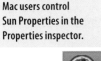

2. Select the ribbon's Visualize tab if it is not already selected. Click the Sun Status toggle in the Sun & Location panel. The sun is on when the toggle is highlighted in blue. Choose Keep Exposure Settings in the Lighting – Sunlight and Exposure dialog box that appears.

Mac users control Sun Properties in the Properties inspector.

3. Expand the Sun & Location panel, open the Set Location menu, and select From Map. Choose Yes when asked if you want to use online map data. In the Geographic Location dialog box that appears, zoom into a hypothetical site anywhere in the world you would like. Right-click the map and choose Drop Marker Here. A red pin appears on the map at that location (see Figure 18.13).

The time zone is selected automatically in the Geographic Location dialog box, but you can adjust it if it is incorrect.

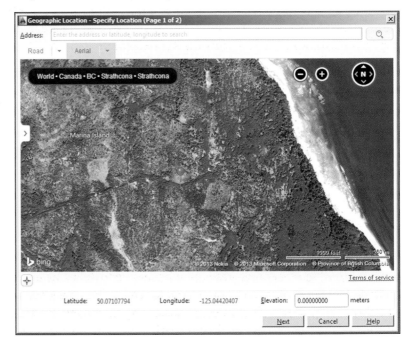

FIGURE 18.13 Specifying the geographic location of the site

4. Click Next in the Geographic Location dialog box and Select Inches (or Meters for metric) from the Drawing Unit drop-down menu. Select the first coordinate system in the list in your chosen system of units and click Next.

5. Click anywhere in the drawing canvas to select a reference point for the geolocation data. Press Enter to specify the North direction as up by default. By specifying North on the plan you are establishing the building orientation on the map.

6. Select the Visualize tab on the ribbon; open the Sky Background menu in the Sun & Location panel and select Sky Background And Illumination. AutoCAD automatically manages the color of the sky and degree of sky illumination based on your chosen time and space coordinates.

Your model should now resemble `Ex18.3-end.dwg`.

Dragging the Date and Time sliders automatically repositions the sun as it would in the real world at the chosen time coordinates.

Sky Background and Illumination

Create Renderings

Rendering is the process of converting the geometry, materials, and lighting settings into pixels. Rendering can be a time-consuming process because it typically requires a lot of computation to perform. There are no rendering options in AutoCAD for Mac (just the RENDER command), and the resulting rendering quality isn't as realistic as that available in AutoCAD for Windows, where you have many advanced options. AutoCAD has a rendering engine called Rapid RT that produces high-quality imagery with few user-configurable parameters.

Exercise 18.4: Make Realistic Renderings in the Cloud

In the following steps, you will use AutoCAD's advanced render settings for Windows to progressively create more realistic renderings. To begin, open `Ex18.4-start.dwg` from this chapter's companion files. Preview renderings are free on the Autodesk® A360 cloud-based service. Cloud credits can be purchased to render high-resolution images up to 4000×4000 pixels on the Autodesk network of servers. Using A360 to render final images can be much quicker than rendering locally, even considering time spent uploading the drawing and downloading the final rendering, because the job is rendered on a large network of render servers that far exceed the computational power of any one personal computer. Another practical benefit of rendering in the cloud is that your local computer remains usable for other tasks while rendering.

You can also upload DWG files to https:// rendering.360 .autodesk .com to render in the cloud.

1. Switch to the 3D Modeling workspace if it's not selected already in the Quick Access toolbar.

2. Select the ribbon's Visualize tab. Click the arrow in the lower-right corner of the Render panel or type **RPREF** and press Enter to open the Render Presets Manager. You will begin by making a preview render in the cloud. Select Low from the Current Preset menu (see Figure 18.14).

If you chose to render locally, you will be prompted to install the Medium Images Library (700 MB) of texture maps. For the purposes of this book, you do not need to render locally.

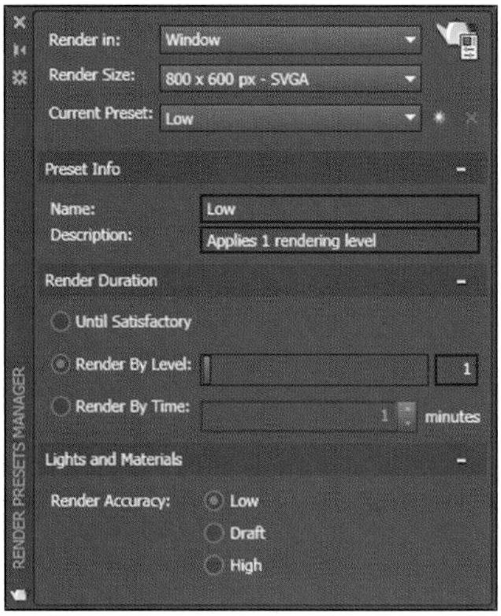

FIGURE 18.14 Render Presets Manager

Depending on A360's rendering load, your rendering job might go in a queue. If so, the A360 site gives notification of the estimated wait time.

3. Save your work as Ex18.4.dwg. Click the Render In Cloud button in the A360 panel. Select Camera1 as the Model View in the A360 dialog box (see Figure 18.15) and click the Start Rendering button.

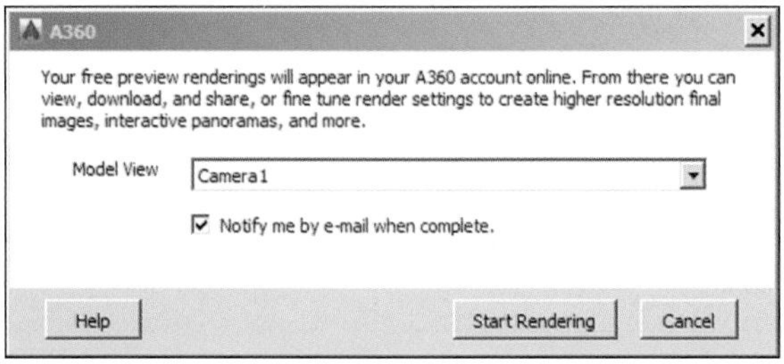

FIGURE 18.15 Selecting a model view for a preview render in the cloud

4. Click the Render Gallery button to launch your default browser and go to the Autodesk A360 site. After a few moments, your preview rendering will appear as a thumbnail (see Figure 18.16), rendered by the Autodesk network of servers.

FIGURE 18.16   Rendering in Autodesk A360

5. Click the menu that appears on the rendered thumbnail image and choose Adjust Exposure. Change Exposure Value to 8.88 and Shadows to 0.5 and click Apply (see Figure 18.17). Your thumbnail image is automatically re-rendered and will appear shortly.

Click the blue FAQ link in the Render Settings dialog box to learn more about cloud credits.

FIGURE 18.17   Adjusting exposure of rendering online

6. After the new thumbnail image appears, open the thumbnail menu and choose Re-render With New Settings to open the Render Settings dialog box in the browser. Choose Field for Environment, set Render Quality to Final, and choose Large as the Image Size. Exposure will say Customized because of what you did in the previous step; no more changes are needed. You can optionally check to be emailed when the job is complete (see Figure 18.18). Click Start Rendering; you will see a progress bar as the rendering is processed on A360.

Render Settings		⊗
View Camera1 ⏱ 6 minutes 3.3 MB		

Environment	Field		Image Size	Large (2.25 Mega Pixel)
Render Quality	Final		Aspect Ratio	4:3 Presentation
Exposure	Customized		Width	1500 px
File Format	JPEG (High Quality)		Height	1125 px
	☐ Alpha (Transparency Background)			

Cloud Credits FAQ

| Required | Available | Left | Estimated wait time <10 minutes |
| 2 | 23 | 21 | ☐ Email me when complete   Start Rendering |

FIGURE 18.18 Rendering a final image in A360

Figure 18.19 shows the final rendering. This particular image took about 10 minutes to complete.

FIGURE 18.19 Final image rendered on A360

Document Models with Drawings

AutoCAD has a set of model documentation features that allow you to generate 2D plans, elevations, sections, and/or details directly from solid and surface models. These features are not available in AutoCAD LT®.

Exercise 18.5: Document Models

In the following steps, you will open a 3D model of a gear and project multiple 2D drawings from it. To begin, open Ex18.5-start.dwg from the companion files (see Figure 18.20).

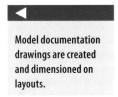

Model documentation drawings are created and dimensioned on layouts.

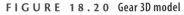

FIGURE 18.20 Gear 3D model

1. Select the 3D Modeling workspace from the drop-down menu on the Quick Access toolbar. Select the ribbon's Home tab.

2. Select the Base tool in the View panel on the right edge of the ribbon and choose From Model Space in the drop-down menu. The command line reads as follows:

   ```
   VIEWBASE Select objects or [Entire model]:
   ```

   Select the gear object and press Enter.

You can also link Autodesk Inventor® base models into AutoCAD in order to generate dimensioned shop drawings.

3. The command line reads as follows:

   ```
   VIEWBASE Enter new or existing layout name to make current
   or [?] <24x36>:
   ```

In this case, there is already a layout called 24×36, so press Enter to accept this default layout. AutoCAD switches to the 24×36 layout, and you are prompted to specify a location for the base drawing. Click an arbitrary point in the lower-left corner of the layout (see Figure 18.21).

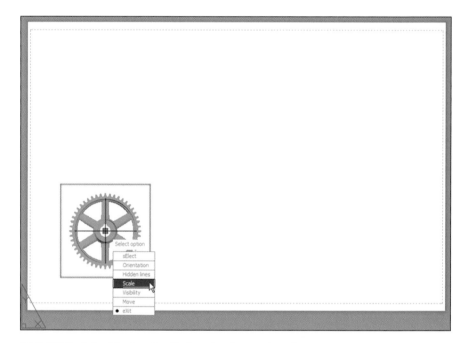

FIGURE 18.21 Locating the base drawing on a layout

4. The drawing is too small, so you will adjust its scale. The command line reads as follows:

```
VIEWBASE Select option [select Orientation Hidden lines
Scale Visibility
Move exit] <exit>:
```

Select Scale from the dynamic prompt menu. Type **1** and press Enter again. It just so happens that several views of the gear fit on the page with the gear at actual size.

5. Press Enter to accept the default Exit option, and you will see that the VIEWBASE command continues.

6. Click a point above the base plan drawing to locate a second projected view of the top of the gear.

7. Click a third point at a 45-degree angle with respect to the base plan to locate an isometric projection and press Enter to end the command. The drawings display in wireframe view showing hidden lines with a dashed linetype (see Figure 18.22).

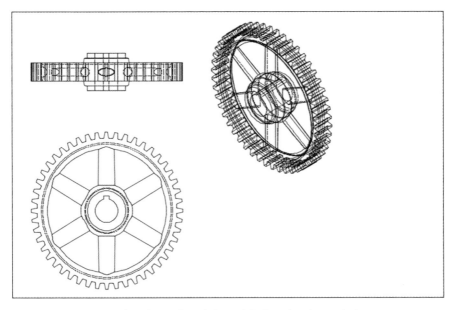

FIGURE 18.22   Locating projected views of the base drawing on the layout

8. The isometric view is a bit large. Select it, and you will see a special border appear around the view object. On the temporary Drawing View tab that appears, click Edit View. Change the scale to **1:2** in the drop-down in the Appearance panel. Open the Hidden Lines drop-down and select Shaded With Visible Lines (see Figure 18.23). Click OK in the Edit panel.

9. Select the original base view of the gear object in the lower-left corner of the layout. Click the Section tool in the Create View panel.

You can move the view objects to better arrange them on the layout.

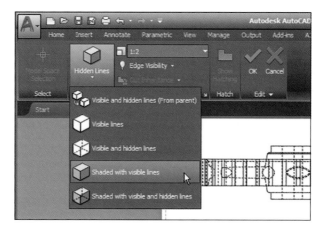

FIGURE 18.23 Changing a view's display properties

10. Toggle on Ortho in the status bar. Click points A and B shown in Figure 18.24 to draw a section cut line and press Enter. Click point C to locate the section view and press Enter to end the VIEWSECTION command.

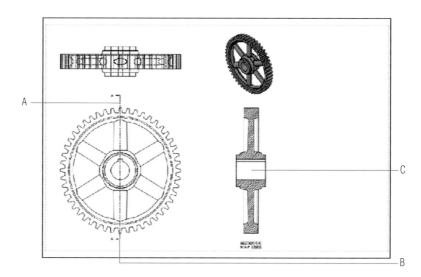

FIGURE 18.24 Creating a section of the base view

11. Select the original base view of the gear object in the lower-left corner of the layout yet again. Open the Detail drop-down on the Create View panel and select Rectangular. Toggle off object snap in the status bar. Click points A and B shown in Figure 18.25 to draw the detail area and press Enter. Click point C to locate the detail view and press Enter to end the VIEWDETAIL command.

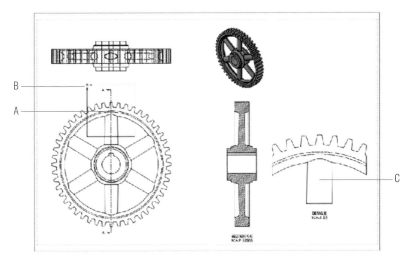

FIGURE 18.25 Creating a detail of the base view

12. Toggle on object snap in the status bar. Switch to the Annotate tab on the ribbon and select the Linear tool in the Dimension panel. Dimension the features shown in Figure 18.26. These dimensions are associated with the section and detail views, which in turn are associated with the base view, which is in turn associated with the model. If you were to change the gear geometry in model space, views and dimensions would automatically update on the layout.

Your model should now resemble Ex18.5-end.dwg.

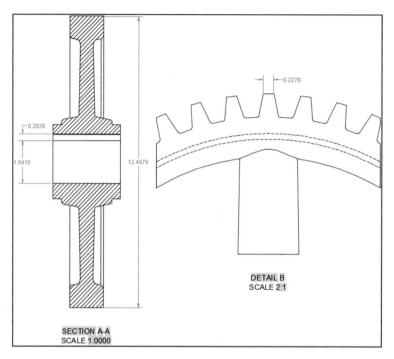

FIGURE 18.26   Associating dimensions with section and detail views

Now You Know

In this chapter, you learned how to assign materials to 3D models, place and adjust virtual lights, create photorealistic renderings, and document 3D models with 2D drawings. Now you know how to create presentation imagery that you can use to show off your future designs.

Making Isometric Drawings

Long before the AutoCAD® program existed, architects and engineers used isometric projection as a method to visually represent 3D objects on 2D paper. You can replicate this traditional method in AutoCAD by making 2D isometric drawings as a simpler alternative to true 3D modeling (with its complex feature set and corresponding learning curve).

One practical advantage of using isometric projection is that you can measure any side of an object and it will always be true to scale. In fact, the word *isometric* means "same measure." The three isometric axes (left, top, and right) are equally scaled in isometric and always appear with a common 120-degree angle between them, as shown in Figure A.1.

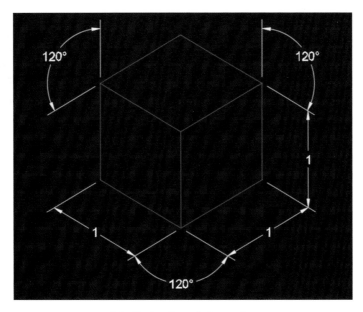

FIGURE A.1 Cube illusion drawn in isometric

The chief limitation of isometric drawings is that they are purely 2D illusions drawn on the xy plane, so you cannot ever change your vantage point like you can with true 3D models or the illusion will be revealed. Figure A.2 depicts a 3D solid cube viewed from the SE Isometric vantage point (the UCS icon in the lower left shows the viewing angle with respect to the three spatial axes). This 3D cube looks identical to the 2D cube shown in Figure A.1.

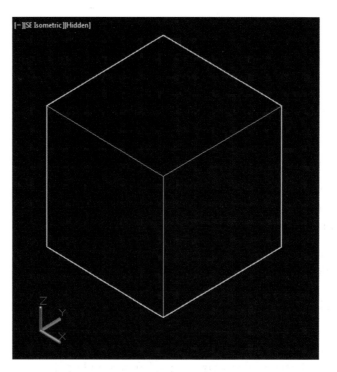

3D models can be shown in perspectives, renderings, and animations. 3D objects have centroids, mass, moments of inertia, and volume properties, and they can be exported to other 3D programs.

FIGURE A.2   3D cube viewed from the SE Isometric viewing angle

If you orbit into any custom viewing angle, the isometric illusion drawn on the xy plane is revealed. Figure A.3 shows both techniques side by side from a custom viewing angle. The isometric illusion on the left is blown because its dimensions are distorted, and the 3D model on the right is simply depicted from another, equally valid viewing angle. Isometric drawings are composed of 2D elements that must always be viewed from the Top viewpoint, looking straight down on the xy plane to be valid 3D representations.

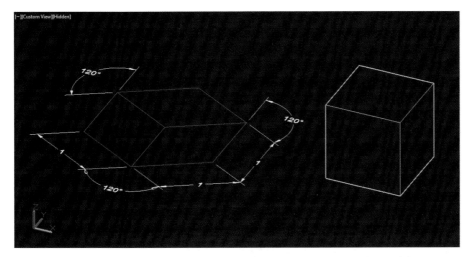

FIGURE A.3 Comparison of a 2D isometric drawing (left) and a 3D model viewed from a custom angle (right)

In the following steps, you will make an isometric drawing:

1. Create a new blank drawing and click the Customization button on the status bar. Toggle on Isometric Drafting if it is not already selected from the menu that appears.

2. Click the Isometric Drafting button, which will show the Isoplane Left icon by default. Clicking this button toggles the icon from gray to a similar green and red icon. This is a visual indication that you have entered isometric drafting mode.

3. Press the F5 key repeatedly and watch what happens to the Isometric Drafting button on the status bar. Each time you press F5 (or Ctrl+E) you cycle through three different *isoplanes*: left, top, and right. Notice the corresponding changes to the cursor in the drawing window and to the icons on the status bar (see Figure A.4).

You can manually toggle isometric drafting mode with the ISODRAFT command.

4. Click the Layer Properties button on the Home tab of the ribbon. Create a new layer called Isometric and color it red. Set this new layer current.

5. Press F5 until the cursor (and status bar) are set to Isoplane Left. Click the Line tool in the ribbon's Draw panel and start drawing the line from an arbitrary point near the top of the drawing window.

Isometric cursor

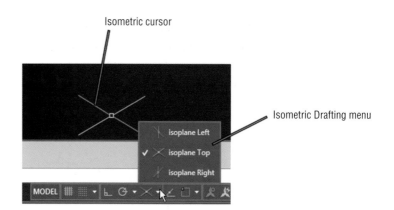

Isometric Drafting menu

FIGURE A.4 The cursor changes to match the currently selected isoplane (top in this example) selected in the Isometric Drafting menu on the status bar.

With Ortho mode on, lines are constrained along the cursor's isometric axes.

6. Toggle on Ortho on the status bar if it is not already on. Move the cursor down and type **1** to draw a vertical line of 1 unit in length. Move the cursor to the right and observe that the cursor is constrained to a 30-degree angle. Type **1** and press Enter to draw another line segment (see Figure A.5).

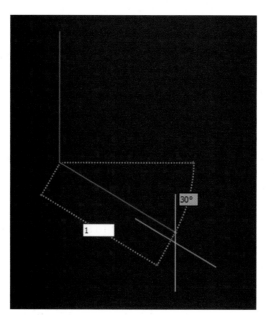

FIGURE A.5 Drawing lines in isometric with Ortho on

7. Move the cursor up, type **1**, and press Enter. Type **C** (for Close) and press Enter to end the LINE command.

8. Press F5 once to toggle into Isoplane Top mode. Draw another parallelogram representing the top of the cube with 1-unit edges to match Figure A.6. Use endpoint object snap to connect the three new lines to the lines you have already drawn.

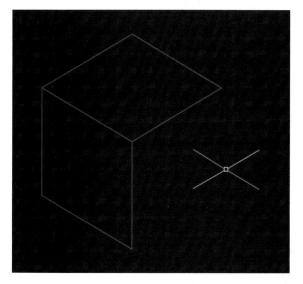

FIGURE A.6 Drawing the top of the cube in Isoplane Top mode

9. Press F5 again to switch into Isoplane Right mode. Complete the 3D representation of the cube by drawing two more lines that snap to the endpoints of the existing lines.

10. Using the Layers drop-down, set layer 0 current. Draw two white lines snapping to opposite endpoints, as shown in Figure A.7.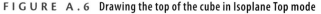

11. Press F5 until you toggle into Isoplane Top mode. Using the Layers drop-down, set layer Isometric current. Type **EL** (for ELLIPSE) and press Enter. Press the down-arrow key and select the Isocircle option from the Dynamic Input menu. Using midpoint object snap, click the midpoint of the top white line. Type **0.25** to specify the radius of the isocircle and then press Enter.

Use the ELLIPSE command's Isocircle option rather than CIRCLE to draw circles in isometric.

12. Press F5 twice to switch into Isoplane Left mode.

13. Press Enter to repeat ELLIPSE. Press the down-arrow key and select the Isocircle option as before. Click the midpoint of the other white line, type **0.25**, and press Enter. Select both temporary white lines and press the Delete key to remove them.

14. Click the Isoplane Left icon in the status bar to toggle off Isometric Drafting mode. The icon turns gray, and the cursor returns to its

normal white appearance representing orthogonal axes. Figure A.8 shows the cube with two circles drawn in isometric with the cursor returned to its normal appearance.

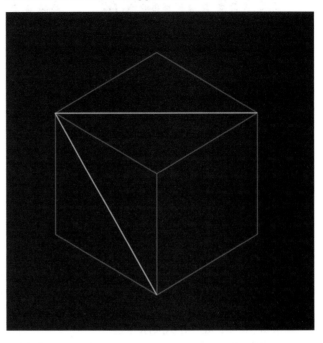

FIGURE A.7 Drawing temporary construction lines on layer 0

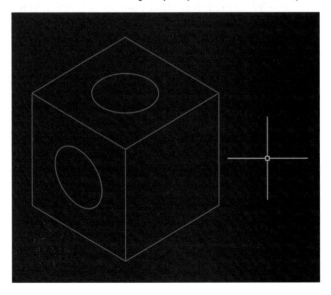

FIGURE A.8 Isometric cube and circle drawing

15. Save your work as Isometric.dwg.

Autodesk™ AutoCAD™ 2018 Certification

Autodesk® certifications are industry-recognized credentials that can help you succeed in your career, providing benefits to both you and your employer. Getting certified is a reliable validation of skills and knowledge, and it can lead to accelerated professional development, improved productivity, and enhanced credibility.

This Autodesk™ Official Press guide can be an effective component of your exam preparation. Autodesk highly recommends (and we agree!) that you schedule regular time to prepare, review the most current exam preparation road map available at www.autodesk.com/training-and-certification/certification, use Autodesk Official Press guides, take a class at an Authorized Training Center (find ATCs near you here: www.autodesk.com/atc), and use a variety of resources to prepare for your certification—including plenty of actual hands-on experience.

Certification Objective

To help you focus your studies on the skills you'll need for these exams, the following tables show objectives that could potentially appear on an exam and in what chapter you can find information on that topic—and when you go to that chapter, you'll find certification icons like the one in the margin here.

Table B.1 is for the AutoCAD® 2018 Certified User Exam and lists the topics, exam objectives, and chapter where the information for each objective is found. Table B.2 is for the AutoCAD 2018 Certified Professional Exam. This book will give you a foundation for the basic objectives covered on the Certified User exam, but you will need further study and hands-on practice to complete and pass the Certified Professional exam.

T A B L E   B . 1   AutoCAD 2018 Certified User Exam sections and objectives

Topic	Learning Objective	Chapter
Apply Basic Drawing Skills	Create, open, and publish files	1
	Draw circles, arcs, and polygons	2
	Draw lines and rectangles	2
	Fillet and chamfer lines	4
	Select objects	4
	Use coordinate systems	2
	Use Dynamic Input, direct distance, and shortcut menus	3
	Use inquiry commands	4
Use Drawing Aids	Work with grid and snap	3
Edit Entities	Create selection sets	4
	Stretch objects	4
	Use grip editing	4
	Use Offset and Mirror	4
	Use Trim and Extend	4
Work with Curves	Draw and edit curved polylines	5
Control Object Visibility and Appearance	Alter layer assignments for objects	7
	Change object properties	7
	Control layer visibility	7
Use Blocks and Xrefs	Define blocks	9
Use Hatching and Gradients	Apply hatch patterns	8
Create and Edit Text	Create text styles	10
	Write lines of text	10
Dimensioning	Create and apply dimension styles	11
Layouts and Annotative Objects	Use the Window command	13

Topic	Learning Objective	Chapter
	Use viewports	13
Printing and Plotting	Set printing and plotting options	14

TABLE B.2 AutoCAD 2018 Certified Professional Exam sections and objectives

Topic	Learning Objective	Chapter
Apply Basic Drawing Skills	Create, open, and publish files	1
	Draw circles, arcs, and polygons	2
	Draw lines and rectangles	2
	Fillet and chamfer lines	4
	Select objects	4
	Use coordinate systems	2
	Use Dynamic Input, direct distance, and shortcut menus	3
	Use Inquiry commands	4
Use Drawing Aids	Use object snap tracking	3
	Use Ortho and Polar Tracking	3
	Use PolarSnap	3
	Use running object snaps	3
	Work with grid and snap	3
Edit Entities	Create and use arrays	4
	Create selection sets	4
	Use grip editing	4
	Use Move and Copy	4
	Use Offset and Mirror	4
	Use Rotate and Scale	4
	Use Trim and Extend	4

(Continues)

TABLE B.2   *(Continued)*

Topic	Learning Objective	Chapter
Work with Curves	Blend between objects with splines	5
	Draw and edit curved polylines	5
Control Object Visibility and Appearance	Alter layer assignments for objects	7
	Assign properties by object or layer	7
	Change object properties	7
	Control layer visibility	7
	Manage layer properties	7
Use Blocks and Xrefs	Define blocks	9
	Reference external drawings and images	9
	Work with global blocks	9
Use Hatching and Gradients	Apply hatch patterns	8
Create and Edit Text	Create text styles	10
	Write lines of text	10
Dimensioning	Create and apply dimension styles	11
	Use multileaders	11
Layouts and Annotative Objects	Create annotative styles and objects	13
	Create layouts	13
	Use the window command	13
	Use viewports	13
Printing and Plotting	Set printing and plotting options	14

These Autodesk exam objectives were accurate at publication time. Please refer to www.autodesk.com/training-and-certification/certification for the most current exam road map and objectives.

Good luck preparing for your certification!

INDEX

Note to the Reader: Throughout this index **boldfaced** page numbers indicate primary discussions of a topic. *Italicized* page numbers indicate illustrations.